STATE OF THE KINGDOM ADDRESS

GOD'S WAKE-UP CALL TO THE SLEEPING CHURCH

By David Newby

Copyright © 2018. David G. Newby. All rights reserved.

No part of this publication may be reproduced or transmitted in any form or by any means, electronic or mechanical, including photocopy, recording, or any information storage or retrieval system, without the expressed written consent of the publisher.

To my love, and Light, Jesus Christ, without whom, none of this would be possible. All praises to the Most High. To my supporters: Family who stuck with me and helped me through some of the toughest times ever. To my friends, who held me down through thick and thin. To my fans and supporters, for all your faithfulness and encouragement. I am forever grateful.

To the *Kingdom Kids*, who partnered with me in this amazing work, not just the book, but the work of the Almighty God on earth. Much love and respect to you all.

You inspire me to write and do more for the world than ever. "Thanks" is not enough. But it's all I can say to express my gratitude. I'm forever indebted to you.

TABLE OF CONTENTS

FOREWORD 1
   My Call To Write 1
CHAPTER 1: "BEHOLD, I COME QUICKLY!" 3
   The Night Before 6
   The Dream Interpretation 8
   "Today" 8
   Get Ready 11
CHAPTER 2: ACT TWO: THE RAPTURE 13
   April 3, 2014: Journal Entry 13
CHAPTER 3: THE GLOBAL REVIVAL 20
   A Nehemiah Vision 24
   10 Basic facts about the revival 26
   Biblical Revivals 30
   7 Mountains of Revival 42
   The Global Renaissance 63
   Revival Comes to the World 64
CHAPTER 4: END-TIME REVELATION 68
   Blown to Hell 70
   The Exorcist 71
   Body Slamming Satan 73
   Lion Territory 74
   Servants of the Devil 81

The Cross	82
The Devil's Harvest	83
Council of Wickedness	85
The Drifting Face	87
God's Pride of Lions	90
Wealth Transfer	93
A Prophetic Word: Exodus Back to God	94
CHAPTER 5: SATAN'S SATIRE	**96**
Schoolyard Bully	98
The Devil Is Mocking You	100
Great Cities Have Great Defenses	101
Unleash the Beast Within You	102
Transformation to the Church	103
The World Is Not Ready	105
Let's Evangelize Like Never Before	107
Reverse the Course of Battle	107
CHAPTER 6: SOUNDING THE ALARM	**109**
Raising End-Time Warriors	110
Four Blood Moons	111
The Third Temple	112
A History of the Temple	113
Temple Institute and Others	115
Preparation Underway	117
Ark of the Covenant	118

- The Red Heifer 119
- World Events 121

CHAPTER 7: SPIRITUAL REALITY 127
- The Spiritual Reality 132
- My Spiritual Encounters 135
- Warning Against False Spirits 156
- Revelations of Hell 158
- Supernatural Power Manifested 171

CHAPTER 8: SAGE STRATEGIES FOR SUPERLATIVE LIVING 173
- Give More to Get More 177
- Practice the Spiritual Fundamentals 179
- Vision, Values, Mission 188
- Strategy, Planning, and Goal-Setting 190
- Execute the Plan 194
- Managing and Monitoring Results 195
- Make Continual Improvements 196
- Create Bigger Plans and Goals 197
- Rinse and Repeat the System 198
- Self-Management 198
- Succession Planning 199
- Follow the Strategies 201
- About My Training and Speaking 201

CHAPTER 9: A CLARION CALL TO LEADERS 202
- Leadership in God's Eyes 203

Leadership In the Church 207

A Five-Fold Call to Action... 208

Developing a Glorious Church 226

Other Christian Leaders 236

Developing a Better Government 237

Business 256

Family 258

Community 259

Other Issues for Christian Leaders 261

CHAPTER 10: RAISED FROM THE DEAD 266

A Wake-Up Call for Individuals 267

Reassess Your Life 291

CHAPTER 11: ARMED FOR BATTLE 292

You Have Everything You Need 292

Move Into Your Greatness 305

CHAPTER 12: BEAUTIFICATION 307

It's Time To Wake-Up 308

How to Prepare for Jesus 309

Prayer of Release: 314

CHAPTER 13: THUS SAITH THE LORD. 315

About the Author 320

Sponsorship Opportunity 322

Permissions 323

Share This Information with Others 324

The Red Heifer 119

World Events 121

CHAPTER 7: SPIRITUAL REALITY 127

The Spiritual Reality 132

My Spiritual Encounters 135

Warning Against False Spirits 156

Revelations of Hell 158

Supernatural Power Manifested 171

CHAPTER 8: SAGE STRATEGIES FOR SUPERLATIVE LIVING 173

Give More to Get More 177

Practice the Spiritual Fundamentals 179

Vision, Values, Mission 188

Strategy, Planning, and Goal-Setting 190

Execute the Plan 194

Managing and Monitoring Results 195

Make Continual Improvements 196

Create Bigger Plans and Goals 197

Rinse and Repeat the System 198

Self-Management 198

Succession Planning 199

Follow the Strategies 201

About My Training and Speaking 201

CHAPTER 9: A CLARION CALL TO LEADERS 202

Leadership in God's Eyes 203

Leadership In the Church 207

A Five-Fold Call to Action 208

Developing a Glorious Church 226

Other Christian Leaders 236

Developing a Better Government 237

Business 256

Family 258

Community 259

Other Issues for Christian Leaders 261

CHAPTER 10: RAISED FROM THE DEAD 266

A Wake-Up Call for Individuals 267

Reassess Your Life 291

CHAPTER 11: ARMED FOR BATTLE 292

You Have Everything You Need 292

Move Into Your Greatness 305

CHAPTER 12: BEAUTIFICATION 307

It's Time To Wake-Up 308

How to Prepare for Jesus 309

Prayer of Release: 314

CHAPTER 13: THUS SAITH THE LORD. 315

About the Author 320

Sponsorship Opportunity 322

Permissions 323

Share This Information with Others 324

- JV and Affiliate Partners 324
- Leave your Mark, Establish Your Legacy 325

Give and It Shall Be Given 326

Join the Movement 326

Book David for Speaking 328

FREE Personal Development Tools, Tips, Strategies, and Information 329

SOKA Success Strategies 90-Day Challenge™ 331

Acknowledgements 332

Set Apart By God - A Very Special Thank You 335

SOKA Success Seminars™ 339

Work with David Newby and His Team 341

- Training Programs 341

Get Huge Discounts on the *State of the Kingdom Address*™ Book or the Audio Program When you Buy in Bulk for Your Employees. 345

COMING SOON 347

- Stay Tuned for Upcoming Releases... 347
- Also Look Out for These SOKA Sequels... 347

Let's Connect Further... 348

Additional Resources for Success 349

- Training Programs 349

Apostolic Movement International (AMI) Fivefold Training 350

ET the Hip Hop Preacher 351

100-Day Challenge 351

DaniJohnson.com 352

Robert Kiyosaki 352
Other Resources 353
   The Bible 353
   Movies 353
   Books 354
   Communities 354
Notes and References 355

FOREWORD

MY CALL TO WRITE

What's the purpose of writing a parody of the United States annual State of the Union Address? Is it to mock the government? Were you called to write this? Who are you, anyway? What makes you an authority and gives you the audacity to write this? Shouldn't you have gone to some other church leaders to get their opinion on this before you attempted it? If God really called you to do this, what exactly did He say to you? How come you're the only one doing this; why aren't others in the church involved?

There is only one sufficient answer to those questions and ones like them: God wanted *me* to write SOKA. The work has been on my mind for years, and I constantly felt the pull of the Holy Spirit on me to write this book. What pressure! And I second your thoughts: "Who am I, God? I'm not worthy to do this. What will people think of me?" Nevertheless, the mandate of God never departed from me. The LORD required me to write this work—perhaps because I'm the biggest fool ever. Maybe it's because I came up in God outside of church and in an unconventional way, and He needed someone different to break the mold, so to speak. Maybe it's because He taught me to write pretty well and that was one of my gifts. Maybe it's because I had been growing in him for several years now, and developed enough spiritually where I could write it wholly dedicated to the process. Maybe it's because I have a high calling. Maybe it's because I have a heart for God…or maybe……just because. When God calls you, you never really know why He chose *you*. That's for Him to know, and it's for you to do whatever it is He asked.

Despite the fact that I delayed, and delayed, and delayed getting started on SOKA, with the 2014 U.S. State of the Union Address occurring just a couple of days before I started the book, I was reminded exactly of what God wanted me to do. God told me that he wanted me to publish SOKA. So here I am. The LORD told me when I first started the book that each and every day for the entire year, He wanted me to spend at least one-hour a day working on SOKA (until it's published). And I fearfully, anxiously, boldly did it—not having a fear of man, but of God. I certainly did not want to be the one that failed to get it done on time, do it wrong, or miss a single day of working on it. I prayed that God would guide me, and *that* He did.

Again, is SOKA intended to mock the U.S. government? Not necessarily. What it is intended to do, however, is to show the country, and the world that the real state, or status of anything that we need to be most focused on is the status of God's Kingdom. The LORD still reigns. And it is by His hand that man is either blessed or cursed. My goal with this book is to help the world become blessable. SOKA is a vehicle used by God to get people to Heaven, save their souls, get them in alignment with His will, wake them up, get them in position for great blessings, wealth, and abundance, and to bring them closer to Him. The Kingdom of God is superior to every kingdom on earth. This work is to help you—whether you are a believer or not—become informed about the times we're living in, as it pertains to God's Kingdom. You must become aware of the LORD's will, plans, and the status of His Body. That way, you may not only thrive in the present and the times to come, but also help others do the same. But above all, you and your household—family, friends, colleagues, associates, network, affiliates, and so on will be saved, capable of making it to Heaven one day through Jesus Christ. Man has gotten away from God. However, for God to make His Church without spot or wrinkle and fit to receive Jesus, upon His return, God has to make some changes. There is a gap between where God wants us, and where we are currently. That gap must be mended before God's perfect plans on earth can be completely fulfilled. This is an analysis of that gap. This is the *State of the Kingdom Address*.

CHAPTER 1: "BEHOLD, I COME QUICKLY!"

But the day of the Lord will come as a thief in the night; in the which the heavens shall pass away with a great noise, and the elements shall melt with fervent heat, the earth also and the works that are therein shall be burned up. -2Peter 3:10

He was fast-approaching. Slowly, yet the fear that overcame me seemed to speed up the time and decrease the distance between us. I wasn't ready. Surely, I signed up for the program, but I just wasn't ready for this much. It was too much, too fast, and too soon. "Wait. Who are you, and why won't you go away?" I thought. <Pause> No answer. I repeated myself, "Who are you, and why won't you go away?" Again, there was no answer.

Furious that he had the audacity to refute me, my face became enraged, and I rebuked him again: "You dirty, rotten devil! In the name of Jesus I command you to GO. GO. GO. Get out of here, devil!"

Nothing. He didn't say a word, but kept on drifting toward me.

He was no ordinary devil. This must have been Satan himself—more powerful than his subordinates. I rebuked his followers with no problem, but Satan was different, stronger. He just wouldn't go. Even the name of Jesus wasn't enough to drive him off. I knew people talked about the name of Jesus in church. I knew I fought many devils and cast them out in the name of Jesus. I knew I heard of miracles—people being raised from the dead, diseases departing, exorcisms, and the like—being done in the name of Jesus.

But all of that was wrong. It went right out the window when I stood face to face with who I knew was *Satan*.

How could I be bowing to Satan—on one knee, the thickness of the clouds surrounding me? The clouds were white, whiter than any white on earth. The entire background was illuminated, in the same white as the clouds. There was light coming from somewhere, but I couldn't see the source of it. I gazed at *Satan* as he approached me, drifting on the clouds as if he was on some sort of conveyor belt positioned under the clouds. I was about chest high in the cloud. "Where am I? Is this Heaven? If it is, why is Satan here?" I reasoned.

"You don't belong here, devil! What are you doing here?" I thought. He kept approaching me, drifting, not saying a word, drifting. Then suddenly, he seemed like he was about 100-feet away from me. I saw his red robe, another sign to me that this was none other than Lucifer—that fallen angel whom the world associated with the color red.

"The audacity of this devil!" I said to myself. "What red!" There is no red like this on earth. It is the red of all reds. It is the red that created reds. It is the color red from which all reds on earth were derived–bright, yet dark, dark, yet bright. It was magnificent in every characteristic of red that a red could be—the darkest, brightest, purest, richest, dullest red imaginable. How is it that this rotten, dirty devil adorns himself in a rich, red robe, as if he was a king? How is it that he has been given license by God to be in Heaven? How?

He drifted, still. The *devil* came even closer, and my entire situation began to unravel. I was scared, more afraid than I had ever been.

State of the Kingdom Address

Either God was going to have to deliver me, or the devil would destroy me. I couldn't do anything with him; he was too powerful.

As I stood in between the balance of fear and anger, I gave in. "I'm all yours. Go ahead, destroy me" I thought. I couldn't move. I couldn't budge. I couldn't stand up. I was in a trance—frozen in fear, amazement, awe, reverence, and submission—down on one knee.

I went from being afraid of being destroyed to being afraid of *Him* that caused me to kneel. And the anger that I had changed to calm and peace. I gazed at him. His gold crown was like none I had ever seen. It was pure gold, yet simple in nature. This crown had no jewels in it like many of the ones I had seen, or the ones I've heard about in the Bible. It was pure, solid gold, and flat, having no texture. It fit his head perfectly. I could see the points of the crown poking upward. I saw his brown hair, shiny and long, pressed down by the crown and reaching down to his shoulders. It shined, as if He was anointed with oil. His facial hair was also brown, and very neatly trimmed—exceedingly neat. "Wow, I guess they must have a nice barber here" I could have just as easily blurted out to him. What a sharp beard—and a very handsome man.

He was tall, and strong. But the most impressive thing about him was that he was powerful. I could feel His power and majesty radiating off of Him. "He must be a king", I figured. There was glory. There was honor. There was peace. There was compassion. There was forgiveness. There was protection. There was deliverance. There was provision. There was holiness. There was righteousness. There was love. All of this came from this man, whom I presumed to be Satan.

The closer He got, the more of His power and glory I felt. I felt His essence. I felt like I found the heart of God. I was living through Him, and He was fully in me. I was enveloped with Him, and no part of me was hidden. I was exposed and vulnerable. He could see my inward parts and he knew my heart. Yet, I felt comfortable. I developed a reverential fear of him. And despite the fact that I had on priestly garments, I could not stand up in the authority He had given me on earth. I had to kneel before the power of the LORD. I was at His mercy.

I woke up without him getting any closer to me than about 50 feet. I guess I was dirty, unprepared, immature, unfit, unworthy to meet Jesus face-to-face. I was young spiritually, and pretty uncommitted to Him. Yet, the one thing I knew from that dream was that if I called on the Lord, and asked Him to come and minister to me in my sleep, He would come. He knew me. He loved me. He heard me. And He answered my prayers.

THE NIGHT BEFORE

I went to bed the night before dealing with deep spiritual battle. I had devils all around me. They tormented me, trying to invoke fear in my heart, and drive me off of God's work. They knew the LORD's plan for me. Satan was bent on stopping me before I got in the power that I have now, and that I will get in the time to come. I fought him constantly, and became a master swordsman. I learned spiritual warfare because I had to; God trained me up in secret. He taught my hands to fight. Yet, I still wanted rest. I could fight, yes. But sometimes you just want to sleep in peace.

I prayed that night for the Lord to come and protect me. I asked Jesus specifically to come and minister to me, to comfort me, to watch over me as I slept. I asked Him to deal with me in whatever

State of the Kingdom Address

way He wanted. I gave my all to Him—at least for that night. And I went to sleep, in the heat of spiritual battle, in the midst of one of the most intense spiritual struggles of my life, in one of the most evil environments I had ever been in, within the walls of the enemy's territory, in the stronghold of the devil. Yet, I prayed to the Lord, and I found peace. I knew He would come to me and be with me.

Within a few minutes I was asleep, and eventually found myself being sucked up to Heaven. It was as if my body and spirit were separated. However, my body catapulted itself to Heaven at the same rate of speed as my spirit. And they both met up in Heaven to reconnect.

The deep spiritual battle that I had been in with Satan and his devils that week had convinced me that I was fighting him, yet again. I mean, I was casting out devils left and right that week—big devils, small devils, women devils, men devils, cat devils, orbs, voices, shadows, taunting devils, Satan himself, swarms of devils, solitary devils, groups of devils, all types of devils. I was going through some really intense, high-levels of spiritual warfare.

Naturally, when I was pulled into Heaven by the Spirit of the LORD, I figured the man in the red robe was Satan. He managed to overcome me, and put my body in a trance like on many other occasions. Though, I was wrong. I stood before Jesus Christ. Correction, I kneeled before Jesus, and I finally had peace in a situation where there was none.

Jesus is the King of Kings and Lord of Lords. Nobody, not even His saints, can stand before Him, unless He gives them permission. If someone tells you they stood before Jesus, it's only because He picked them up from off of their knees. Either that or He explicitly gave them permission. Your default position in the Lord's presence is on your knees or on your face, prostrate before Him.

THE DREAM INTERPRETATION

God gave me the interpretation of my dream. He showed me that Jesus is getting ready. The Lord is coming back to earth in full glory and judgment. He had on a red robe in my dream, which represents the blood, the redemption of the saints, war, impending judgment, and an urgent call for preparation from the saints. The dream signified the Lord's Second Coming.

I've had visions of Jesus coming down from Heaven wearing a white robe. That's indicative of the Rapture. Nevertheless, this dream was not so. He was wearing a red one.

The time of the Lord's return is fast approaching us. He showed me that His Kingdom is so imminent, that He already has His clothing on for His Second Coming. The Church is scarcely prepared for the Rapture. They are most certainly not prepared for His Second Coming, when He returns for war against Satan and his army, and for destruction.

It's for this cause that I write to you today. The Kingdom of Heaven is at hand. What are you doing to prepare yourself and your household for Jesus' return?

"TODAY"

One day I struggled with the doubt I had as to why God chose me to write *State of the Kingdom Address*. I thought for a moment about how I should write the book—what was the driving force behind it? Suddenly, I got an idea: "Write the book as if Jesus was coming back tomorrow." What do you want people to know? How can you help get them saved? How can you help people avoid hellfire? Who is in danger of falling into the abyss and how can you lift them up? Whose life is spiraling downhill and what would you tell them if you just had five minutes to talk to them face to face about God's will in their lives? "That's what I will do" I thought. Write the book as if Jesus was returning tomorrow!

Immediately as that thought danced around in my head, God corrected me with a powerful, undeniable word of rebuke: "No! No! No! ***Today***, David. Write the book as though I am coming back today!" I knew without a doubt that Jesus could return any minute. It wasn't simply a matter of days, months, or years. It wasn't even a matter of minutes, seconds, or milliseconds. It was a matter of moment to moment, time to time, situation to situation, uncertainty to uncertainty, and breath to breath. Jesus could return anytime He wanted, and the world was clearly not ready!

God needed the Church and the world to know that the imminent return of Jesus is upon us. People had to be ready to spend their eternity either with God in Heaven or with the devil in hell. Time is of the essence. And I now had a new perspective from which to write: I will write with urgency, boldness, bluntness, full conviction, and honesty. I will love the people to lead the people. I will not hold back from what God has me to say. No matter who this book empowers or offends, I will speak the truth of God's word as the Holy Spirit leads me. It's better for me to hurt feelings than hurt souls by allowing people to perish.

1Thessalonians 4:17 says, "Then we which are alive and remain shall be caught up together with them in the clouds, to meet the Lord in the air: and so shall we ever be with the Lord." It's apparent from this scripture, that the Lord is coming back to rapture His people. Nevertheless, many will be left behind.

According to Matthew 24:36, The Lord can come back to earth to rapture His Body of believers at any time: 'But of that day and hour knoweth no man, no, not the angels of Heaven, but my Father only.' In fact, many of the Biblical prophecies, which are said to be precursors of His return have already been fulfilled. Examples include the establishment of the country of Israel (1948), wars and rumors of wars, an increase in natural disasters, signs and wonders in the heavens, such as the four *blood moons* in 2014-2015, and the like. Even the building of the Third Temple in Jerusalem, another prerequisite of Jesus' return to earth (at least in the case of the Second Coming), is currently being organized by many of the Jewish people in Israel, particularly the lineage of the Levites (the ancient priesthood of Israel, consecrated by God to make sacrifices on behalf of the people). For example, all of the gold vessels for the temple have been created, priestly garments have been made, and the dimensions of the Third Temple have been laid out in accordance with the book of Leviticus. The Ark of the Covenant is also said to have been found—another required article of the *Third Temple*. The Third Temple, of course, is supposed to hold the gates that the Lord walks though when He returns to earth in the Second Coming. Find out more about the rebuilding of the temple at templeinstitute.com.

I've had at least three specific dreams where I saw Jesus face to face, in what appeared to be either the Rapture or the Second Coming. I described one of those dreams here in the opening chapter. I will detail another one in Chapter 2.

State of the Kingdom Address

The bottom line is this: the day will soon come when everyone has to see Jesus face to face—either for redemption or for destruction. Even if you don't believe Jesus is coming back, or coming back soon, you will do well to prepare just in case. At least you will be saved if He does come back at a time you least expect. If for any reason He doesn't return, all you will waste is time preparing. Alternately, if Jesus does come back and you're not prepared, you could lose your very soul.

GET READY

Get ready. As suddenly as Jesus left the earth, being taken up from the disciples, He can reemerge just as quickly. Do what you have to do to prepare yourself and your household for salvation. People often think about salvation in terms of where they will go when they die—with hopes of getting to Heaven. Yet, there aren't too many occasions that I hear of people talking about the return of Jesus. What if He returns even before you die a natural death? Are you ready?

I am reminded of the story of the ten virgins from Matthew 25:1:

> Then shall the kingdom of heaven be likened unto ten virgins, which took their lamps, and went forth to meet the bridegroom. And five of them were wise, and five were foolish. They that were foolish took their lamps, and took no oil with them: But the wise took oil in their vessels with their lamps. While the bridegroom tarried, they all slumbered and slept. And at midnight there was a cry made, Behold, the bridegroom cometh; go ye out to meet him. Then all those virgins arose, and trimmed their lamps. And the foolish said unto the wise, Give us of your oil; for our

lamps are gone out. But the wise answered, saying, Not so; lest there be not enough for us and you: but go ye rather to them that sell, and buy for yourselves. And while they went to buy, the bridegroom came; and they that were ready went in with him to the marriage: and the door was shut. Afterward came also the other virgins, saying, Lord, Lord, open to us. But he answered and said, Verily I say unto you, I know you not. Watch therefore, for ye know neither the day nor the hour wherein the Son of man cometh.

Nobody knows the day or the hour in which the Lord will come. In less than the blink of an eye, He can be here to rapture His Church. It's time to take life seriously. If you've been living separated from God and not living in conjunction with His will, it's time to wake-up. Eternity awaits you. Whether that's in Heaven with the LORD, or in hell with the devil, it's your choice. Don't proceed to the next chapter without making sure your soul is saved. Please pray this prayer:

Dear God,

I come to you as a sinner. I know that I was born in iniquity, and there is nothing I could have done myself to save me from my sins. LORD, I know that it's by your grace, and only through your Son, Jesus, that I am saved. Jesus, thank you for dying for me. I accept you as my Lord and Savior. God, forgive me for all of my sins. Teach me how to be a disciple. Help me live a life that is pleasing to you. And show me how I can help you spread the gospel. In Jesus Christ's name. Amen.

CHAPTER 2: ACT TWO: THE RAPTURE

In a moment, in the twinkling of an eye, at the last trump: for the trumpet shall sound, and the dead shall be raised incorruptible, and we shall be changed.
-1Corinthians 15:52

APRIL 3, 2014: JOURNAL ENTRY

The Trumpet

I woke up at 2AM the other morning after going to bed around 10PM. I couldn't sleep. I had to let the people know what just happened. So I went to my social media accounts, and this is what I wrote:

> Shaken. Up early. I just had a dream of the Rapture or Second Coming. Weird. A large angel was in the sky and blew a trumpet. Jesus appeared next to the angel in a bright light and white robe. The plot of His return unfolded right in front of my eyes. I looked up and begged Jesus, 'Nooooo, Lord! Not yet. Nooooo!' He faded out but the angel was still there. Jesus came back a second later in the light again. He was dressed in a white gown. I waved at him with my hands as if to stop Him. I cried, 'Noooo! Please stop.' He faded out again. The angel was still there. Jesus came back in the light

again. I was scared and panicking. Everybody was scared, trying to run away.

I didn't elaborate much beyond that on social media, as that wasn't the forum for it. But this is. I had been living in sin, away from where God wanted me spiritually. It's a tough thing to love God, and want to serve Him with all your might, and do right all the time, and put forth your best effort, yet fall short of the mark. I felt like God was not only dealing with me and my walk with Him, but He was dealing with the Body as a whole, wanting me to share my experience with the people of the LORD. He could return as instantly as He did in my dream. And it's an event that, when it unravels, will shake up the heavens to its core.

We hear a lot about the Rapture or God's judgment. However, the amount of sheer fear that came over me in that dream is indescribable. To see the LORD appear in the sky with the archangel blowing the trumpet is something you can never be ready to see. You can't muster up enough strength to be totally prepared to witness Jesus appearing in the sky with the archangel, even if every fiber of your spirit, soul, and body worked 24/7 for the rest of your life to get ready for Him. It's like going from your regular everyday life to being immediately propelled into a spiritual drama at the highest level possible. Jesus' return is that Great Play, that Act in God's classic story of love and judgment, good and evil, natural and supernatural, mortality and immortality, the divide between what we know and the unknowable that supersedes everything in life and the afterlife. It's that one event that God, Heaven, hell, the world, the heavens, angels, saints, Satan, devils, and everything on earth and the universe are waiting for. And in my dream, it all happened, suddenly. Epic. Terrifying. God glorifying.

I saw people running away from Jesus in fear. Pure pandemonium set in—cars and traffic fleeing from Him. Chaos. Everywhere. Even I, as a firm believer and devout Christian, was fearful of my own

State of the Kingdom Address

salvation. In my dream, as the Lord was in the sky, I cowered in fear under what seemed to be a rock, as Jesus was in the midst of returning. I still begged for Him to delay what was transpiring. Some may say, "Well David, if He was coming in the Rapture, why were you afraid? Maybe He was going to rapture you? Or maybe you were afraid because you weren't going to be raptured? Or maybe it wasn't the rapture that you saw, but His Second Coming, in which He judges the earth? Perhaps that's why you were afraid?" To that, I say, I'm pretty certain the dream represented the Rapture, as an archangel appeared with a trumpet, in accordance with 1Thessalonians 4:16. Nonetheless, when Jesus is in the sky, with all power, glory, and authority to judge the earth, you don't question whether or not it's the Rapture or Second Coming when it's occurring. You are overcome by reverential fear. And you try to evade His wrath. That's exactly what happened to me in the dream. I tried to plead with Him to give us time, and to spare us, while also trying to hide from the presence of who He was.

That was the first part of the dream. As I mentioned earlier, in the post I shared in my spiritual journal, and on social media, Jesus appeared several times in the *light*, in perfect synchronization with the angel's blowing of the trumpet. As the angel blew, Jesus appeared in a bright white light. The angel was also in the light, but Jesus' was much brighter than his. I prayed for Him to not come yet. He faded out and disappeared. He came back in the light, and as I prayed again, He disappeared. He came back once more in the light, and I prayed again. He then dimmed out, and disappeared. Some say, anytime the LORD does something three times, it's a sign of judgment. That may very well be true. Though, whether or not He ended up judging the earth in my dream, since He appeared three times in it, is beside the point; He eventually faded out and spared us. Nonetheless, Jesus is undoubtedly coming back real soon to judge us in actuality, in real time. And only a remnant of the people will be safe from the horrors, trials, and tribulations that are coming on earth and the inhabitants of it. It's much better to be a pig and get to Heaven than be an unsaved human being in these times. I now move onto Part Two of my dream that night, which describes the desperation that will come over us as we try to get on that last *train* to salvation before God's swift and decisive judgment is poured out upon the world.

The Train

Part Two of my dream occurred from inside of a train. I was a passenger on a train that was trying to escape from the wrath to come. The scene from Part One quickly shifted from night to day, and I was in an entirely new location. Yet, I was still experiencing the coming of the Lord, which I again, believe was the Rapture. I firmly believe that the LORD placed me in different scenarios to really understand how pervasive the return of Jesus is. Everyone will experience it, whether they are in America or Australia, whether it's daytime in one place and night in another, whether they are at home, or at work, conducting business, or buying lunch at a local restaurant. It will be one event that all people will simultaneously experience all over the world, and no one will be able to escape it.

In any event, I would describe that train in Part Two of my dream that night, as the *Rapture Train*. The only people that were onboard were those that, by God's grace, were able to be raptured by the LORD and escape the seven years tribulation to come. Let me just say that there were very few people on the train, but a whole lot of people off of it. In short, the vast majority of the world will not be raptured by the LORD. Unfortunately, many will die in the seven years of tribulation, which takes place after the Rapture. Others will die in the destruction on the earth during the Rapture, for example, when people are suddenly taken up to the sky to be with the LORD. Can you imagine driverless cars, as the saints of God are plucked from their automobiles? Think about airplane crashes that are likely going to occur as a result of Godly pilots being removed from earth in the Rapture. What about the spikes in crime, such as murders, terrorism, genocide, government coups, martial law, and similar things taking place as a result of law enforcement officials being

State of the Kingdom Address

raptured? Things like that are going to be occurring on every continent and in every country. Some will also die as martyrs during the 7 years of tribulation, because they will refuse to take the mark of the beast or worship his image, which is an entirely separate story in and of itself. However, those martyrs will be saved and able to enter Heaven, for not accepting the mark of the beast. After Jesus' coming, only a select few of those remaining on earth will be able to be saved, provided they survive the tribulation. Again, this is assuming that they are not raptured. That's why it's so important to make sure we're rapture-ready. If you're a lukewarm Christian right now, and barely serving the LORD when things are easy, as compared to how they will be, how much less are you likely to serve Him when tribulation sets in and the antichrist reigns? Think of all the persecution that will be upon believers. Think about how the Holy Spirit will not be on earth during the reign of the antichrist. People will not walk in His fruit, which is love, joy, peace, longsuffering, and others (See Galatians 5:22). Evil will rule the earth. Also, think about the pain, affliction, torture, and torment upon people who will profess the name of Jesus as their Lord during a time when the antichrist will rule the planet:

> Therefore rejoice, ye heavens, and ye that dwell in them. Woe to the inhabiters of the earth and of the sea! for the devil is come down unto you, having great wrath, because he knoweth that he hath but a short time (See Revelation 12:12).

Moreover, think about the punishment that the antichrist will inflict upon people that do not worship his image, the *abomination of desolation* (See Daniel 12:11).

It's better to get into God's Kingdom now and accept Jesus as your Lord and Savior, than to have to endure the difficult times that are coming upon the world during the tribulation. Becoming saved during the tribulation means you would have to leave it up to martyrdom to enter Heaven, as opposed to accepting Jesus and being raptured. Remember, nobody that accepts the mark of the beast will be saved; they are eternally damned, and headed for hell (See Revelation 14:11). That's why the Rapture is so significant. It's our only way out of the tribulation looming on the horizon.

In returning to my dream, the train was speeding by every train stop, and I felt like it was going at least 120 mph. Each stop had a number of passengers outside, waiting to get onboard. Yet, the train did not stop. They were screaming for it to stop, some were even throwing their hands up in disbelief as the train passed them. They were shocked that the train was speeding pass every stop, not even slowing down.

Some of the people already on the train were trying to get the train to stop and let other people on, but to no avail. Even as they attempted to open the doors while the train went by the stops, other passengers fought with them to prevent them. One guy on the train was fighting with everybody that got near the train doors to let on other passengers. It was like he was begging the engineer to go faster, or to keep going. We were all afraid of what was approaching us. We felt like the train was the only way we could escape that thing that was pursuing us so fast. We needed a fast mode of transport to dodge it. The train was it.

At one point on the ride, I tried to let other people onboard the train. However, the same man that was attacking everybody else also attacked me. We began fighting, and ended up on the ground wrestling. He would not let me open the door, and the train kept speeding forward. The train in my dream represented salvation, a way out of impending doom for the people on earth. Take heed. Get your train ticket in advance. Get to the train station. Get on the train. Get right with God, or get left behind.

Even up until that dream, I thought I was in a close relationship with God. I thought I was saved and knew how to get to Heaven. I presumed I was safe and "Rapture-ready". Despite that, I was not even prepared for Jesus to come back, according to the dream. I found myself in danger of being left behind or facing His wrath. I was terrified throughout the dream. If I, being a believer and dedicated servant of the LORD, found myself barely escaping judgment, how much less the wicked and unsaved?

Pretribulation Vs. Post-tribulation

There is general agreement in the church that the rapture will occur. However, the time that it will occur is debatable. Some believers follow the "Pretribulation theory". That's the belief that the church will be raptured before the seven years tribulation begins. The pre-trib theory is where the phrase "Left Behind" derived. In other words, if you're not raptured, you will be "left behind" to face the tribulation.

Other Christians subscribe to the "Post-tribulation theory". The consensus with post-tribulation is that the church will go through the seven years tribulation and be raptured right after Daniel 9:27 and Matthew 24:15.

I personally follow the pretribulation theory. I believe those that are saved and living in accordance with God's word at the time of Jesus' return will be raptured. Everyone else remaining on earth will experience the tribulation. However, even those facing the tribulation will still have the chance to become saved. They will more than likely need to become martyrs, enduring the difficulties of the seven years tribulation, while denouncing the anti-Christ.

Again, this is my personal opinion. Whatever view you follow, know that you are ultimately responsible for your own salvation.

CHAPTER 3: THE GLOBAL REVIVAL

Moreover there are workmen with thee in abundance, hewers and workers of stone and timber, and all manner of cunning men for every manner of work. Of the gold, the silver, and the brass, and the iron, there is no number. Arise therefore, and be doing, and the LORD be with thee. -1Chronicles 22:15-16

Underway is revival a. Reading that backwards, you get "A revival is underway." I wrote it backwards because that's how the Body of Christ, in large part, has been thinking when it comes to revival. We think, feel, act, and move backwards. Just as well I open this chapter with a backwards sentence!

We have been doing it all wrong. We wait and wait, and beg God to bring in revival:

> ➤ "LORD bring us revival."
> ➤ "Bless us with a revival God."
> ➤ "When revival comes..."
> ➤ "Give us revival Jesus."

You say that to God, but God is saying this to you:

"You are the revival!"

God sent you the revival over 2000 years ago. His name is Jesus Christ, and hopefully He lives in you. I said hopefully, because some people don't allow Him to live in them. Revival occurs when we adopt His mindset, His Spirit, His disposition, His character, and His victory over the devil, His heart, His passion, His drive, dedication, commitment, sense of purpose and responsibility, and self-sacrifice for the greater good. It occurs when we allow Jesus to reign in us, because that's the only way we can get those things I just mentioned.

We've been fighting God. He says, "Revival is now", we say, "Not now God, later". He says, "Do my will". We say, "Not thy will, but mine be done, God." He says, "Let me live in you; give me full control." We say, "Just take that part of me in the far right corner, LORD. That will be enough for you." He says, "Go left." We say, "I will go right, God." He says, "Start this business, ministry, or program." We say, "I will do this one instead, God." He says, "Write this book." We say, "I'm not really a writer, God. I'll just wait for somebody else to do it." How can we ever expect revival if we don't hearken to the voice of the Holy Spirit? We must let go and let God take us higher! We have to fully and completely give in to His will. We do that, and He will lead us to a spiritual revival so great that it would make all the ones in the past look like child's play. So again, I turn back to my opening statement of chapter 3. This time, I'll write it the right way, since we're beginning to think correctly: A revival is underway. And in particular, it's underway for the Body of Christ.

There is likely to be a clear distinction between the people of God and the people of the world. That's right. The Church, the true people of God (not the building) will progressively grow better and brighter, as the world grows worse due to rebellion against God. As the Church prospers spiritually, rededicating our lives to God, sanctifying ourselves, and obeying His word, so will our works prosper outwardly. Collectively.

Call this an overly optimistic view, but I believe God wants to come back to a Church where there is not one weak or feeble one among us. That's because we will all be blessed, glorious, successful, highly productive, effective, and caring for each other, the Body. Where there is lack, the abundance in the Church will reach it. Where there is abundance, the lack will request it. The revival that I speak of is indicative of the people of God stepping up to becoming that Church without spot or wrinkle (Ephesians 5:27) that He designed us to be. The 'perfecting' of the saints described in Ephesians 4:12 will compel believers to spiritual development. This, in turn, will enable them to discover their calling and fulfill their destinies as ministers of Jesus Christ.

The Church will set the tone for international revival. We will lead the way. It's not so much about a universal utopia, far from that. In fact, the world will spiral downhill in accordance with Matthew 24 and 2Timothy 3. In addition, much of the Church will suffer affliction, as Jesus describes in Matthew 24:9. Nonetheless, the Church, in general will still be advancing against the kingdom of darkness. We will serve as a beacon of hope, a safe-haven for people to run to during the difficult times in the world. Business failures? Run to the Church for help. Government problems? Talk to a spiritual leader in the Church. Marital issues? Go seek advice from the Church. Need some good Godly counsel? Reach out to the Church. Notice the capitalization of the word *Church*. Again, the church is not the institution. Get out of that mindset. The Church is you and me!

That's why we must step up in holiness, righteousness, and sanctification. We have to get ready for the influx of people that will be flocking to us in droves to get help. They will need us to lead them to God. And who in their right mind would follow the direction of a broke, busted, disgusted, sinning-comfortably-without-conviction, so-called member of the Body of Christ? Not many! If you're broke, you'd be hard pressed to get anybody to trust you to lead them to wealth and abundance. Our mindsets have to change in order for the revival to take effect. And that's what's going to occur...right now, in Jesus' name.

As a result of that new mindset, and the paradigm shift in our thoughts and behaviors, we will begin to move like Christ. We will really be His hands and feet. Then, and only then, will we be that City set on a hill that people will rush to in order to see and become a part of us! God wants to graft them into His Body! And when that happens, we will be the center, a well-respected and admired center, of human growth, development, success, and advancement. As the floodgates open, and the world storms into the Body of Christ, our primary duties are to embrace them, help meet their basic necessities (food, water, shelter), minister to them, lead them to salvation through Christ, and build them up in the Body of Christ through the word of God.

God will indeed glorify the Church to bring the world to the Cross. Keep in mind, I mean the true Church, not the institution, but the Body. There is some of His Church in church, but there is some of His Church outside of the church. Not all of the church is His Church. But all of His Church is His Church. It's important we make that distinction because the church will continue to spiral downhill with the world, but the true Church will be transformed and will glisten as a diamond in a room full of coal. Be sure you aren't just playing church, but are really living for Jesus and are a part of His Body. The LORD knows His people.

The Church will, doubtless, be a glorious people that Jesus will come back to—glorious in spirit (walking in faith, hope, love, unity, peace, power), and glorious in works, with blessings, signs, and wonders following. It's in this context—revival to the Body of Christ (and revival to certain facets of the world by way of our work)—that I proceed with this chapter.

A NEHEMIAH VISION

I was riding around in Baltimore a couple of years ago. I couldn't help but notice the run-down condition of many of the neighborhoods. Several of the houses and buildings were dilapidated. Being my hometown, I felt compassion for Baltimore, and for the people that lived there. I felt like Nehemiah in the Bible when he saw the fallen state of Israel, and the broken down wall of Jerusalem. Nehemiah wanted a revival for Israel. I wanted the same for Baltimore, for every major city in the U.S., and for the nation and world as a whole.

As I was meditating on the issue, God spoke to my heart and told me that Baltimore will be built up. And that we are living in the end-time revival. The LORD began speaking to me about how the Church has *it* all wrong. We think the revival is just a spiritual movement of God on earth to usher in the return of Jesus. That's part of it, and the most important part, of course. But God began showing me the unique, unprecedented times in which we're living.

It's interesting that long before Baltimore gained a national spotlight for the death of Freddie Gray at the hands of Baltimore City police officers, God already showed me that a revival was coming to the city.

A couple years after God told me that the neighborhoods would be renewed, the Freddie Gray incident occurred, with ensuing riots, media coverage, and plans to rebuild the city shortly thereafter. The government began taking a closer look at the ghetto, not just in Baltimore, but in other parts of the country, especially where people died unjustifiably at the hands of police. Ultimately, plans to develop Baltimore City, with new houses, shopping centers, community programs, and work opportunities in many of the impoverished neighborhoods, were well underway. In fact, I attended the Congressional Black Caucus sometime around July 2015 to discuss social issues like minorities dying unjustifiably by the hands of police officers. Congressmen, in conjunction with local business owners, church leaders, community organizations, and Baltimore citizens, were coming up with plans to improve the city, both economically and socially (relations between citizens and law enforcement). The goal was to fix issues like poverty, crime, and civil injustice, things that had long been overlooked by the masses, at least until an incident like the Baltimore riots of 2015 occurred.

A national revival is in the making. Unfortunately, sometimes it takes tragedy, disorder, and destruction for us to open our eyes, and say, "We have to change things." In Baltimore, God used the negativity associated with the Baltimore riots to bring people to the understanding of just how deep the underlying problems of our cities and communities run. We, indeed, need revival.

As I toured Baltimore City that day, a couple years before the Baltimore riots, God ministered to me about what *revival* was, what it meant, and how it would affect the world. Suddenly, I began to get revelation after revelation from the Holy Spirit as to what people could expect during the end-time revival.

David Newby

10 BASIC FACTS ABOUT THE REVIVAL

#1 - Unprecedented Times

You are living in unprecedented times! Can you believe it? You are a special child of God! Your birth and life have been divinely scheduled for the greatest moment in history. God made you a part of His End-Time Church. You could have been born in 1000 B.C., or 27 A.D., or 995 A.D. or any other period in history. However, you are right here, right now—smack-dab in the middle of a mighty awakening that God has placed on the earth to usher in the return of Jesus: 'You have come to the Kingdom for such a time as this'. You are an *end-time saint*, soldier, warrior of God. Can you imagine the number of miracles, signs, wonders, blessings, Godly projects, and victories for the Kingdom of Heaven that will be wrought through your hands? God, Jesus, the Holy Spirit, angels, and the great *Cloud of Witnesses* from Hebrews 12 watches. You have an audience of heavenly spectators, and they're pulling for you.

#2 - Biblical Signs and Wonders Will Occur

In the context of the end-time revival, the world will see signs and wonders performed by God's Church at a level they have never seen. And the world will marvel. People will begin seeing Biblical-like miracles take place on earth through the hands of believers. For example, Elijah rained fire from the sky in the book of Kings. Such miracles will occur in these end-times as well. There will be public displays of God's miracle-working power in the same way that Moses parted the Red Sea, or how Joshua parted the Jordan River, or how Joshua caused the sun and moon to stand still, or how Jesus walked on the water. I would not be surprised if saints of the Most High caused mountains to be literally and figuratively cast into the sea, to command storms to cease, to raise the dead, and to walk on water. In fact, I would be surprised if those things didn't happen during our lifetime.

#3 - The Church Will Do Greater Works Than Jesus

The miracles in the Bible were already done in the past, and many of them are being done today. But Jesus came and gave us more power. He sent us the Holy Spirit as well as Jesus' name. And when Jesus was amongst the disciples, He told them, "There will be greater, later!": Verily, verily, I say unto you, He that believeth on me, the works that I do shall he do also; and greater works than these shall he do; because I go unto my Father. -KJV John 14:12

#4 - The Revival Is Spiritual

God will pour out His Spirit on all flesh. The revival is spiritual in nature. It's intended to advance God's Kingdom from the inside out (from the spiritual to the physical). God will give us new power, new revelation, new wisdom, new spiritual gifts, new knowledge, new favor, and more. He will also help us build our lives in sanctification to Him. In other words, He will revive us spiritually as we wholly dedicate our lives to His will.

#5 - The Revival Is Physical

Why do people of God only believe that God will usher in a spiritual revival? This is plain wrong thinking. God is a God of creation, beauty, and magnificence. Heaven is His home and earth is His footstool. Earth was meant to be a microcosm of Heaven—just a small taste of what Heaven is like. We see this from the Garden of Eden before Adam fell. As I drove by that decrepit neighborhood in my hometown of Baltimore I told you about earlier, God told me that He would restore things (buildings, homes, offices, organizations, businesses) to beyond their former glory. The Lord told me that man will do the natural (Ex. Rebuild the homes, communities, buildings, etc.) but He will do the supernatural (revive us spiritually, and others)! As it will be in Baltimore, so will it be around the world in every city and community (particularly as it relates to God's people and the work of their hands). While the world around them may be falling apart, their homes, buildings, communities will be blessed. Consequently, as a results of God's grace and favor on His people, their businesses will flourish, ghettos and rural areas will be revived, nonprofits and charities will be built up and expanded, bank accounts will overflow, His resources will flow through the Kingdom, and soldiers in the Kingdom will share with each other like He originally intended it to be. Love will be exercised through the works of His saints. Believers will help God beautify the world. They will be largely responsible for showing off His spirit within them (love, patience, charity, etc.) and doing the works to back it up (starting Godly businesses, etc.). If you thought that all the great revivals throughout human history (like the Renaissance, the Harlem Renaissance, etc.) were something, they can in no way, shape, or form compare to the times in which you are living.

#6 - International Repentance and Turning Back to God

The U.S. and other countries around the world will return back to the Godly values that they were founded upon. They will return to their first love: 'Nevertheless I have somewhat against thee, because thou hast left thy first love' (See Revelation 2:4). In fact, I had a prophetic dream in March of 2012, which I discuss a little later, signifying this same event in the U.S. (the return back to our former values). Nations around the world will experience the same type of return back to God. Unfortunately, many of the evil events occurring around the world (terrorism, bombings, etc.) will cause people to seek God more and repent of their wrongs, ultimately returning back to His ordinances.

#7 - Glory to God

God will be glorified in the site of the entire world. The Lord will get His glory, and He will share it with no man, no government, no system, or anyone else. The entire earth, including the inanimate objects will once again glorify their Creator.

#8 - Glory to the Church

God will say to the world, "Look. This is my Body, my beloved, my anointed! Aren't they pretty? Look at my Spirit upon them. They look just like their *Daddy*. Look at them walk in my power and my victory!" Currently, the Church is far from being what God wants it to be. I'm here to tell you, God is about to change some things. He is about to change His Church. And He will altogether kick sin out of it.

#9 - Saints Will Receive Partial Blessings

You're not getting partially blessed. You're getting blessed partially. God is blessing you in partiality. He's being biased with you. He's separating the sheep from the goats, the wheat from the chaff, the righteous from the evil-doers. And He is going to show you off by blessing you in a real biased type of way. The LORD wants the world to know what they're missing by not serving Him. You are about to be blessed, just so God can be glorified. Your blessings will provoke the world to jealousy. The favor of God upon you will make you an enviable entity to those around you. Look at how Jacob's cattle were blessed and Laban's weren't in the book of Genesis (See Genesis 30). God will bless your stuff and mess your enemy's stuff up! He will separate you from their troubles and turmoil in the same manner that He separates light from darkness. Your hand will be blessed and your enemy's hands and works will be cursed by God (See Psalms 1:1-4)! He also blesses those that bless you and curses those that curse you (See Genesis 12:3).

#10 - The Wake-Up Call

Ever received a wake-up call from a hotel? Well, that's exactly what God is going to do to the world concerning His revival on earth. He's going to give unbelievers one last chance to hear the Word, and witness signs and wonders, and see the Saints of God being blessed by walking in oneness with the Lord. The unbelievers will hear the gospel, and they will have a chance to receive Jesus as their Lord and Savior. Many will be converted, and secure their spot in Heaven.

BIBLICAL REVIVALS

According to Reverend Robert Evans, *revival*, in the Bible, means any remarkable improvement in devotion to God by God's people (Source: Evans, 2016). For the purposes of shedding a little more light on revivals, as it relates to the Word of God, let's look at a number of revivals that occurred throughout Biblical history.

Jacob leads a revival

The first indication of revival that Jacob received from God was at Bethel. There, the LORD showed Jacob the ladder to Heaven and told him that he and his seed would be given all the land that he saw in his dream (See Genesis 28). The next occasion of a revival looming occurred for Jacob right before he was reunited with his brother, Esau in Genesis 32, where he also wrestled with God for a blessing:

State of the Kingdom Address

> And Jacob was left alone; and there wrestled a man with him until the breaking of the day. And when he saw that he prevailed not against him, he touched the hollow of his thigh; and the hollow of Jacob's thigh was out of joint, as he wrestled with him. And he said, Let me go, for the day breaketh. And he said, I will not let thee go, except thou bless me (See Genesis 32:24-26).

From Genesis 35, we see the consummation of a revival from the earlier preludes, as God instructs Jacob to build an altar to Him at Bethel, where Jacob first fled from Esau:

> And God said unto Jacob, Arise, go up to Bethel, and dwell there: and make there an altar unto God, that appeared unto thee when thou fleddest from the face of Esau thy brother. Then Jacob said unto his household, and to all that were with him, Put away the strange gods that are among you, and be clean, and change your garments: And let us arise, and go up to Bethel; and I will make there an altar unto God, who answered me in the day of my distress, and was with me in the way which I went. And they gave unto Jacob all the strange gods which were in their hand, and all their earrings which were in their ears; and Jacob hid them under the oak which was by Shechem. And they journeyed: and the terror of God was upon the cities that were round about them, and they did not pursue after the sons of Jacob (See Genesis 35:1-5).

God appeared to Jacob again, confirming His promises to him:

> And God said unto him, Thy name is Jacob: thy name shall not be called any more Jacob, but Israel shall be thy name: and he called his name Israel. And God said unto him, I am

God Almighty: be fruitful and multiply; a nation and a company of nations shall be of thee, and kings shall come out of thy loins; And the land which I gave Abraham and Isaac, to thee I will give it, and to thy seed after thee will I give the land (See Genesis 35:10-12).

Samuel leads Israel to revival

Samuel leads Israel to return to the LORD with all their heart:

> And it came to pass, while the ark abode in Kirjathjearim, that the time was long; for it was twenty years: and all the house of Israel lamented after the LORD. And Samuel spake unto all the house of Israel, saying, If ye do return unto the LORD with all your hearts, then put away the strange gods and Ashtaroth from among you, and prepare your hearts unto the LORD, and serve him only: and he will deliver you out of the hand of the Philistines. Then the children of Israel did put away Baalim and Ashtaroth, and served the LORD only. And Samuel said, Gather all Israel to Mizpeh, and I will pray for you unto the LORD. And they gathered together to Mizpeh, and drew water, and poured it out before the LORD, and fasted on that day, and said there, We have sinned against the LORD. And Samuel judged the children of Israel in Mizpeh (See 1Samuel 7:2-6).

King Asa leads a revival during the split of Israel and Judah

King Asa righted many of the wrongs committed by King Solomon, who had gone after other gods to appease his foreign wives. Asa also instituted many laws to turn the people back to God, at a time that he was blessed with peace, prosperity, and protection from foreign invasion (See 2Chronicles 14-15):

> And Asa did that which was good and right in the eyes of the LORD his God: For he took away the altars of the strange gods, and the high places, and brake down the images, and cut down the groves: And commanded Judah to seek the LORD God of their fathers, and to do the law and the commandment. Also he took away out of all the cities of Judah the high places and the images: and the kingdom was quiet before him. And he built fenced cities in Judah: for the land had rest, and he had no war in those years; because the LORD had given him rest. Therefore he said unto Judah, Let us build these cities, and make about them walls, and towers, gates, and bars, while the land is yet before us; because we have sought the LORD our God, we have sought him, and he hath given us rest on every side. So they built and prospered (See 2Chronicles 14:2-7).

Elijah brings revival during a drought

Then we see the revival brought forth by Elijah. Elijah pronounced a drought during the time of King Ahab. Three and a half years later, rain came according to the word of God through Elijah. God wrought a miracle through the hands of Elijah in the sight of King Ahab, Israel, and the prophets of Baal (See 1Kings 18):

> And it came to pass at the time of the offering of the evening sacrifice, that Elijah the prophet came near, and said, LORD God of Abraham, Isaac, and of Israel, let it be known this day that thou art God in Israel, and that I am thy servant, and that I have done all these things at thy word. Hear me, O LORD, hear me, that this people may know

that thou art the LORD God, and that thou hast turned their heart back again. Then the fire of the LORD fell, and consumed the burnt sacrifice, and the wood, and the stones, and the dust, and licked up the water that was in the trench. And when all the people saw it, they fell on their faces: and they said, The LORD, he is the God; the LORD, he is the God. And Elijah said unto them, Take the prophets of Baal; let not one of them escape. And they took them: and Elijah brought them down to the brook Kishon, and slew them there. And Elijah said unto Ahab, Get thee up, eat and drink; for there is a sound of abundance of rain (See 1Kings 18:36-41).

Jonah leads a revival

A revival also occurred through Jonah. God told him to prophecy to Nineveh that God would destroy their city. They immediately repent, and obey God, turning the LORD's wrath away from them (See Jonah Chapters 1 - 4):

> And Jonah began to enter into the city a day's journey, and he cried, and said, Yet forty days, and Nineveh shall be overthrown. So the people of Nineveh believed God, and proclaimed a fast, and put on sackcloth, from the greatest of them even to the least of them. For word came unto the king of Nineveh, and he arose from his throne, and he laid his robe from him, and covered him with sackcloth, and sat in ashes. And he caused it to be proclaimed and published through Nineveh by the decree of the king and his nobles, saying, Let neither man nor beast, herd nor flock, taste any thing: let them not feed, nor drink water: But let man and

State of the Kingdom Address

beast be covered with sackcloth, and cry mightily unto God: yea, let them turn every one from his evil way, and from the violence that is in their hands. Who can tell if God will turn and repent, and turn away from his fierce anger, that we perish not? And God saw their works, that they turned from their evil way; and God repented of the evil, that he had said that he would do unto them; and he did it not (See Jonah 3:4-10).

Revival of King Jehoshaphat of Judah

Following King Asa, Jehoshaphat became King of Judah. He reigned at the same time that Ahab reigned in Israel, during the time of Elijah and Elisha, who were prophets of Israel, and not Judah (See 2Chronicles 19 and 20). King Jehoshaphat was influenced by Jehu to return to God:

> And Jehu the son of Hanani the seer went out to meet him, and said to king Jehoshaphat, Shouldest thou help the ungodly, and love them that hate the LORD? therefore is wrath upon thee from before the LORD. Nevertheless there are good things found in thee, in that thou hast taken away the groves out of the land, and hast prepared thine heart to seek God (See 2Chronicles 19:2-3).

Afterward, Jehoshaphat brought righteous judgment back to Israel by empowering the Levites, judges, priests, and chiefs of the fathers of Israel to judge the people:

> Moreover in Jerusalem did Jehoshaphat set of the Levites, and of the priests, and of the chief of the fathers of Israel, for

the judgment of the LORD, and for controversies, when they returned to Jerusalem. And he charged them, saying, Thus shall ye do in the fear of the LORD, faithfully, and with a perfect heart. And what cause soever shall come to you of your brethren that dwell in their cities, between blood and blood, between law and commandment, statutes and judgments, ye shall even warn them that they trespass not against the LORD, and so wrath come upon you, and upon your brethren: this do, and ye shall not trespass (See 2Chronicles 19:8-10).

In 2Chronicles 20, Jehoshaphat led Israel to worshipping God, which led them to victory over their enemies, Moab and Ammon:

> And Jehoshaphat bowed his head with his face to the ground: and all Judah and the inhabitants of Jerusalem fell before the LORD, worshipping the LORD. And the Levites, of the children of the Kohathites, and of the children of the Korhites, stood up to praise the LORD God of Israel with a loud voice on high. And they rose early in the morning, and went forth into the wilderness of Tekoa: and as they went forth, Jehoshaphat stood and said, Hear me, O Judah, and ye inhabitants of Jerusalem; Believe in the LORD your God, so shall ye be established; believe his prophets, so shall ye prosper (See 2Chronicles 20:18-20).

King Hezekiah of Judah

From 2Chronicles 29 - 32, King Hezekiah of Judah led God's people to revival, following a number of kings before him leading the people of Judah away from God. Hezekiah took the throne when justice and spirituality had declined dramatically in Judah. Hezekiah was in office at the time when Israel was destroyed by foreign invaders, which prompted him to ensure the same fate would not be seen in Judah. So he worked to rededicate the nation back to worship of God:

> And he brought in the priests and the Levites, and gathered them together into the east street, And said unto them, Hear me, ye Levites, sanctify now yourselves, and sanctify the house of the LORD God of your fathers, and carry forth the filthiness out of the holy place. For our fathers have trespassed, and done that which was evil in the eyes of the LORD our God, and have forsaken him, and have turned away their faces from the habitation of the LORD, and turned their backs. Also they have shut up the doors of the porch, and put out the lamps, and have not burned incense nor offered burnt offerings in the holy place unto the God of Israel. Wherefore the wrath of the LORD was upon Judah and Jerusalem, and he hath delivered them to trouble, to astonishment, and to hissing, as ye see with your eyes. For, lo, our fathers have fallen by the sword, and our sons and our daughters and our wives are in captivity for this. Now it is in mine heart to make a covenant with the LORD God of Israel, that his fierce wrath may turn away from us (See 2Chronicles 29:4-10).

The revival during Hezekiah's days helped Judah gain an increased level of God's protection from their enemies, as evidenced in 2Chronicles 32:22: 'Thus the LORD saved Hezekiah and the inhabitants of Jerusalem from the hand of Sennacherib the king of Assyria, and from the hand of all other, and guided them on every side.'

King Josiah ushers in revival in Judah

King Josiah led the last great revival during the times of the kings of Israel and Judah. I have elaborated on the revival through King Josiah in other sections of this book. So, for that reason I will omit it here. However, revival through Josiah epitomizes what God is doing on earth in this day. He is bringing in the last great revival of our times through righteous men and women of God placed in positions of leadership. You can find out more about Josiah in 2Kings 22 – 23.

Daniel and intercessory prayer

Through intercession, Daniel learned to bring in new blessings from God. During the 70 years exile of the Jewish people into Babylon, Daniel studied the writings of Jeremiah, which declared a return back to God. Daniel became committed to prayer in order to see prophecy fulfilled as discussed in Daniel 9:

> In the first year of his reign I Daniel understood by books the number of the years, whereof the word of the LORD came to Jeremiah the prophet, that he would accomplish seventy years in the desolations of Jerusalem. And I set my face unto the Lord God, to seek by prayer and supplications, with fasting, and sackcloth, and ashes: And I prayed unto the LORD my God, and made my confession, and said, O Lord, the great and dreadful God, keeping the covenant and mercy to them that love him, and to them that keep his commandments; We have sinned, and have committed iniquity, and have done wickedly, and have rebelled, even by departing from thy precepts and from thy judgments: Neither have we hearkened unto thy servants the prophets, which spake in thy name to our kings, our

princes, and our fathers, and to all the people of the land (See Daniel 9:2-6).

Haggai and Zechariah show signs of revival

In Haggai 1, God instructs Israel to rebuild His house after it had been lying waste:

> Then came the word of the LORD by Haggai the prophet, saying, Is it time for you, O ye, to dwell in your cieled houses, and this house lie waste? Now therefore thus saith the LORD of hosts; Consider your ways. Ye have sown much, and bring in little; ye eat, but ye have not enough; ye drink, but ye are not filled with drink; ye clothe you, but there is none warm; and he that earneth wages earneth wages to put it into a bag with holes. Thus saith the LORD of hosts; Consider your ways. Go up to the mountain, and bring wood, and build the house; and I will take pleasure in it, and I will be glorified, saith the LORD (See Haggai 1:3-8).

Zerubbabel, Joshua the son of Josedech, and the remnant of the people

> And the LORD stirred up the spirit of Zerubbabel the son of Shealtiel, governor of Judah, and the spirit of Joshua the son of Josedech, the high priest, and the spirit of all the remnant of the people; and they came and did work in the house of the LORD of hosts, their God, In the four and twentieth day of the sixth month, in the second year of Darius the king (See Haggai 1:14-15).

In Zechariah 1:1-6, the word of God came to Zechariah expressing displeasure with the people:

> The LORD hath been sore displeased with your fathers. Therefore say thou unto them, Thus saith the LORD of hosts; Turn ye unto me, saith the LORD of hosts, and I will turn unto you, saith the LORD of hosts. Be ye not as your fathers, unto whom the former prophets have cried, saying, Thus saith the LORD of hosts; Turn ye now from your evil ways, and from your evil doings: but they did not hear, nor hearken unto me, saith the LORD. Your fathers, where are they? and the prophets, do they live for ever? But my words and my statutes, which I commanded my servants the prophets, did they not take hold of your fathers? and they returned and said, Like as the LORD of hosts thought to do unto us, according to our ways, and according to our doings, so hath he dealt with us (See Zechariah 1:2-6).

God then gives Zechariah His plan for revival to His house

> So the angel that communed with me said unto me, Cry thou, saying, Thus saith the LORD of hosts; I am jealous for Jerusalem and for Zion with a great jealousy. And I am very sore displeased with the heathen that are at ease: for I was but a little displeased, and they helped forward the affliction. Therefore thus saith the LORD; I am returned to Jerusalem with mercies: my house shall be built in it, saith the LORD of hosts, and a line shall be stretched forth upon Jerusalem. Cry yet, saying, Thus saith the LORD of hosts; My cities through prosperity shall yet be spread abroad; and the LORD shall yet comfort Zion, and shall yet choose Jerusalem (See Zechariah 1:14-17).

State of the Kingdom Address

Revival through Nehemiah after the Jewish exile to Babylon

Zerubabbel, Ezra, and Nehemiah experienced signs of a revival during the times that the Jews were returning from exile in Babylon. However, Nehemiah ushered in a more significant revival than the other two. We see in Nehemiah 8 that Ezra brings the Jews back to the law of God:

> And Ezra opened the book in the sight of all the people; (for he was above all the people;) and when he opened it, all the people stood up: And Ezra blessed the LORD, the great God. And all the people answered, Amen, Amen, with lifting up their hands: and they bowed their heads, and worshipped the LORD with their faces to the ground (See Nehemiah 8:5-6).

Earlier in the book of Nehemiah, we see Nehemiah initiate the rebuilding of the wall of Jerusalem, which signifies a spiritual rebuilding of proper worship to God:

> We have dealt very corruptly against thee, and have not kept the commandments, nor the statutes, nor the judgments, which thou commandedst thy servant Moses. Remember, I beseech thee, the word that thou commandedst thy servant Moses, saying, If ye transgress, I will scatter you abroad among the nations: But if ye turn unto me, and keep my commandments, and do them; though there were of you cast out unto the uttermost part of the heaven, yet will I gather them from thence, and will bring them unto the place that I have chosen to set my name there (See Nehemiah 1:7-9).

These revivals throughout Biblical history are clear evidence that every so often, God does something powerfully profound to us spiritually that changes the face of the globe. A present-day revival is in the making, and God is using this generation to bring it forth.

7 MOUNTAINS OF REVIVAL

Imagine what a revival would look like in the world, if things just exponentially improved for all of us, in all areas. People think of revivals based on our past experiences or what happened in history. I assure you, the revival that's coming to earth will blow your mind. It's God's revival. He will do things His way, in His power, in His wisdom, with His ultimate plan in mind—to glorify the Church in these last days. God will cause a spectacular shift in the *7 Mountains* (7 areas in which life can be divided into): Religion, government, business, family, media, education, and arts & entertainment.

Let's explore how a revived world would look in all of these major areas of life.

#1 - Religion

God builds up our spirit:

People will be built up spiritually, no longer walking around in shame, discouragement, hopelessness, and things of that nature. Instead, they will walk in faith, hope, and love (See 1Corinthians 13:13). The peace of God will overtake them and it will reassure them that God is with them.

State of the Kingdom Address

People will come closer to God and experience a real relationship with Him:

People are still walking around as if the veil of the Holy Temple had never been rent when Jesus died for them (See Matthew 27:50-51). They act like they're separated from God, as if He's some mystical being that will pounce on them if they dared to come before His throne. They know God and believe in Him, but the close level of intimacy with the Father is often missing. Christians should see God as a loving Father who wants to comfort and console us. He is personable, desiring for believers to go to His throne boldly and even with the innocence and freedom of children.

People will learn to walk in power:

"Go in this thy might, and thou shalt save Israel from the hand of the Midianites", said the angel of the Lord to Gideon in Judges 6:14. Believers will walk in the power they are given—in the name of Jesus, in the Holy Spirit that dwells in you, in the weapons of warfare, in the grace of God.

The devil will be exposed and people will learn how to effectively battle him:

Satan hates to be exposed for who he is. He likes for Christians to fear him, underestimate him, overestimate him, or be oblivious to him. As more people get revelation from God about the traps and tricks of the devil, they will begin to share that information with other believers. It's like an army, where all the soldiers in it share intelligence with their comrades about the weaknesses, strategies, and tactics of the enemy. The devil will be exposed and the attacks of the Church on the forces of evil will be more effective as a result. They will be hitting Satan in his soft spot, where there is no armor or protection.

Spiritual rebirth will trickle down into worldly successes:

"Seek ye first the kingdom..." will be lived by the saints of God. Consequently, prosperity will flourish in the physical world for them. God will make those that are anchored in Him the head and not the tail. They will become the envy of all men.

Hidden Warriors will arise:

There is an obscure army in God's Kingdom. This army is full of warriors or *warriors-in-training*. These men and women of God have been trained in secret. They have undergone much more than just boot camp; they received training in the special forces of God's army. They are revolutionaries, conquerors, commanders, and leaders. They have learned battle in the highest degree. They know their spiritual weapons by name and by function. They know how to use their weapons and they are familiar with when to use what. They know what types of damage the weapons can inflict upon the enemy.

These people have been built up in many ways, and toughened, spiritually, mentally, emotionally, psychologically, socially, and physically. They know how to be hungered or at thirst. They are able to fight in any circumstance, and their success does not depend on their condition, but on their faith and determination.

They can be clean and well dressed, or dirty and *naked*. They can have much, or have little. They can be served, or hunt for their food. They can be warm or cold. They can be rich or poor. They can abase or abound. They can fight in the jungle or in a cave. They can battle in a business meeting or on a street corner. They can fight the devil or one of his subjects. They fight physical manifestations of Satan, or they can just fight his spirit. They can fight spirits directly, or they can bring under control a man possessed by spirits. They can overcome with

State of the Kingdom Address

love, or they can overcome with boldness, and the power of their actions and decisions. They are not just soldiers, but warriors of God. They are members of the LORD's elite forces, who can battle anywhere, anytime, and in any way for the glory of God and to advance His Kingdom on earth. They were trained up by God, and it's through His spirit that they were made effective soldiers for the Kingdom.

Men like Joshua, David, Elijah, Paul, Peter, Gideon, Samson, and Elisha exist today. Women like Deborah and Jael from the book of Judges, are alive today. They are warriors and rebels of the Most High God. They are sent out to stir up trouble against the forces of darkness and destroy the works of the devil. They will walk in the spirit of their warrior ancestors. The full power of God Almighty will be resident in all of them. And Jesus will be the name that they use to prevail against their enemies.

High levels of spiritual warfare will occur between good and evil. It will not be a surprise for God's elect to see plain sight manifestations of Satan himself. They will see his face. They will see his body. They will recognize him when he shows up, and they will know that they are in the heat of the battle. This deeper level of battle is for God's warriors. They have by and large been trained outside of the church. They are not a part of the status quo. They may have attended church, and may still even go to church regularly. However, their real spiritual training occurred outside of the church. God brought them up Himself, in unconventional ways, through hurts, pains, challenges, and situations in which the world over cannot relate. They are His leaders, and will be responsible for teaching God's Church how to fight. They will impart their skills and knowledge onto church parishioners. They will teach them how to have faith, walk in the power of God, use their weapons of warfare, identify the devil, take land from the enemy, and destroy his works.

This rising army is not a part of "church as is". Quite frankly, if that were the case the army of God wouldn't advance much. We would continue to be doing the same things we've done for decades. To see a change, God has to raise up revolutionaries with revolutionary mindsets. These people are just different. And no matter what they do, what they say, how they act, how they talk, what they wear, they simply do not fit in with everyone else. God made them different intentionally, and He refuses to allow them to conform to the norms of church and society. They are set a part to be leaders of a spiritual revolution on earth.

Help for the lost:

The world is lost. Many people are running around looking for God, but are finding Him in all the wrong places. They are becoming vulnerable to the many religious philosophies out there that leads them away from the truth. The troubles that will come on the followers of the world will demonstrate to them that they are not servants of the Most High. They have been duped into believing the lies of the devil, and they will pay for it dearly.

Nevertheless, God will send for them. He will send His true servants to them in order to reveal to them the gospel. Leaders of God will be as servants once again. They will humble themselves, and they will go to the pits, valleys, caves, prisons, dungeons, troubles, pain, and difficulties of those in need. And they will sit with them and help them get to know God and His word. The lost will be found, and God will not let one of His sheep be taken by the devil. Whom the LORD marked as His will be His; and no man or devil shall take them away from Him: 'And I give unto them eternal life; and they shall never perish, neither shall any man pluck them out of my hand' (See John 10:28).

The Church will grow tremendously as nonbelievers start to pour in, hungry for a relationship with God. Church attendance, public displays of praise and worship, and a love for God will increase, astounding the world. Former sinners will develop a zeal for God and become the agents of change in their communities and amongst their friends. God will be preached about more in every area of life, and in every industry. He will once again be glorified in this world.

#2 Government

God will bring *His* political leaders back to His will:

Expect God's political leaders to consent to the ways of God and begin to shape their policies around godliness. In viewing the U.S. State of the Union Address a couple years ago, I couldn't help but notice the words, "In God We Trust" on the wall behind the president. A year later, during another State of the Union Address, the same words were visible on the wall in the backdrop: "In God We Trust". Year by year, I suppose that same background remains during SOTU (See image here: http://rol.st/1M8atVF). How ironic. The U.S. has been a witness against itself by using those contradictory words in one of the most popular and important annual speeches in the world. "In God we trust", but *from* God we turn. In the SOTU speech in 2014, the president went on to promote gay marriage. Like many political leaders, the president is often a product of his environment, of that formidable political system that sucks the spiritual life and ambition out of our leaders. You can be somewhat Godly, says the system; but not enough to deviate from the mainstream way of thinking. It's a matter of live by the system, die by the system. If you give your very heart and soul to the system to get elected, chances are you're going to have to continually serve it to stay in office. It's time for a spiritual transformation in world leadership. We need leaders to counter the system, step up, and represent God the right way:

> Cry aloud, spare not, lift up thy voice like a trumpet, and shew my people their transgression, and the house of Jacob their sins. Yet they seek me daily, and delight to know my ways, as a nation that did righteousness, and forsook not the ordinance of their God: they ask of me the ordinances of justice; they take delight in approaching to God (See Isaiah 58:1-2).

The nations will be changed by its leadership:

God will place into office more Godly leaders who will lead forth a spiritual revival on earth. Wicked people in high places will be brought down. The world has seen it happen throughout the earth, in Iraq with Saddam Hussein, in Libya with Kaddafi, and in Afghanistan with Osama bin Laden, to name just a few. New leaders will emerge in government and they will precipitate a change to their respective countries.

A spirit of Godly solidarity will sweep across the globe:

Government leaders will help bring about solidarity throughout their nation by promoting spirituality. From country to country, despite any political, economic, or social differences between nations, the common thread of faith will bring people together. People will be on the same accord—to improve the world by serving and obeying God.

State of the Kingdom Address

National Day of Revival:

After hearing so much about the National Day of Prayer here in the U.S., I thought it only appropriate to create a National Day of Revival™. The National Day of Revival™ is an event, much like the NDP, with its spiritual focus. However, the NDR brings people together for the sake of reviving the world spiritually, economically, and socially. The NDR will kickoff sometime around or before 2020 in the United States, more than likely at one of our historic landmarks or parks. Examples include Fort McHenry (the birthplace of the U.S. National Anthem), not just because I'm a Baltimore native, but because Fort McHenry is a historic landmark as well as a patriotic symbol of solidarity for U.S. citizens, in that we are united by the U.S. anthem. Another location we are expecting to launch the NDR is at the Washington Monument in Washington, D.C., for many of the same reasons as Fort McHenry. My goal with the National Day of Revival™ is to help improve the spiritual state of the country, which would result in a greater dedication to God, a greater love and service of country and fellow citizens, more outpouring of love and peace on people around the world, and greater blessings in the country, through greater efforts, responsibility, commitment, work, sacrifice, and productivity by all. In short, people would step up and work harder to do better for God, for their country, for their families, for their fellow citizens, and for themselves. Such a movement would transfer to the world, as people all over the planet would begin to see that we are all citizens of the earth, placed here to be good, productive, and prosperous people. The National Day of Revival™ is coming soon. It won't just be in the U.S. And it won't just be a one day thing. It will occur in countries all around the world.

Pumpkins falling out of the sky:

The National Day of Revival™ brings me to a dream I had a few years ago. The dream, which I'll describe in a little more detail in Chapter 4, was of Pastor Rod Parsley of World Harvest Church in Columbus, Ohio, leading the U.S. back to its heritage. Pumpkins were falling out of the sky, and the pastor was telling everybody to eat the fruit of the land, and to enjoy it. The pumpkin is a sign of harvest, and national heritage here in the U.S. People in the U.S. celebrate thanksgiving, and much of our history and how the country was founded seems to revolve around the pumpkin. To make a long story short, the pastor was helping to lead the nation back to its roots, its foundation, the spiritual principles in which it was founded. The National Day of Revival™, and the dream of the pastor go hand-in-hand. God is going to start a major revival in America. It could very well start from one of its historic land marks, like a Fort McHenry.

#3 Business

Better financial stewardship:

Good financial stewardship will be more important to business owners than it was in the past. People will begin to see how their wasteful spending has cost them the ability to meet their basic necessities. Luxuries will be a thing of the past for some who were used to it. Their disrespect of money will lead them to poverty: 'He that loveth pleasure shall be a poor man: he that loveth wine and oil shall not be rich' (See Proverbs 21:17).

Alternately, people that are wise with money will be blessed. God will reward those that do good with their finances, and punish those that do bad. As a result, the wealth of the wicked and unwise will end up in the bank accounts of God's wise and faithful servants. This is the *wealth turnover*.

State of the Kingdom Address

The 'new' wealthy will come from everywhere, from every industry, background, location, socio-economic status, race, culture, and denomination. Believers will get exalted very quickly due to their faithfulness with the little in which God entrusted them. They will also be used by God to confound the wise, prudent businessmen, and bring them to envy. The world will see that it's individuals that know how to operate spiritually that will have the greatest wealth on earth.

Moreover, many businesses, big and small will simply cease to exist. They will fall. They are, especially those businesses that knew to do right, were warned of their ways, but never gave in to God. Their penalty is to be destroyed. Millionaires and billionaires who have gotten money by building businesses without God in them, will see their enterprises lost. In most cases, the righteous will be the new owners of the *property*. It will be supernaturally turned over to them. Many business empires built on pornography, drug dealing, extortion, stealing, bribery, theft, prostitution, fornication, drunkenness, gossip, sex, violence, and any type of crime and ungodliness will be brought down. The financial gains from them will end up being divinely transferred to Godly businesses, movements, and programs that will be used to glorify God and spread His word throughout the earth. Much of the world's wealth is already laid up for the just. However, in these end-times, the people of God will take it by force. And they know how to take it by force, the spiritual force of faith and powerful, unfathomable works following. These people are spiritual giants, operating very effectively in the spiritual realm and proficient at spiritual warfare.

Additionally, God's wise and faithful servants who get entrusted with the wealth of the world will use much of it to do God's work. There will be an inconceivable surge in charitable giving. There will be an increase in the number of community organizations being built around the planet. There will also be a spike in the number of humanitarian social movements around the world. That's because the 'newly rich' will begin to express their compassion toward the needy through their giving. It's a case of them putting their money where their heart is.

Even some well-known wealthy people who are in the secular world will become converted into Christians. As a result, their wealth and influence will be used to help more people around the world with issues like hunger, poverty, sickness, and disease. Big names in entertainment, sports, and business will be at the forefront of a social revolution—one intended to improve living conditions and the state of humanity all across the globe. Imagine if a Bill Gates, Warren Buffet, Richard Branson, or other billionaire business mogul suddenly became a devout Christian. That would more than likely lead to them tithing a percentage of their income specifically for God's work on earth. For instance, 10% of Bill Gates' $80 billion net worth is about $8 billion. Much of that money could be used to resolve some of the world's biggest problems, such as famine, sickness, and homelessness, not to mention spread the gospel.

Clearly, these individuals already give an extraordinary amount of money to charity. However, I would argue that by them becoming Christians and giving their money to charity, they will have a bigger impact on the world. One reason is because they would have more of God's favor and blessings upon them and their lives as a result of being in the Kingdom and working exclusively for the LORD. That would equate to more money for them, which means they could sow even more money. Second, they would more than likely give to Christian organizations that operate according to God's will. Their financial gifts would be able to further those organizations' mission and reach around the globe, which would help save the lost. Third, their money would be used strictly to back causes in line with Kingdom advancement. For example, they would not support movements like homosexual marriages and similar issues that are contrary to God's word. They will not be wasting money on unnecessary causes. Instead, their money will be used to fund important God-ordained movements, businesses, and projects. Think of all the billions of dollars that are essentially wasted around the world, from country to country, by nonbelievers supporting ungodly causes. As money is spent right, the right results will come.

Another thing concerning the revival in business is that God will beautify his Church through business and wealth accumulation. In other words, many believers, whether or not they are proficient in business, will emerge as business moguls in every area of life, whether in real estate or trading stocks. God will show off His Church with great wealth and business successes. The luxurious lifestyles that are lived by many of today's wealthy in the secular world will be seen in the Church. Faithful saints of God will be comfortable, no longer poor and destitute, but blessed financially. Hungry people will be full. Thirsty people will be quenched. This is the inheritance of God's people. The fatted calf will be slim, and the thin cattle will be fat (See Ezekiel 34:17-23). God has judged the fat, according to the book of Ezekiel. The LORD will redeem all of those found thin and wanting in His Kingdom. They will inherit the wealth on earth, and live rich lifestyles that were once enjoyed by many of the unrighteous.

Likewise, God will pour out new ideas, creativity, power to create wealth, wisdom, knowledge, and understanding upon His saints like never before. New minds will arise. Exceedingly wise business owners will emerge from the abyss. The LORD will shock the world by raising up those that should not be in business, according to the world. But He will make them prosperous, so that He may get the glory. Businesses in the Kingdom will thrive. Every industry will be affected by the increase in the number of businesses, nonprofits, charities, projects, productions, products, and services of saints of the Most High popping up all over the place. Countries, states, cities, towns, and communities will thrive because of the increase in profitable business by the children of God. They will carry the heart of the LORD and give back to the world as a result. Money will be in the right hands, and not wasted.

Still, God will add even more wealth and abundance into the hands of His elect. The world's bank accounts, finances, houses, cars, property, land, ideas, businesses, jewelry, food, water, furniture, luxuries, and more will be moved to the hands of the righteous. God will laugh at the world when this occurs. Yes, He will mock those that mocked Him. And He will bless those that love His word and keep His commandments. Though his anointed are full, He will bless them yet the more. He will give them more businesses, and more ideas, and more property—even that from the wicked—and He will cause His shower of blessings to fall upon them. The LORD's servants will not be able to keep up with the flow of financial blessings. Their cup will run over, and their excess will be given to those that are without and who do not have a part in the LORD. Strangers, orphans, widows, and the poor will be well taken care of by God's children. The lame will rejoice, even as Mephibosheth rejoiced when David invited him as a guest to His palace. The poor will be adopted by the righteous rich. They will eat and be fully satisfied because of the grace of God on those He loves.

However, the wicked will be famished. They will work hard and be short of finances. They will sow seeds and reap weeds. They will not prosper, and they will be greatly ashamed for turning their backs on the LORD, and for failing to repent. Even so, this will not be enough to quench God's wrath. In the same way that He blessed the children, He will curse their enemies. He will send plagues upon the households of all those that hate God's anointed. Unless the wicked repent, God's wrath will continue to be poured out upon them. Some of the wicked will die, taking their own lives for the pain, agony, and shame of poverty, lack, and loss. Others will die natural, untimely deaths due to their greed and obsession with the spirit of *Mammon*. However, God will show mercy to those that humble themselves and repent of their sins. He will restore to them what was lost. Nevertheless, they will suffer some consequences of their sins. Those that do not repent will feel the fire of God Almighty. Their staff of bread will be broken. Even so, the faithful and righteous will thrive financially and be blessed.

#4 Family

God will restore the structure of the family unit to one that honors God and operates in righteousness:

Families will be built on adherence to the word of God. The LORD will begin to save entire families, bringing them to the Cross of salvation. The LORD always had a redemption plan for entire families. However, we have gotten out of alignment with reaching Heaven, with many people not accepting Jesus as their Savior. Even so, God is about to change things, making families right with Him, and positioning them for Heaven and for blessings on earth. Households will be saved and will be living examples of God's grace and mercy for those He calls unto Him.

The sanctity of marriage will be restored:

God-appointed marriages will thrive. Husbands and wives will fall more in love than ever before; it will be a Godly love. People will also begin to respect the institution of marriage the way God designed it, between one man and one woman. As a result of this restoration in marriages, families will thrive, being supported by Godly men and women who raise their families and run their households with virtue and integrity. The home will be a safe-haven, a place that no matter what happens outside in the world, the devil will have a hard time getting into the homes of believers. The doorposts will be marked by the blood of Jesus.

Parents will raise their children in righteousness:

Parents will become more responsible, teaching their kids about holiness and righteousness. Children will be raised up with a deep desire to know and love God.

Men will lead the family in godliness:

Men will be better leaders than ever. They will lead as God shows them how. They will protect, provide for, support, and love their families as unto God. They will be an example for their families to follow.

Women will support their husbands and manage their households right:

Women will begin to trust their men, and give them the respect they deserve, as men of God. Men will earn this respect by the protection, love, and support they provide to their spouses and family. But women will receive men as the servants of God, heads of the household, and leaders of the family. They will trust the work and the vision that God gave the men to lead their families. Women will feel very secure and protected by the man of God. They will naturally consent to his leadership, and trust that God is clearly with him as he guides his family to God's blessings.

Men build houses, women build homes:

"Men build houses, women build homes" is a concept that I came up with recently. That's to say, men build houses. They are often given the dream, the vision, the blueprint, the divine mandate to lead their family to victory. It's not saying that women don't get the vision or the blueprint from God, because they do. It's saying that in terms of the family unit, God often selects the men to lead their families, thus giving them the way to do it. So in order to "build houses", men need a plan from God. The houses represent the life, the vision, the dream that God gave the man for success. His entire job in life is to build that house, that vision, that blueprint for his work, breakthrough, victory, so that he can provide for, and protect his family. The man is still the head of the house: 'Therefore as the church is subject unto Christ, so let the wives be to their own husbands in every thing' (See Ephesians 5:24). "Women build homes" refers to the fact that women provide support for the family. They build the home, that sanctuary, that environment conducive to love, growth, peace, and comfort. The women of God will become better at building Godly homes, in support of their men who go out to build the houses and the vision that God gives them. Again, this is not to say that the roles cannot be reversed, where men build homes and women build houses. It may be in some cases. Though, keep in mind, God is restoring the family unit. And His Kingdom always operates in order. Wherever there is a family, God will expect the man, if available, to lead it, and the woman to support him, as unto God.

Families will become productive:

Fruitful units of blessing and productivity will be the new identity of Godly families. Everyone works, supports each other, gives back to the world, and serves God. Those types of things will be what define the new spiritual family in these last days.

Family members will love, respect, honor, support, and provide for each other.

People will live by 1Timothy 5: 'But if any provide not for his own, and specially for those of his own house, he hath denied the faith, and is worse than an infidel'. They will provide for their immediate family, their extended family, their communities, neighbors, countries, and spiritual families, including the people around them in need.

#5 Media

Increased interest in faith-based issues:

News media will gain an increased interest in the things of God. Stories about faith will become commonplace.

Media helps increase public interest in religion:

Public interest in God will be heightened as a result of hearing the many testimonies of faith on the news and in newspapers and magazines.

Spirituality and religion will no longer be an issue of privacy:

Spirituality will come to the forefront of conversation as people will discuss it in the same way they discuss the top breaking news stories of the day in other areas like politics, entertainment, and business. Imagine that. Spirituality and God replaces other news at dinner tables.

Media will help reduce the reluctance of the public to embrace religion:

The media will show people it's okay to discuss their faith in public.

People that are living apart from God will desire a deeper relationship with Him as a result of what they're hearing and seeing on TV:

Instead of being ashamed of the gospel, people will start to become ashamed for not being a part of this new spiritual awakening on earth. People affected by the media will seek a closer relationship with the God they hear about or see on the news.

#6 Education

Public schools, colleges, and universities will be more receptive to learning about God and living a life that is pleasing to him:

Forget about God not being taught in schools. That's all about to change, not just because of some new law. It's because people will want God to be taught to their children. A light bulb will go off in many of the lawmaker's heads that says, "This God-thing is making our nation more prosperous. People are more cordial to one another. It's having a positive impact on society. Our economy is growing. People are getting better jobs. Why not make spirituality a part of the curriculum, or at least available as subjects in public schools, colleges, and universities even more than they are now?" Be forewarned: the educational system is about to change, and God will be at the head of it.

Teachers and professors will build their curriculum around righteous topics:

Righteousness will be the rule of the day in classrooms around the world. Teachers and professors will begin to teach on subjects, or teach subjects in ways that put God first. For example, business classes will be taught in ways that teach students 'how to start a Godly business', or 'how to make sure God is in your business' in addition to teaching the practical principles that are already being taught in schools. God's ways of doing business, for instance, will be placed first, worldly business concepts and ideas, second.

The Word of God will become an essential part of the school system:

The Bible will be a critical part of the school system. It's currently shunned in most public schools, as being inappropriate or divisive, but God will change things. As more people become spiritually enlightened, common sense will tell them to place the Bible in schools to have their children and their citizens learn the life-changing and world-changing truths of God's word.

The educational system will teach students to put God at the foundation of life:

God is the key to our success. It's not just education or work. It's God, who blesses the works of our hands, and establishes the desires of our heart as we follow Him. The educational system will teach students to have God as the foundation of their lives. Teachers will show students that everything they do for God and His glory will work out fine and be blessed. Education will be viewed as simply a vehicle by which one glorifies God.

Continuing education deepens people's walk with God and enables them to be prosperous masters of their respective trades (i.e. God blesses the work of their hands):

Adults will pursue continuing education courses that develop them spiritually. They will want to learn more ways to grow their faith, walk closer with God, hear God's voice, build Godly businesses, teach God's word, incorporate faith-principles into their everyday life, and similar things. A revival is coming to the education system! Can't you just feel it?

#7 Arts & Entertainment

People will tap into their hidden genius and become aware of unique skills and talents they never knew existed:

What if God just delved deep into you, and pulled out all of the hidden talents you possessed? You would probably discover some artistic abilities you never imagined existed—writing, drawing, producing music, singing, cooking, dancing, acting, sculpting, directing, producing movies, and others. Well, that's what this end-time revival will look like. God is raising up artistic geniuses. He will beautify this world through the amazing forms of expression they create with their hands and their minds. Their works will glorify Him.

Deeper desire to explore and express themselves will result in more people rising to the top of the world of the arts:

You will see *nobodies* all of a sudden become *somebodies* in the field of arts and entertainment. As more and more people become free in their life, living as unto God, in full self expression, God will live vicariously through them. Think of King David. He was a king, a warrior, a soldier, a servant, a priest, an apostle, a psalmist, and he played the harp extremely well! Can you imagine that? Here is this strong, powerful leader, who God so endowed with the gift of creative genius, that he wrote the book of Psalms and played the harp for King Saul to soothe him. God is raising up people in these days in the same way He did with David; these people will become very successful in life. Yet, they will not forget the beauty of life. Their successes and joys in life will be witnessed in their outward expression through art and entertainment.

People will revel in the beauty of human artistry:

Beauty. That's the best synonym to describe the types of works that will be available for the world to see. Think Michelangelo, Shakespeare, Da Vinci, and many others like that. In these last days, God is bringing *them* out all at the same time. God's people will rise up creatively, having the skills and wisdom of the many men and women that went before them. An outpouring of God's spirits will enable people to complete artistic projects that eclipse those of their predecessors.

Greater appreciation for the arts will spread worldwide:

People will simply love the arts. They will flood museums to see the latest paintings. They will flock to bookstores to pick up bestsellers from emerging authors. They will go to restaurants to experience 3-star meals from some of the best chefs around, and those, Godly men and women. God will teach people to do the impossible in every area of art and entertainment.

Celebrities will be used for God's glory:

God will bless Christian celebrities who are in the field of art and entertainment. And even many celebrities in art and entertainment, who have become successful through worldliness, will be transformed to Godliness. Don't count out those worldly actors, singers, comedians, athletes, rappers, and others just yet. God is going to change them in broad view, for the whole world to see. They will bear witness of His love and grace. They will continue their careers, develop even more professionally, and begin to put out more positive work, or at least do their work in such a way that glorifies God. The LORD placed them where they are for a reason. He will graft them into His Kingdom, and use them to prepare the way for His return.

The art industry will boom:

I can't help but imagine how magnificent the world must have been to see the likes of Beethoven and Bach thrive during the Renaissance from the 14th to 17th centuries. People of those days probably witnessed some of the best artistic works of all-time as these creative geniuses led the world into a rebirth. That was then—and done without all of the latest technologies that exist at present. For example, today, high definition cameras, computers, and the Internet allow us to take the field of art to an entirely different level. Aside from that, the most important thing is that in these end-times, God will be here with us to make this the greatest renaissance of all time. He will show us how to be the absolute best at everything we do. The reason is He wants to be glorified as much as possible through us in order to bring as many people as possible to Him. God will use arts and entertainment to bring forth a mighty revival on earth. The arts industry is His tool to beautify His people, glorify His name, and save souls while there is still time remaining before judgment.

THE GLOBAL RENAISSANCE

Many renaissances have occurred throughout history, and in many parts of the world. One of the most known, at least in my country, has been the Harlem Renaissance of the 1920s and 30s. However, that one pales in comparison to the renaissance that God is preparing.

His will be the greatest of all time—even greater than that that occurred during the period of Galileo, Socrates, Aristotle, Plato, DaVinci, and others.

During our days, believers will exhibit artistic capabilities, business acumen, creativity, and intelligence like the world has never before witnessed. God will pour out His wisdom upon His workers in all genres of life, and cause them to be signs and wonders to those around them. They will do it through the *Global Renaissance* that is upon us.

This Global Renaissance will result in a total rebirth of the Body of Christ. You will see a great awakening across the globe. You will see the talents of artists, musicians, speakers, motivators, builders, innovators, and more emerge. Many people who are under the radar, but are faithful to God, will be brought to the center stage to lead this renaissance. Well goes the old adage: "God doesn't call the qualified; He qualifies the called."

Nevertheless, there will be many things torn down before the renaissance can occur, inclusive of people's thoughts, feelings, lifestyles, and habits. Yet, God will build up His Church in the way that He wants to build it up. And it will be a time of peace, blessings, prosperity, and safety on earth for all the saints in the midst of some of the darkest times for the rest of the world.

REVIVAL COMES TO THE WORLD

The revival is about spreading God's word on earth so that He can get as many of His people in Heaven as possible. It's most certainly a spiritual movement of God, first and foremost. Nonetheless, it is also physical. God will usher in a lot of great things in these last days, and His saints will benefit greatly.

Your job as a believer is to be aware of the times, know your responsibility (spread the Word, do the work, and advance the Kingdom), and ride the powerful wave of the new movement of God on earth. You are in the wave, and it's mighty. Jesus is coming back, like He said He would. And this end-time revival will prepare His way.

I close this chapter with an article that I contributed to a popular Christian magazine about God's revival on earth, and how He's raising up revolutionaries that will lead their fields:

> "Developing the Mindset of a Revolutionary"
>
> Have you ever noticed how different you are from everybody else around you? I mean, you try to fit in. You do everything you know to do to conform to how the world does things, but it just doesn't work. At your job, you stand out like a sore thumb. In business, you think unconventionally, and challenge the way things are done in your industry. At home, you are always the one that thinks outside the box. And in your everyday life, whether at the grocery store, the mall, or at a restaurant, you can't seem to get that 'peculiar' light off of you; people just look at you funny, and with interest and curiosity.
>
> If any of the above sounds like you, you could be a person that God will use to usher in a new movement on earth. He made you different, and rightly so. If you were the same as everybody else around you, the world would continue to do the same things as usual. The church would continue to be

broke. And God couldn't bring forth His end-time revival on earth. He made you and people like you to lead a revolutionary change that will impact the world-over.

Countless Others Have Gone Before You
Think for a second about the many revolutionaries that have gone before you. Start with the Bible. You have Jesus, who established the new covenant between God and man (salvation through His blood, and not by the law). Then you have Paul, Peter, and the other apostles, who helped establish the Church. You have Moses, who led the children of Israel out of Egypt and bondage. You have Joshua, who led the children of Israel into the Promised Land. David helped to establish the Kingdom of Israel. Solomon built the First Temple. Abraham was the father of faith, showing us what it means to trust and obey God. Noah built the ark and established a new world.

Then you have revolutionaries of today, and of modern times. John Rockefeller became a revolutionary oil tycoon, causing the government to have to slow him down with anti-trust laws. On a side note, one of my favorite quotes to this day came from John Rockefeller: 'No man can succeed in any calling without provoking the jealousy and envy of some...the strong level-headed man will go straight forward and do his work, and history will rightly record.'
Martin Luther King, Jr. was a revolutionary civil rights leader, guiding the world to social justice and equality for all. And the list goes on and on. The point is, throughout history, God has always reserved a select group of men and women of faith to be set aside to bring forth a new

movement on earth. And He is doing the same thing today.

God Needs Change Agents

The LORD needs change agents. I'm sorry. Ordinary just won't cut it. God needs you to step up, step out, and be the peculiar, strange people, that He called you to be in order to bring people to Him: 'Let your light so shine before men, that they may see your good works, and glorify your Father which is in heaven' (See Matthew 5:16).

Will you be that light that God wants you to be? Will you step outside of the box and boldly go where the Holy Spirit leads you? Will you do something different from everybody else? If you won't, I have some sad news for you: somebody else will. And those same people that step up are the same ones that God will make the head of His revolution on earth. They will take what you leave behind. And God will magnify them in the sight of the entire world.

CHAPTER 4: END-TIME REVELATION

Behold ye among the heathen, and regard, and wonder marvellously: for I will work a work in your days, which ye will not believe, though it be told you. -Habakkuk 1:5

Somewhere around the summer of 2001 I had one of my biggest epiphanies ever. I was asleep one night and I dreamed I saw Jesus Christ descending from the sky.

In the dream, I was driving my car, and it was as if I was driving away from the Lord as I followed the road. However, He kept approaching me, as if He was the sun. He was so big that it was impossible for me to evade Him. He seemed to be hundreds and hundreds of feet tall. And that was just about from his waist to his head. I could not see him from about his waist down.

I saw His face. His beard was brown and His eyes were fixed on me as I drove the car, looking back at Him through my windows. He had a look of peace upon His face, slightly smiling. However, He exuded full power, as one that could build up or destroy anything He wanted, any time He wanted.

He was dressed in an all white gown. It was glowing and bright. The Lord seemed to be translucent—you could see partially through him as if He was a spirit. Yet, He was still as tangible and real as ever.

State of the Kingdom Address

The sky was dark as it was nighttime. And Jesus seemed to light up the sky and the world around me. He was the light, and the center of life. Life seemed to focus on Him.

I felt overwhelming anxiety, peace, excitement, and awe all at the same time. I felt as if the Lord came for His people, and I was one of them. I felt like at any moment, I would be taken up by Him. In my dream, I knew I was in the midst of the Rapture. Nevertheless, I didn't see anyone else in the dream but myself. That dream could be indicative of how a saint of God will be taken up by the Lord when He comes back to rapture the Church. Each believer will feel like an only child. They will feel like the Lord is the center of the universe, and they are the apple of His eye. They will each have their own, unique experience with Him.

Since that dream almost 15 years ago, I decided to record all of my meaningful spiritual dreams in a journal. I have accumulated a number of profound and prophetic dreams and written them down in my spiritual journal. In fact, the Rapture dream was one of the earliest entries in my spiritual journal. And I have gone on to record some of the most powerful, exhilarating, and revelatory dreams about the Kingdom of God and God's plans for the world.

It's in this chapter that I will discuss in detail some of the most important dreams, visions, and messages I've received from God, as they relate to you. Hopefully, you can glean from the symbolism and events in the dreams to get yourself and your household positioned for salvation and for success in the Kingdom.

I will provide a synopsis of each dream, followed by my own interpretation of the dreams, as given by the Holy Spirit to interpret them. Each time that I have a *spiritual* dream or vision, I either immediately understand the meaning or I pray to God for an interpretation of them. And He gives me their meaning without fail, probably about 90% of the time.

Here are some of those dreams and visions, along with the approximate date in which they occurred.

BLOWN TO HELL

4/9/11

I had a dream last night that I was at home with my wife, or girlfriend. I assume she was a wife because she was half-dressed around me, with just underwear and a small t-shirt on. I am starting to change spiritually, so I can't imagine me being around a woman half-naked unless she's my wife.

The woman was lying down on the couch. And while she was lying down she began to buck, and shake, kind of like she was having a seizure. Immediately, I determined it wasn't a seizure. She was being attacked, or even became possessed by a demonic spirit. When I came to that conclusion, I took a step or two back. I knew I had to rebuke the spirit and I was in no way afraid. But when I stepped back, I taunted the devil, telling him that he was coming out of her and I was going to get rid of him.

So I went forward toward the woman and rebuked the devil several times as I approached her. It was a powerful demon and it didn't come out of her right away. So I put my mouth on her stomach, and sucked the spirit with a deep breath until the demon left her body and came into me. However, it was weak compared to me. It had no strength over me. I easily overpowered it, and it could not possess or subdue me.

I exhaled the spirit and blew it out of me, literally blowing toward the ground. I blew it back into hell with the breath of God.

Interpretation and Lesson

You are starting to grow in God and become powerful. The demons that used to subdue you and torment you have no power. The devil cannot defeat you nowadays with the same demons he used in the past. So, what does he do? He attacks you in other ways. He goes after loved ones and tries to possess, influence, torment, control, and harm them.

As a person of God, you have to walk in the power of the Holy Spirit and allow Him to overcome the devil through you. You are the vessel of God; He lives mightily in you. You are a protector of your house, and a guardian of your family. Stand strong against the devil, knowing that you can defeat him through God.

THE EXORCIST

12/17/11

I had a dream that I was casting out a devil from a little girl. It seemed like I was in a semi-trance by a demonic spirit as I slept. But it wasn't like the trances I usually experienced. In this one, my body and spirit and mind were not completely overcome. I was not possessed. Rather, I was in a position of power. The trance seemed to be a trance of aggression rather than possession. In other words, the trance caused me to be the aggressor and attack the demonic spirit.

The little girl was lying down and she seemed to be possessed by the devil. I performed an exorcism on her. But I didn't even touch her. I pointed my finger at her, and my finger was endowed with supernatural power. I rebuked the devil from the little girl in the name of Jesus. However, I didn't have to touch her, and I rebuked the spirits with my finger. [Note: On December 5th 2015 I came across this scripture from Luke 11:20 in the Bible, which made more sense of the dream: 'But if I with the finger of God cast out devils, no doubt the kingdom of God is come upon you.']

My finger shot out power into the little girl, and as I rebuked the devils, I pointed at her intentionally as to deliberately shoot the power of God into her. At some point, I couldn't get the whole phrase out, as in "I cast you out of her". So I just began saying 'Jesus'. Each time, I pointed at her in a commanding way. Then, I said "Jesus, Jesus, Jesus", several times.

Her body began to jump and levitate each time I pointed at her, rebuked the devil out, and said the name Jesus. It was like I was bouncing her on and off the bed like a basketball. She convulsed each time I pointed. Eventually the devil came out, and I woke up.

Interpretation and Lesson

I take the trance to symbolize the Holy Spirit causing me to cast out devils in the name of Jesus and through the power of God. The power of God is mounting up in me as I grow in Him and develop my faith.

As a blood-bought believer, God's power should be growing in you as well. You can rebuke devils out of people, and in many cases you can do it in word only, without having to literally lay hands on someone. The manifestation of God's power in you can literally cause people to bounce on a bed, be thrown across a room, or the like as you cast out the devils from them.

BODY SLAMMING SATAN

3/24/13

I had a dream last night that I was fighting the devil. In the dream, I was in a large public bathroom at the library. I felt an evil presence around me. This presence is normal for me in real life as well (as the devil tries to taunt and torment me a lot when I'm alone, particularly in bathrooms). In the dream, I felt the same eerie presence that I typically feel in real life if Satan tries to torment me in bathrooms—same type of situation, and same type of vulnerability.

I got mad, and defied him as I would in a real situation, rebuking him. I felt his power try to overcome me as I rebuked him. I kept on rebuking him, and I felt an intense struggle—him struggling to hurt me, and me struggling to overcome him with my words of rebuke. Neither was really winning. It was as if we were both trying to get to each other, but it was a struggle, like a wrestling match.

Then suddenly, my rebukes got to him. My body tussled with his spirit. I couldn't see him, but I felt his spirit. It was like I was wrestling the air, but it was really the devil's spirit. So as I wrestled the devil, I picked him up in my dream and body slammed him on the ground. I was still beating on him while he was down. I was now in control of him.

Next, we were placed on what looked like a bed. I overpowered him on the bed and it seemed like I grabbed his face with both hands. I saw the similitude of a face, or the shape of it, but it still seemed like a spirit. The face was similar to the size of my own, even shaped like a man's face.

I pressed toward the face with my own face, in attempt to eat the devil. I literally tried to devour him, eat his face off. It was a struggle there too, yet I was getting closer and closer. He resisted in fear, but the power of the Holy Ghost was in me, and I was even winning in that battle to eat him. I then woke up, being unable to eat him.

Interpretation and Lesson

The dream possibly meant that God is endowing me with even more power from on high to fight against the devil and overcome him as I go out to do God's work and take territory from the devil.

As you go out to do more and more of God's work, you will have more bouts with the devil. Many of these duels will be one-on-one with Satan instead of just dealing with one of his lower level devils. He will try to resist you and put fear in your heart. Have faith in God. Whether you be in a public bathroom, a cave, or the *valley of the shadow of death*, the devil cannot defeat you if you walk in the power of the Holy Spirit.

LION TERRITORY

3/6/12

I had a dream that I was in some sort of wildlife conservation. A few weeks before this dream, I saw a YouTube video about wild African dogs. I looked that video up to learn more about the wild dogs since they were ranked as the top hunting animal by some measure, because they had an 80% kill rate, as compared to lions or wild cats

State of the Kingdom Address

that average about 30%. I was interested in learning more about them and their hunting tactics. In the video, there were people in their vehicle at a wildlife conservation to observe the wild dogs. The dogs chased an animal, which probably was an impala or gazelle, past the people's vehicle. The dogs came very close to the people, and the people seemed to jump up into the back of a truck as the dogs came close to them, chasing their prey. The people got out of harm's way and the dogs. There seemed to be like 5 or 6 wild dogs that took the animal down. That was the summary of the YouTube video I saw a while ago. Now, back to my dream.

I was in the same place in my dream as the people were in the YouTube video. It looked like almost the same exact setup. Only, in my dream, I seemed to be in lion territory, not wild dogs. I saw lions all around. I was in that place with my brother, my uncle, and there were also many other people there. Numerous lions roamed about. I saw several male lions, but my eyes zeroed in on one male lion with the mane. He was the one that was approaching me as I sat at a picnic table dressed in a priestly suit.

He was running towards me and my brother, as the other lions were running after the other people. The male lion who was after me charged me and my brother, and I told my brother to get up onto the picnic table with me so we can avoid the lion. We were scared, but we jumped up onto the table. The lion ran at us and jumped up onto the table with us. I was terrified, and so was my brother. We both began fighting the lion. My brother fought with him, without actually making any real contact with the lion. I fought him with a knife I had on me.

The lion was aggressively coming against me, but he didn't prevail. He could not eat me, bite me, scratch me, or harm me in anyway, though he tried. He was still coming for me and attacking. I also tried to prevail against the lion (as my brother also resisted him). So I took my knife and began stabbing the lion in the back of his neck as he was attacking me. I made deliberate stabs into his neck to try and kill him. I stabbed him several times, and I saw the puncture wounds (though no blood was actually pouring out). I could feel and hear the squishing sounds I made by stabbing him. I also saw blood in the stab marks. I stabbed him many times, but it did not kill him and he seemed unharmed.

I was scared because he was not dying, but was still attacking me. My uncle began to run away from the other lions that were pursuing him. Then, my brother leaped off the table. He ran in fear. The other lions were chasing the people. I then ran right behind them, in fear of the lion I was fighting. The lion I was fighting chased after me, but passed me without attacking me. He chased hard after my brother, and the others in front of me (who by this time were running up some steps that seemed to be in some sort of building). Meanwhile, I was still running in fear because I still was being chased by another lion, though not the original one I was fighting. I kept running, and so did my uncle, brother, the other people, and all the lions. Everyone was scared.

I eventually ran into the building where the other people had run. I caught up to them, and noticed my uncle had made it to the top of some steps. But my brother was on the steps; the lion that I was originally fighting with had caught him. My brother was trying to fend him off and climb to the top of the steps with my uncle. I was on the steps with my brother, but I was unharmed, though I was chased onto the steps by the other lion. The lion was unable to kill my brother, and I was trying to protect him from it and help him get up the steps. I then woke up.

State of the Kingdom Address

Interpretation and Lesson

The lions in the dream represented Satan, and devils. The male lion that attacked me represented Satan, the leader of the pride, and defender of his territory. In the dream, the lions were defending their territory. Satan knows that his time is almost up, and that Jesus is returning. He also knows that the Church is at war with him, and that God is sending us out to take his territory. He is fiercely defending his land!

Earth, to Satan, may not be the kingdom that he wants. But it's a lot better than Hell and the Lake of Fire. Satan, is defending his territory at all costs. His devils represented the other lions in the land that chased the people out. This is not to exalt myself in any way, but there is a reason that Satan himself came after me. I'm a big threat to him because I'm out doing God's work and in God's power. You may also be one of the biggest threats to the devil, particularly if you're really in God, aware of the truth, a leader in the Kingdom of God, a spiritual warrior, and spread God's message to other people.

Satan goes after the ones that are the greatest threat, just as he went after apostles like Paul, Peter, and many other apostles in the early days of the Church. That's not to say that other people in the body of Christ are safe. They get attacked by other lions (devils) and Satan as well. Even if you're not really in God, or in a close relationship with Him, guess what? You still get attacked! Why? It's because Satan hates you, and so does his other lions. You are a threat to his territory because you are a child of God.

By the way, if you do more for the Kingdom of God, you can expect more attacks to come against you than the average person. Satan will target you more than he targets other people that just dip and dabble in a relationship with God. In the Body of Christ, those that are really committed to God and serving Him are the head—the greatest danger to Satan because they are more than likely fully aware of the truth and walking in it. Satan knows he can destroy the body if he destroys the head. So church leaders, beware of the many wiles of the devil. He is walking about the earth seeking whom he may devour, with lust, pride, fear, bitterness, unforgiveness, and sin in general. If he can't overcome you in battle, his next best option is to weaken you by getting you in sin. Then, you become more exposed to his fiery darts and attacks. Examine yourself consistently and check for any chinks in your armor.

My uncle in the dream represented the average person. He wasn't necessarily saved, yet he wasn't evil. He was the typical person. So being a person, he got pursued by hungry lions (devils) that wanted to destroy him. The devil wants to kill and destroy all of humanity, whether you're in God or not.

The main lion (Satan), though he attacked me, was unable to harm me. God gave me protection from him because I was close to God. As you grow in God, you become stronger in Him. The anointing is like a fiery shield around you. The devil can't penetrate it unless you get caught up in sin and that hedge of protection gets removed. The devil couldn't do anything against me, though he tried. However, I was also unable to prevail against him, though I tried. It was an even battle more or less. That kind of makes me think of the book of Genesis, where God said He would put enmity between man and the devil: he shall bruise his head, and the devil shall bruise his heel.

In any case, it was an even battle. I took that to mean, I was not strong enough in the Spirit to completely overcome the devil. In life, I was still growing in God, perhaps still dealing with some sin and

State of the Kingdom Address

unrighteousness, which separated me from the power of God. God wanted me to give Him more of me. I asked God the day I had the dream to give me more of Him. He responded by saying He wants more of me. So, I knew I had a ways to go in order to become stronger against Satan.

The main lion (Satan) caused my brother to run off. Why? It's because he's my protégé. He was still young in the spirit. At age 23 at the time, and being less experienced than I was spiritually, he was pretty new to spiritual battle. However, for the past 15 to 20 years or so, I've been through many spiritual battles. Consequently, my brother eventually ran off when he saw that he couldn't prevail against Satan.

The stairs of the building represented spiritual development. My brother and I were in a period of spiritual growth in God. In real life, we were both trying to become closer to God and fulfill our purpose. That's exactly where Satan attacked my brother in the dream, on the path of spiritual growth, which was represented by the stairs. Satan hates for people to grow closer to God because that makes them a more formidable opponent.

Note, that Satan also attacked us both when we were on the table, but I couldn't find information as to what the table meant in terms of symbols. It may have meant a meal, such as the word of God, which is often referred to as meat. If you stand on the word, Satan will not be able to defeat you. The picnic table may have also represented a type of fellowship (breaking of bread with other believers), sanctification (setting yourself apart from the world with fellow believers), or communion with God (as in the last supper).

So how does this all relate to you?

You are a member of the End-Time Church. There is an end-time revival coming that will require the saints of God to take back enemy-held territory:

> And Joshua said, Hereby ye shall know that the living God is among you, and that he will without fail drive out from before you the Canaanites, and the Hittites, and the Hivites, and the Perizzites, and the Girgashites, and the Amorites, and the Jebusites (See Joshua 3:10).

There is a spiritual takeover as well as a physical takeover coming! God is causing His Kingdom to come to earth spiritually with Jesus' return. He's also causing the Church to prepare the earth for Jesus to return. There will be a wealth transfer, a revival, an increase in the influence of the body of Christ over a lost world (i.e. increasing our territory), and else wise. God is pushing the devil out spiritually, and physically. More finances, real estate, gold, silver, property, blessings, are coming. But it will only come by it being taken by force from the devil. So, whether or not you want to be a part of the move of God, as we prepare for Jesus' return, you are a part of that move. You have come to the Kingdom for such a time as this. God is raising up mighty conquerors, not just in word, but in action.

Satan is desperately defending his territory, and the battle we face will not be an easy one. Even so, we get the victory by the blood of Jesus. Just as Satan was unable to harm me in the dream, he is unable to harm you because God protects you. The deeper you go in God, the more of His hedge of protection you get around you. Amen.

State of the Kingdom Address

SERVANTS OF THE DEVIL

7/19/12

I had a dream a couple of nights ago where I was in a supermarket of some sort. I was walking and passing several aisles. And on the other side of the store was a man that looked like he was wearing a pharmacist jacket. There was also a girl somewhere in the store near the pharmacist. The man and the girl appeared to be on the same team, and it was as if I was their opponent. They were out to get me, and I was eluding them by going to different aisles. Every time they saw me, I would go to the next aisle. The girl was the one I seemed to be after, but she called on the pharmacist for help. He then was after me. So I was dodging him, as if he were the authoritative figure. It seemed as if I was after the girl, and I wanted to hurt the pharmacist in some way.

Then, I heard a voice over the intercom. It seemed like a powerful voice, yet evil. It was giving me brief instructions on what to do to the man, or harm the girl. The voice seemed inherently evil, yet it spoke nicely.

It was telling me things like "Kill the man.", or "Hurt the girl." But my conscience was telling me otherwise, that the voice was reprehensible. Although, it seemed to have some control over me, which I also hated. I tried to block out the words over the intercom, but I kept hearing them. I put my hands over my ears to block them out. In my dream, I perceived that the voice was the devil. I had been working for him in the dream, and he was controlling me through the intercom.

Interpretation and Lesson

The same night I had the dream, I had committed a sin. If you serve sin and the flesh, you are essentially serving the devil. God had been dealing with me for the longest time to walk in His Spirit. Yet, I sinned at that time. The dream simply told me that when I walk in the flesh, I am serving the devil. Do not serve sin and you won't be serving Satan. He will have no control over you. Sin gives Satan legal ground to harass or buffet us!

THE CROSS

8/21/12

I was taken to Calvary and I was at the Cross while Jesus was being crucified. I saw Jesus on the cross. He appeared to be slightly bloody and marred. His face was handsome, but you could see the helpless look on His face as the soldiers had their way with Him. He had a look of compassion, love, service, selflessness, and innocence on His face. He looked into my eyes with conviction, as to say "I'm doing this for you".

It was about early evening in my dream. It appeared slightly cloudy and the sun didn't seem to be shining. There was just a slight overcast, and Jesus was the light (as all attention was focused on Him and the Cross). He seemed to radiate to the people around Him who watched. I felt all of the commotion around, people talking and moving about. There was a lot of activity.

Yet, Jesus' quiet, still, innocent look caused a certain stillness that seemed to erase the noise and life around Him. I witnessed everything but the actual death of Jesus.

Interpretation and Lesson

I take it the dream signified that God wanted me to get serious with Him. In understanding what Jesus did for me, I needed to present my body a living sacrifice to God as my good and reasonable service.

Jesus wants you to stop taking His death in vain, and trampling on His blood! Stop living a life of sin. Do His will. Help save people around the world by teaching them about salvation and ministering to them about God.

THE DEVIL'S HARVEST

8/21/12

A few days ago, I dreamed I was lying in my bed. It was right next to this curved window that provided a panoramic view of the outside. I looked out the window while I was in bed, and I saw a man wearing a straw hat, who resembled a farmer. The hat was wide and it covered his entire head.

He had a wide mouth, and he was absolutely atrocious! He was one of the ugliest men I had ever seen. And he kept peering at me through my window from outside. He was perverted, vile, nasty, evil, and was smirking at me.

He was intent on trying to harm me (as in molesting a child). He looked at me to let me know he was there, or to make me afraid. I stood there watching, unafraid, daring him to try something against me. It was as if I was saying, "Yea. Come on, try me. You got the right one!" I was ready for a battle. But he kept looking. And eventually I heard a knock at my door.

I supposed it was the man from outside and I was angry, ready for battle, and on the defensive. I was mad that he had the audacity to try me, and to not just look at me from outside, but even to knock on my door. I really wanted to harm him. So I answered the door, and expected to see him. Yet, I saw other people. The man with the straw hat had left.

The people that were at the door were good-natured, innocent, friendly people who meant no harm to me. There was a man in the front of the people, followed by 2 or 3 more people behind him. They were talking outside of my door. I let the man in, and there was no harm to me, whatsoever.

Interpretation and Lesson

I woke up from that dream and thought back on how ugly and eerie the man with the straw hat was. I was trying to interpret the dream, and I couldn't. I asked God for help, and asked Him who the man was and what it meant. He told me that the man was Satan. He told me that he was trying to contend with me, and even make me afraid. That's why he kept peering at me through the window. I was unafraid, so he left.

However, the most important thing about the dream is this: The devil has a harvest of tares, which are sowed amongst Jesus' harvest of wheat, according to the book of Matthew 13: 'The enemy that sowed them is the devil; the harvest is the end of the world; and the reapers are the angels' (See Matthew 13:39). The people who are without Jesus and unsaved are being reaped by the devil. Satan is reaping souls faster than Jesus is reaping them: 'Therefore hell hath enlarged herself, and opened her mouth without measure: and their glory, and their multitude, and their pomp, and he that rejoiceth, shall descend into it' (See Isaiah 5:14).

In the dream, the devil was mocking me to make me feel like the work I was doing for the Kingdom was in vain. As a believer, Satan will contend with you for every single human soul out there. You have to fight for them. Your work for God is not in vain. Heaven rejoices for every person you bring to the Cross of salvation. Work for God with a sense of urgency, knowing that Satan is also working urgently to reap faster than you: 'And let us not be weary in well doing: for in due season we shall reap, if we faint not' (See Galatians 6:9).

COUNCIL OF WICKEDNESS

8/25/13

I had a dream about three weeks ago where I was fighting three dead spirits. They were men, and appeared as death. All three had the same appearance, same clothing, and were split images of each other. They were bald, pale (as in almost green or gray like death) and they wore black, as in a black cloak. They were laughing at me as I contended with them and tried to get them.

I was rebuking them not so much away, but as in a way to get them (to apprehend them). It was as if my rebuke was intended to capture, or lay hold on them. The three men were laughing still, and all the while trying to resist me. They appeared as the man on the movie *Hellraiser*, Pinhead (without the pins). If you don't think a lot of the characters in these scary movies don't come from Satan, and the reality of the spiritual world, you're sadly mistaken. All the evil you see in movies comes from the devil.

Anyway, the three men looked just like Pinhead in terms of their characteristics. They swerved, and floated around me as I tried to get them. They circled me. They drifted around me. They toggled. They switched positions. As I moved closer, they all three kept moving away, shifting, to evade me. All the while, I kept getting closer to all three of them, rebuking them all the while, trying to get all three while they laughed and resisted. They were men, but dead and evil. They were the devil but more specifically the *Council of Wickedness*, Lucifer, Pharaoh, and Apollyon[1]. I first learned about the Council of Wickedness from Apostle Les Crause at Apostolic Movement International (Source: Crause, 2016).

Interpretation and Lesson

I am in a war against Lucifer, the ruler of the three, Pharaoh the ruler of the world, and Apollyon, the leader of the specific attacks against the saints of God (sickness, lust, pride, fear, etc.). My calling requires me to fight high levels of warfare against the Council. I am not afraid of them, but resist them even as they resist me.

If you are called high up in Christian leadership, whether as a Fivefold minister (Apostle, Prophet, Pastor, Evangelist, Teacher) or as a leader

---

[1] The Council of Wickedness refers to the three highest spirits in which Satan operates. They are the chief spirits of the devil, and they mimic the Godhead of God, Jesus, and the Holy Ghost. Only the Council of Wickedness, Lucifer, Pharaoh, and Apollyon do the devil's work. Lucifer is the ruler of the three. Pharaoh is the head of the world's finances and financial systems. And Apollyon is the leader of the attacks against the people of God. If you see lust or pride creeping up into a believer, that attack was facilitated by Apollyon.

in another area such as business, politics, or someplace else, you will be engaged in extremely high levels of spiritual warfare. You will not simply face spiritual battles with everyday devils. No, you will deal with wickedness in high places. Namely, you will have to deal with the prince of this world, and his two partners. You will deal exclusively with Lucifer, Pharaoh, and Apollyon. Think bigger. Think spiritual warfare strategies. Plan. Execute plans. Get deeper in God. And be forever circumspect with your thoughts and actions. The highest level devils are constantly trying to take you out.

THE DRIFTING FACE

1/23/14

I dreamed I was in my family's house. We were playing some popular 70s R&B music, and I was grooving to it. I went down in the basement and it seemed active—music, lights on, a party environment. I decided to lay down and go to sleep, but I wasn't really tired. I didn't have a bed so I laid down in the middle of the basement floor, which was like my bed.

The party atmosphere of music and lights was still alive. I looked up and saw a shadow pass on the wall. It was a man's face, perfectly symmetrical. The face was shaped and sized the same as an ordinary man, only it was a shadow. It floated along on the wall and I watched it and became alert. The face began to grow pointy ears. And it kept floating along.

I looked at it and immediately knew that it was Satan. So as soon as I knew that I started rebuking him. Only, he didn't go away. There was a struggle. So I kept on rebuking him; still he didn't go. I wasn't scared, but angry. I struggled to get rid of him. I don't recall saying the name of Jesus. But I cursed the devil and demanded him to go.

He didn't go. Then, his face stopped floating on the wall (where I just saw the side of his face). Instead, it turned around and looked straight at me, as in 3D, being perpendicular to the wall. The face eventually came off of the wall and looked straight at me in defiance. It was a challenge. I saw his eyes. They were bright, unlike human eyes, but they seemed to shine in an evil way. His face was evil towards me.

I kept rebuking him because I felt him approaching me. So I kept cursing and rebuking, still. I began to mock him. I laughed at him in an evil voice. He could not overcome me, although I could not overcome him. So I laughed him to scorn. I kept trying to rebuke him, and I couldn't understand why he wouldn't go.

I usually have no trouble rebuking the devil. I have many encounters with devils, but Satan is stronger than them. I rebuke them with no problem, but I often had a little more struggle with Satan. So as I kept rebuking, I heard the voice of God say "Relax". I was fighting the devil with my rebukes, but God wanted me to be calm and not worry and receive Him and His Spirit. God fought the battle. I stayed still and watched His salvation.

Interpretation and Lesson

The house represented my life. I was in the basement, which may have signified a struggle or hidden place in my life (such as a sin, or challenge). There was a party atmosphere which could signify comforts, worldliness, or even luxuries in life. The party and music could have also been indicative of sin, worldliness, and separation from God.

State of the Kingdom Address

I tried to go to sleep, or 'get rest' from my situation. But there was no bed. There was no comfort in myself, or my stuff, or what I have. Though, I still decided to go to sleep on the floor. That's where my bed should have been.

The devil was in the *room*, or in my life, as an adversary. I am fighting high levels of spiritual warfare now, such that Satan himself is my primary opponent. He manifested himself on the wall as a shadow, a man. Note, the devil can come to you in just about any form he wants. He can even manifest himself as an angel of light: 'And no marvel; for Satan himself is transformed into an angel of light' (See 2Corinthians 11:14).

In some cases, the devil will even appear as Jesus, Himself. It's incredibly important that you test the spirits! On a side note, I had one particular dream where the devil appeared in my dream as one of my cousins. He had knocked on my front door in the dream and wanted me to answer, telling me that he was my cousin. But my cousin had died several years before the dream! I immediately felt an evil presence, and when I had opened the door, my cousin disappeared, and my body was placed in a trance. It was none other than the devil, who had manifested himself as my cousin in the flesh. What a dirty, sneaky, rotten devil. Beware of his tricks. Anyway, I defeated Satan through the name of Jesus in that dream. I ended up defying his spirit and pursuing him around my house to attack him. I went to my bathroom on the lower level of my house, hoping and expecting to see him in there. I didn't see him. He was hiding. Then, the Spirit of God overtook me. The Holy Spirit came upon me and caused me to raise my two fists up in the air as if I was a champion. As I lifted my hands in the air I felt the power of God ruling over all the powers of the enemy. I then began to parade around my house in the dream saying, "I am the champion. I am the champion." I felt like an ancient gladiator who just won a fight. I kept walking about declaring that I was the champion. I finally woke up. The dream showed me that we are undefeated champions through Christ. We defeat all the powers of Satan when we are walking in the blood and name of Jesus. Now, back to the interpretation of the dream with the face on the wall.

In that dream, Satan was as an equal to me, having the face of a normal-sized man. He came against me, but I could not rebuke him although I tried several times. He then floated toward me. I was not totally dependent on God, but I trusted in my flesh. Satan overcame me, when otherwise I would usually overcome him.

Nonetheless, I laughed at him, still. That showed me I still had God and trusted in my protection from God. Though, I was not totally walking in His spirit. I trusted in my flesh, my abilities to overcome Satan (the flesh represented the sin, or challenges in my life).

God told me to "Relax". In other words, "Stop struggling against the devil in the flesh. You can't win like that." God wanted me to walk in the power of the Holy Spirit, which was my deliverance. I had to walk in the Spirit to overcome the devil. Not by might, nor by power, but by my Spirit says the LORD (See Zechariah 4:6). When I relaxed, and trusted in God's Spirit, I woke up. I overcame Satan by God's grace.

Beloved, your only way to defeat Satan and any sins or challenges you struggle with in life is to walk in the Spirit. Fighting the devil in your flesh is like fighting him on his home turf. The flesh gives the devil the home-field advantage. You must rely on the power of God through the blood of Jesus to win against Satan in a spiritual battle.

GOD'S PRIDE OF LIONS

State of the Kingdom Address

1/17/14

I had a dream a few nights ago after I asked for God to minister to me in my sleep. I slept and was taken back in time, to a prosperous place. It seemed like I was thriving in life and the land and times around me were vibrant. The dream was much deeper than I can remember. But the part I remember best is that I was King Solomon. I was in a cave that had lions in it. The people around me were scared of the lions and tried to get away. But I walked in the midst of them. They were inside the cave. And the deeper I went in the cave, the more lions appeared.

They came toward me, but not in harm, sort of like in familiarity and camaraderie. It was like they knew me or accepted me as one of them. They kept showing up, more and more of them, groups and groups as I walked deeper in the cave. The cave was more bright than dark. There was light and the lions came from glory.

The lions were all big, full grown, maybe adults. And they looked like females without the mane, or maybe even males without mane. They were exotic looking—bright, even white and off-white—not the typical color I've seen of lions. I was an important figure, who had power with the lions. The people around me looked up to me and respected me. They found safety around me. They were afraid and insecure around the lions. I wasn't.

It felt like I was very comfortable in terms of my lifestyle, like I was living in comforts (dress, provision, land, etc.). I even felt like I had a royal gown and crown on, as a king would wear. It was a prosperous time, it seemed. I then woke up.

Interpretation and Lesson

The dream meant that I am a king in God's eyes. I have the ability to inherit the Kingdom—wealth, wisdom, power, grace, faith, favor and other things, just like King Solomon. It's a time in my life where I am really pursuing God and His calling. I am also going hard after my goals and success, working harder and more focused than ever.

I was amongst lions. I often refer to myself as a lion in real life; it's a part of my branding. So God put me in the midst of lions. But they were friendly lions, as if they were on my side. Those lions were exotic, beautiful, but strong. They represented men and women, the people of God who are on my side. They came from the light, from God's glory. Caves are usually dark, but they emerged from the light. That's goodness. They are with me and are going out to conquer the land with me.

They will inherit God's promises with me. There were many of them. And the deeper I went into the cave the more showed up. The cave may have meant life (the world), God (the light), or my calling. I'm commonly comparing myself to King David, but God showed me that I was as Solomon also. Solomon is known for wealth and wisdom.

I have long pursued God. He is letting me know that the dreams, words, visions that He's shown me over the years are true. He is letting me know that I am well on the path to inheriting riches, wisdom, favor, comforts (something I don't have right now, and haven't for years), and honor. Amen.

As a child of the Most High God, you are a joint-heir of the promises of God through Christ. You have the right and calling to reign as a king. Every promise of God is yes and amen. God is building up His army of lions to send them out against the forces of darkness and take the wealth of the wicked. You are a critical part of that army. Satan likes believers to believe they are the only ones going through something. He likes to isolate them through his 'divide and conquer' war strategy. However, don't fear him, or buy into his tricks. Don't fear doing your work or conquering the land that is before you. You have help! You have God, and also a team of other lions by your side. These Kingdom lions may not always be visible, but they are still there and facing the same enemy as you. They engage the devil in battle in the same way as you. It's one people, the exact same army, just fighting from different battalions.

I have an important side note to include in this chapter. It's about a great wealth transfer that is about to occur on earth.

WEALTH TRANSFER

Pastor Benny Hinn at bennyhinn.org, once described how he felt a wealth transfer is in the making. It will be much like the wealth transfers of Biblical days. They took place in the lives of many of our great patriarchs:

#1 Abraham

In Genesis 12:10; 13:1-2, the Pharaoh of Egypt gave Abraham wealth.

#2 Isaac

Isaac experienced another wealth transfer from king Abimelek during a famine in Genesis 26:1.

#3 Jacob

Jacob went through a wealth transfer when he took the cattle from his uncle Laban in Genesis 31: 6-9.

#4 Joseph

Joseph received a wealth transfer when Pharaoh entrusted him with his stuff and made him ruler over Egypt, from Genesis 41:39-44.

#5 Israel

In Exodus 3:19-22, God promised Israel that it would leave the land of Egypt and bondage, laden with the wealth of Egypt.

#6 Solomon

God gave King Solomon the wealth of one nation, plus the wealth of the nations of the world in 1Kings 10:23.

#7 You

A great wealth transfer is coming to you, as a child of God, in these end-times. Proverbs 13:22 mentions how the wealth of the wicked is laid up for the just. Do not be surprised if all of a sudden you see ungodly businesses begin to fall, and those same establishments being converted to righteous enterprises by God's people. The LORD needs the finances to be in the right hands to finance the gospel: "Though he heap up silver as the dust, and prepare raiment as the clay; He may prepare it, but the just shall put it on, and the innocent shall divide the silver" (See Job 27:16-17).

A PROPHETIC WORD: EXODUS BACK TO GOD

State of the Kingdom Address

The spiritual void in people's lives will cause them to return back to God in the same way the children of Israel returned back to God after the exodus from Egypt. There will shortly be an incredible spiritual movement of people around the world seeking to serve the LORD!

Want to hear many more of my prophetic dreams and visions like the ones in this chapter to help you strengthen your walk with God? Stay tuned for my upcoming book, *Diario Spirituali*™ ("My Spiritual Journal"), tentatively scheduled for December 2016! Please review the Additional Resources page at the end of this book for info about *Diario Spirituali*™, and other upcoming releases.

CHAPTER 5: SATAN'S SATIRE

They that see thee shall narrowly look upon thee, and consider thee, saying, Is this the man that made the earth to tremble, that did shake kingdoms; That made the world as a wilderness, and destroyed the cities thereof; that opened not the house of his prisoners? -Isaiah 14:16-17

A middle-aged woman with blond hair was driving her car the other day. She was talking out loud, apparently rebuking the devil. She was naming and claiming her victory. She was telling Satan where he had to go and how. She was demanding that her blessings came into her life immediately, and that the devil let go of everything he was holding of hers. I was on the outside of the car on the passenger's side, sort of floating in spirit, but keeping up with the car. I could see everything that was happening.

I was amazed that she was so bold, speaking to the enemy with conviction. Suddenly, as she spoke, and drove her car along on the highway, the devil appeared in her passenger seat. He was not there in theory, but in the flesh. He had the appearance of death. He was pale, sort of greenish, with a bald head. He had on what looked like a black robe. And as the woman continued to rebuke him, not noticing him yet, he spoke to her: "How dare you rebuke me! You don't know who I am. That is not faith that you have. Now, I am here. Let me see you send me away." The woman screamed in horror, "Aaaaaaaaaaaaaaaaaaaaaaaaaaaaaaaaah!" as she held her face with both hands, as to cover her eyes in horror. She could not believe that the devil showed up in her life and she saw him face to face. She could not believe he was that real, and could appear to her right in her car. I have news for you: Satan can appear to you anytime anywhere he wants, provided God allows him. The devil appeared to Jesus in the wilderness for 40 days. Jesus also saw him fall from Heaven as a bolt of lightning, as I mentioned in previous chapters. Jesus had several real-life encounters with the devil, and that will hold true for believers in these last days. God is beginning to open up our eyes and let us see the spiritual realm like never before.

Anyway, as the lady with blond hair screamed, I stood there totally unafraid. It was as if I knew who the man was, and I fought him several times. I was used to seeing him. Unfortunately, most of the world wasn't used to it. My dream continued with the lady screaming in fear. I eventually began facing Satan.

The scene switched to the bathroom. I was at the bathroom shower, where I was looking for the devil, expecting to see him hiding in the tub. I couldn't find him. He was gone. I eventually woke up.

Many Christians in the world are much like that woman in my dream. They rebuke Satan in church. They claim they are full of faith. They memorize Bible verses and the whole nine. However, they don't consider the depths of spiritual warfare. If Satan appeared to them face to face, most of them would pee their pants. That, in part, is why the devil mocks the Church. He knows what we will inevitably have to face in the near future. We will have to face him, the one who is on our property. How can we conquer land for the Church if we are unable to engage the devil? Fear, lack of faith, unfamiliarity with spiritual warfare, lack of knowledge about our spiritual arsenal, and inexperience in using our weapons of warfare will keep us from getting the victory over Satan. A warrior in God's Army should be able to battle on all fronts, against any enemy, in any condition, and in any location. The sad thing is the Church is not quite ready for battle. But that will change, and change soon. God is going to fix us.

SCHOOLYARD BULLY

Remember that school yard bully from when you were younger? He was always picking on somebody smaller than him—taking their lunch, pushing them around, knocking their books out of their hands on the way to class. He knew he was just too intimidating for someone to even dare try to resist him. But every so often, someone with a little bit of courage stares the bully in the face and decides to push him back. They stand up to him. Then, what does the bully often do? He backs off them and picks on somebody else.

You see, the Church is much like that little puny kid who the bully (the devil) harasses. We are beaten up, mocked, teased, afflicted, mistreated, and then some. Just like the kid being bullied, we take much of what the bully dishes out at us—not just because we may be scared to push back. It's because most of the Church does not know how to push back, how to effectively engage in warfare with the devil. Even worse, the saints that do step up to contend with the devil, do so haphazardly, weakly, and without the power, faith, and courage necessary to overcome the forces of evil.

Unlike the kid that stepped up and challenged the bully in the schoolyard situation, the Church fails to tap into its inner strength, consequently failing to defeat the devil when they encounter trying times. The schoolyard child often defies the bully with his courage, and things of a worldly nature. You, as a child of God can only thoroughly challenge the devil by mastering your weapons of warfare, namely the name of Jesus, your faith, prayer, worshiping God, applying the Word, rebuking the devil, and the countless weapons of warfare discussed in Ephesians 6. Believers are much more intent on waiting for God's deliverance than to step up and use what God has already given us to defeat our adversary. Sure, God is our only way to win the fight. But the fight must often be fought through Him. We have to not only learn how to use our weapons, but to use them. I hear many believers saying, "I will just keep my eyes fixed on Jesus." I say to you, "Jesus is keeping His eyes fixed on you, waiting to see if you walk in that power that He has given you through His blood and His Word!" Sure, the Lord will personally deliver you out of many situations. On those occasions, you will simply stand still and see the salvation of the LORD. Though, there will also be situations that He expects you to deliver yourself with the arsenal He has given you— the name of Jesus, the Word of God, declarations, rebukes, the shield of faith, and others. If you would never have to battle the devil, what's the purpose of spiritual weapons—to use them on yourself? Of course not. We must learn to beat the devil, through God and the arsenal He has provided.

The problem with the Church is this: our weapons of warfare have collected dust. Saints are walking around in *lion* territory with an "Eat me" sign on their backs, parading around as if they have already won some battle. The truth is the Body of Christ has scarcely won anything. A victory through Jesus is only the victory if you walk in it. The devil and his troops are sitting there in wait, laying smack dab in the middle of the path to your victory, daring you to come try and push them off the path. Why does Satan stand there waiting for us? It's because He knows that in our present state the Church does not have the level of mastery of our spiritual weapons that's required to cause him any harm. We talk a good talk, but our walk is pitiful: 'For our gospel came not unto you in word only, but also in power, and in the Holy Ghost, and in much assurance; as ye know what manner of men we were among you for your sake' (See 1Thessalonians 1:5). We have to learn to be demonstrations of power, as discussed in 1Corinthians 2:4, not just in speech, but in action as well.

Pathetic. Ridiculous. Weak. Faithless. Unprepared. Choose your synonym. Any one of them accurately describes the Church in its present state. It's nowhere near that 'glorious Church…not having spot, or wrinkle', according to Ephesians 5:27, that God envisions the Church being one day. So Satan laughs at us. We're a complete and utter satire to him, a comedy.

THE DEVIL IS MOCKING YOU

Beloved, the devil is mocking you! Satan is saying to himself, as the weak, lethargic, ill-prepared Church—the army of God—approaches him, "How dare they come against me! They are not prepared to do battle!" As a battle-hardened, fellow soldier in Christ with you, I tell you, "Do not challenge the devil until you're truly ready for battle. And do not take spiritual clashes with the devil lightly." You need not look any further than the story of the seven sons of Sceva, from Acts 19:14 to understand that if you're not prepared to war with Satan, you'd best not be on the battlefield. You could possibly end up getting hurt, or even worse. Spiritual warfare is no game, and the enemy you're up against is not to be taken as a joke.

The Church is sent headlong to advance God's Kingdom against a strong opponent—the devil. Satan and his army are prepared for the Church. But the Church is not prepared for him. People don't know about many fundamentals of faith: how to hear God's voice, how to walk in the Holy Spirit, how to pray, how to make declarations and decrees, how to activate angels to work on their behalf, how to bind up Satan, how to *resist* the devil, and other things. How then can they go up against Satan? It's time we became the warriors that God made us to be.

Again, Satan has made this end-time movement of the Church a satire, a comedy. He is enjoying the show, as the Church, in its current state, prepares itself for defeat. No longer should the devil be allowed to mock God's people. And no longer will he. God will be glorified through us. He will develop an incredible, terrible army with banners that represents Him well in battle: 'Who is she that looketh forth as the morning, fair as the moon, clear as the sun, and terrible as an army with banners?' (See Song of Solomon 6:10). By the grace of God, that banner that we will be wearing is the name of Jesus Christ and the victory in His name. Amen.

GREAT CITIES HAVE GREAT DEFENSES

Consider this. How long have you toiled in life to overcome problem after problem to get what you have, the position, faith, income, property, relationships, and much more? I bet those things cost you a great deal of blood, sweat, and tears to attain, right? Now imagine this. What you have acquired in life thus far is only a very small fraction of the bountiful blessings that God has in store for you. Sure, you probably stole some stuff back from the devil, but he is still holding the majority of your breakthrough in his hands. That's why you're probably not a millionaire yet. Satan gave you a little bit of your things back, but he's a crook, a thief, a liar. Therefore, what he gave you back pales in comparison to what he has yet to give you back. There are greater cities to be conquered than the ones you have already. And great cities have great defenses because their inhabitants don't want you in their land: 'Now Jericho was straitly shut up because of the children of Israel: none went out, and none came in' (See Joshua 6:1).

Now, think about this. You worked hard to get where you are. And I'm quite sure you had to overcome a lot of devils to get there. If Satan and his army of devils fought you so diligently for the little bit of wealth, health, land, possessions, position, and blessings you have, how much more do you think he will fight you for the land and blessings that God has yet to give you, especially for the inheritance of the Kingdom of Heaven? What you don't have is greater than what you do have! God told Joshua there was much more wealth to get, and He's telling you the same exact thing today: 'Now Joshua was old and stricken in years; and the LORD said unto him, Thou art old and stricken in years, and there remaineth yet very much land to be possessed' (See Joshua 13:1).

Satan will gladly allow you to hold onto what's already in your hands. That ain't a blessing. That's what remained after Satan took the lion share from you—greater wealth, health, relationships, marriages, and others. You got the short end of the stick, and the devil laughs because you call that a breakthrough. Don't allow the devil to play games with you. Pronounce a *holy robbery* upon him, and take your stuff back.

UNLEASH THE BEAST WITHIN YOU

Here's a word of warning. In order to get the true victory that God has prepared for you during these end times, you have to take the land. It has to be stolen from the devil, and Satan has to be knocked flat on his butt by some end-time, battle-ready, warrior-saints. Your victory has to be taken, and Satan is well prepared for an advancing army of God. You have to be ready for him, or else you are facing a losing battle. Get serious with the devil because he commands an elite army. Learn your weapons of warfare, and master them!

All throughout the Bible, God talks about loving your enemies. Well, this is the one time you can freely destroy your enemies and release all your pinned up aggression on him. Let your battle ax fly. Give the devil hell to pay, and let him know you will no longer tolerate him robbing you blind and destroying your life. Mount up in the power of the Holy Spirit and let the kingdom of darkness see, recognize, and bow down to the Godly warrior in you.

TRANSFORMATION TO THE CHURCH

God will not allow the Church to be defeated by Satan. The Church will win the battle, and God's Kingdom will advance on earth, allowing billions of people around the world to hear the gospel. However, a transformation within the Body of Christ must occur for God's Kingdom to be ushered in on earth the way that He wants it to be. God is raising up warriors in these end times to serve on the frontlines of His army. These warriors will demonstrate *faith-power* by destroying the works of the enemy through their faith. They will be a sight for the world to see.

In fact, you could very well be one of the end-time warriors. If that's the case, know that God is shaping you. He is teaching you to have stronger faith, more dedication, more courage, less fear, more selflessness, greater loyalty to the Kingdom, more anger against the forces of darkness, and a greater desire to witness to the world about Jesus. Consequently, Satan's *comedy* that I mentioned earlier will be a comedy indeed—only he will be the brunt of the joke.

Following are a few disheartening statistics of why it's so important for the Church to get right. If we don't spread the gospel, and get people saved, who else will? Keep in mind that our chief assignment as believers is the Great Commission, to spread the gospel. Evidently, spiritual battle is as much about spreading the gospel and saving souls as it is about engaging the enemy to "take territory." Satan will fight with us to prevent us from spreading the gospel. The territory we seek to take is not so much physical territory just for the sake of having physical territory. Every acre of land we take is to spread the gospel and bring glory to God. In other words, physical territory (land, finances, neighborhoods, communities, social media, and others) is used in the Great Commission. Likewise, there are unsaved souls on some of that physical territory. There is also the spiritual territory to speak of, which represents the principalities and powers we contend with in the spiritual realm. Going back to my earlier point, that our job is to spread the word and get people saved, it's easy to see that any land we get, either physical or spiritual, will be highly contested by Satan. So, if we have trouble battling him for that contested land, we will also have trouble stepping up to our purpose, and effectively living it, which is, in some way to minister to lost souls. In sum, spiritual warfare is not just a pretty term that God threw out there to have us spar with the devil. It is an essential part of salvation for a lost world. We must fight to get the word out!

It should go without saying that Satan not only laughs that we are ill-prepared for battle against him (not that we don't have the arsenal, but that we are not thoroughly using it). He is also probably pretty amused that we are not as effective as we should be at spreading the gospel.

Those are the reasons I stressed the importance of spiritual battle in this chapter. I will not labor the point on spiritual warfare in this book.

State of the Kingdom Address

Hopefully, you at least know you have some spiritual weapons at your disposal, including living free from sin, repentance, the name of Jesus, the Bible, faith, prayer, and praise. The subject of spiritual warfare is beyond the scope of this book. I will provide a more thorough discussion of it, along with defining what it is, what it entails, and what strategies and tactics you can use for victory in my upcoming book **Spiritual Warfare Manifesto.** You can find out more about the **Spiritual Warfare Manifesto** at the end of this book in the references section.

THE WORLD IS NOT READY

Here are some things we must change as the Body of Christ. Consider a few of these dismal statistics. The world is clearly not ready for Jesus to return...

> - 14.5 million Jews that practice Judaism (not Messianic Jews) don't believe Jesus is the Messiah
> - 1.6 billion Muslims, roughly 23% of the world's population don't believe Jesus is the Messiah
> - 550 million Buddhists worldwide don't believe the world will ever end, the possibility that people are saved by grace, or that Jesus' death at the Cross is an important part of humanity
> - 1.2 billion Roman Catholics in the world don't believe in the Rapture
> - 161 million atheists in the world don't believe in God

> 38% of Christians polled believe that Jesus will definitely not, or probably not return in the next four decades (Source: Mosbergen, 2013)
> An average of 232,876 people are dying every day in this world. The vast majority of these people are going to hell. It's estimated that less than 1% of professing believers make it to Heaven, much less for an unbelieving world (Source: Stewart, 2016).
> 85,000,000 humans will die every year on average. Few make it to Heaven: 'Strait is the gate and narrow is the way that leads to life, and few there be that find it', according to Matthew 7:14.
> 2.18 billion Christians are in the world, and the vast majority is not positioned to go to Heaven. Satan would love for believers to think that everyone goes to Heaven. What a lie! Heaven is a holy place, and it takes more than church attendance and believing that God exists to get a spot there.
> Two-thirds of the world is not Christian, and is likely unsaved. Peter's words ring loudly here: 'If the righteous scarcely be saved, where shall the ungodly and the sinner appear?' (1Peter 4:18)
> The average church has less than 1000 members (much more like 200 members in the U.S.). At 1% saved, only 1 member or less, per average church is really positioned for Heaven.

You don't have to look too deep into these statistics to see why the devil laughs at the Church. We're doing a poor job getting people saved, and Satan is reaping a lot of souls as a result. Even many church members, some being church leaders, would probably not make it to Heaven if they died today. Some are backslidden, some serve the world and not God, and others haven't repented.

I go back to my dream in Chapter 4, where I saw Satan posing as a farmer. He had a rake, or some other sort of harvesting tool in his hand. He was preparing to reap his harvest (the *tares*, or souls of the unsaved, as discussed in Matthew 13:25). The ministerial effectiveness of the Church has to be improved. Otherwise, many more people on earth will be lost to the hands of the devil.

LET'S EVANGELIZE LIKE NEVER BEFORE

Evangelizing is what all those statistics are about. We must evangelize as if our lives depended on it. We need to spread the word of God and lead people around us to salvation. If we want to put a dent in the problem, we have to get off of our couches and get into the streets. We have to avoid talking about change on social media, and pound the pavements to bring the change to the people. If we aren't a part of the solution, we are a part of the problem. You don't have to go far to tell people about salvation. It starts right from where you are, in your own sphere of influence.

REVERSE THE COURSE OF BATTLE

So what can we do to reverse Satan's comedy into a tragedy (for him)?

Well, it starts with leadership. Are you a church leader? If so, I'm encouraging you to get right with God. Work harder, sacrifice more, improve your ministry, preach about hell, expose the devil to the

Church, and return to God so that He may use you to save more people. Many church leaders have become stale, and it's time for them to get their fire back. Preach boldly and with conviction in order for God to save the lost.

You are in leadership for a reason—because many others were not fit for the job. God is placing the onus of preparing His saints for battle on you. You have to take your work more seriously and totally burn out for the cause. I will talk more about church leadership in Chapter 9.

For now, let's turn to the next chapter, where I will give you some perspective on the present times.

CHAPTER 6: SOUNDING THE ALARM

When it is evening, ye say, It will be fair weather: for the sky is red. And in the morning, It will be foul weather to day: for the sky is red and lowring. O ye hypocrites, ye can discern the face of the sky; but can ye not discern the signs of the times? -Matthew 16:2-3

As one of my famous sayings goes, "Everybody has something to say, but not everybody's saying something." Discernment of the times, and the words of people, is more important than ever. We must be aware of what God is doing on earth, in the heavens, and in Heaven to prepare us for the things to come. God is sounding the alarm, calling us to rise up to a higher level of spiritual awareness as well as higher levels of sanctification, commitment, and service to Him.

Do we understand how God is moving on earth? That's to say, are we Kingdom-aligned, appropriately positioned, or as I like to say, "ahead of the curve", which is ahead of the world around us? Do we study our Bible, and are we in tune with end-time prophecy? Do we stay in prayer and meditation, asking God what He wants from us and how our part affects His grand plan? Are we listening to the right people, those especially chosen by God, anointed to guide us, and/or gifted in eschatology, or *end-time studies*? It seems everybody and their momma has a prophetic word these days. Do we pay attention to the signs in the sky, the moon, the sun, the stars, or even the natural phenomenon, weather patterns, and disasters which affect our lives on earth? Do we listen to the still, small voice of the Holy Spirit, Who ushers us along to effectively fulfill our purpose on earth and reveals to us the nature of God and His plan? Are we getting our lives, our families, our countries, our communities, our businesses, and our households in order, to spiritually prepare us and our family and our friends for eternity? Last, but certainly not least, are we becoming increasingly more dependent upon God to meet our needs, and less dependent on the world system, which will eventually topple? These types of questions must be answered if we want to ensure our safety, success, and salvation as God's Kingdom progresses on earth.

RAISING END-TIME WARRIORS

Apostolic Movement International (AMI) is a ministry that has been given a mandate by God to prepare the Body of Christ for the final move of God, asserts that God is preparing end-time warriors, apostles, to lead a movement of God on earth. This movement, according to AMI, will take the Church into the Promised Land that God has; it's a time and place where every believer will be walking about as a City set on a hill (Source: Apostolic Movement International, 2016).

AMI believes that the End-Times Apostolic movement started at the turn of the century, but became clearly evident in 2001. Just as Christ set aside his select 12 apostles in order to train them up and ultimately release them into the world to create a revolution, God is doing the same thing today with apostles. These 'hidden warriors' are being trained up in secret, in obscurity, to be placed into the world as leaders of this final move of God.

I find AMI's ministry particularly interesting, in that they are focused on bringing up apostles as well as other Fivefold ministers. We know that God brings in His great movements on earth through apostles, and other ministers. So it's critical that we keep our ears to the ground and be ahead of the curve. In addition, you should know whether you are called to the Fivefold. And AMI will be able to help you determine that. Check out AMI at http://apostolic-movement.com when you can. Even if you're not called to be a leader in the Church, it would behoove you to view yourself as an end-time warrior, and allow God to use you to bring glory to His name.

Through AMI and many other people and organizations on the forefront of God's End-Time Army, the LORD is sounding an alarm. He is using leaders in His Body to mobilize His Church into greater action and effectiveness in spreading the gospel.

FOUR BLOOD MOONS

On *Joni Table Talk*, a Christian television talk show on Daystar TV, Pastor John Hagee, of Cornerstone Church in San Antonio, Texas, discusses the importance of the four *blood moons* as they relate to the judgment of the world[2]. (See the full interview here: http://bit.ly/1TqXn7h).

I agree with Hagee on his final points:

You should "stop looking to Washington for your solution. Look up; the answer is coming from Heaven."

---

[2] Hagee believed the four blood moons were a new prophetic revelation for the Body of Christ from the word of God. Hagee explained how God uses the heavens as His billboard, and through the blood moons, God is pronouncing judgment upon the earth, in accordance with Genesis 1:14: "And God said, Let there be lights in the firmament of the heaven to divide the day from the night; and let them be for signs, and for seasons, and for days, and years."

"The world is going to get worse and worse, but the church is going to get brighter and better".

A Great Shaking in the U.S.

On a similar note, Rabbi Jonathan Cahn, author of *The Harbinger*[3], believes a great shaking in America is coming, and it could lead to a major catastrophe such as a famine in the land. We must pay attention to the signs of the times, whether they be in Heaven, the heavens, or on earth, because God is undoubtedly speaking through them.

THE THIRD TEMPLE

Founded in 1987, The Temple Institute is a nonprofit organization, located in Jerusalem, dedicated to building the Temple of God on Mount Moriah in Jerusalem (Temple Institute, 2016). As you may know, there has already been a First and Second Temple. In short, the Temple Institute is committed to constructing the Third Temple, the one that is supposed to prepare the way for Jesus' return.

The Third Temple is a prerequisite to the Lord's return to earth, as He is supposed to touch down in Jerusalem and walk through the Temple gates. Some Jewish scholars believe that 2240 CE is the

---

[3] In *The Harbinger*, James Cahn describes Biblical signs determining America's future. Cahn claims that the harbingers, 'the warning of judgments', which are 9 in all, tells us what is going to happen to the U.S. Cahn says that one of the warnings of judgments, the *shemitah* (i.e. release, fall, collapse, or shaking in Hebrew), which is an ancient mystery that goes back over 3000 years to the times of Moses on Mt. Sinai, is affecting everything from the 911 attacks to the rise and fall of the U.S. economy and the plummeting value of the dollar, to the crash of the stock market, and the rise and fall of nations.

deadline year for the Messiah to arrive. The Third Temple is likely to be built before then, since they are working to have it up before Messiah returns to earth.

The Third Temple, or The Holy Temple, or Ezekiel's Temple, as prophesied in the book of Ezekiel (Chapters 40-42), is a precursor of the Great Tribulation that will come upon the earth during the reign of the anti-Christ. I will expound upon the Temple Institute shortly. But let me first provide a little bit of background about the history of the temple and how it will play a pivotal part in the winding down of eternity.

A HISTORY OF THE TEMPLE

The Third Temple is described by Ezekiel as 'an eternal edifice and permanent dwelling place of the God of Israel on the Temple Mount in Jerusalem.'

In Jewish tradition, the building of another temple to replace the First and Second Temples is sacred, and is a common request of Jews through the *Amidah* prayer—praying three times a day done by Orthodox Jews.

Animal sacrifices, according to many Orthodox scholars and Rabbinic authorities, are said to resume in the Third Temple as a form of worship to God in conjunction with the rituals of the First and Second Temples. Can you imagine how much controversy would arise out of animal sacrifices in the modern world? Animal rights activists would be enraged.

Other activities expected to resume in the Third Temple are the incense offerings, psalms the Levites used to sing in the temple, and preservation of *tumah*. The tumah were rules of purity that only allowed people who were ritually purified from all uncleanliness, for example, contact with the dead, menstruation, contact with non-kosher animals, people who had certain diseases, to enter the holy temple.

There have been several attempts to rebuild the Temple throughout the ancient ages. They obviously failed. One particular attempt occurred in 363 CE where gentiles, under the guidance of Roman emperor, Julian (361-363 CE) tried to rebuild the temple, yet were scared off by balls of fire that shot up from within the earth as well as earthquakes:

> Julian thought to rebuild at an extravagant expense the proud Temple once at Jerusalem, and committed this task to Alypius of Antioch. Alypius set vigorously to work, and was seconded by the governor of the province; when fearful balls of fire, breaking out near the foundations, continued their attacks, till the workmen, after repeated scorchings, could approach no more: and he gave up the attempt.

Divine intervention prevented the gentiles from rebuilding the temple. It's to be done by the Jewish people. Julian was ultimately killed in battle a short time later.

Subsequent attempts to rebuild the temple were made in medieval times:

610 CE: The Sassanid Empire drove out the Byzantine Empire and gave control of Jerusalem back to the Jews, who reinstituted animal sacrifices and the rebuilding of the temple. The Persians eventually gave the area to Christians, which turned the partly built structure into a garbage dump. Soon after, the Byzantines took the area back.

State of the Kingdom Address

7th Century CE: During the Siege of Jerusalem in 637 CE by the Arabs, The Jews and Arabs were feuding over religious differences, when a man of the "sons of Ishmael" gave a sermon to unite the Jews and Arabs under the banner of their father Abraham and jointly enter the Holy Land. The Jews began reconstruction of the temple, until the Arabs expelled the Jews and designated the area for their own prayers. The Jews purportedly built another temple in a different location.

1267: During the Mongol raids into Syria, Nahmanides, A medieval Jewish scholar wrote this letter to his son in reference to the land and the Temple:

> What shall I say of this land...The more holy the place the greater the desolation. Jerusalem is the most desolate of all...There are about 2,000 inhabitants...but there are no Jews, "for after the arrival of the Tartars, the Jews fled, and some were killed by the sword. There are now only two brothers, dyers, who buy their dyes from the government. At their place a quorum of worshippers meets on the Sabbath, and we encourage them, and found a ruined house, built on pillars, with a beautiful dome, and made it into a synagogue...People regularly come to Jerusalem, men and women from Damascus and from Aleppo and from all parts of the country, to see the Temple and weep over it. And may He who deemed us worthy to see Jerusalem in her ruins, grant us to see her rebuilt and restored, and the honor of the Divine Presence returned.

TEMPLE INSTITUTE AND OTHERS

Despite, the Orthodox Judaism belief that the Third Temple will be completed after the return of the Messiah, and also left up to divine providence, many organizations have been focused on rebuilding the temple in current times, prior to the return of the Messiah. Examples include the *Temple Mount and Eretz Yisrael Faithful Movement* and *The Temple Institute*. Both of these organizations are committed to rebuilding the Third Temple on the Temple Mount (Mount Moriah), which is currently under Muslim control.

The Temple Institute, for instance, "is dedicated to every aspect of the Holy Temple of Jerusalem, and the central role it fulfilled, and will once again fulfill, in the spiritual wellbeing of both Israel and all the nations of the world" (Source: http://templeinstitute.org/).

Currently, two historic Islamic structures including the *Dome of the Rock* and *Al Aqsa Mosque*, both being about 13 centuries old, are the biggest obstacles for the rebuilding of the temple by the Jews on the temple mount. The Dome of the Rock is said to be the exact location of where the temple used to stand.

Israel has consented to preserving these two buildings as part of international agreements:

> Any efforts to damage or reduce access to these sites, or to build Jewish structures within, between, beneath, beside, cantilevered on top of, or instead of them, would lead to severe international conflicts, given the association of the Muslim world with these holy places (Source: Temple Institute).

Some scholars believe that the Dome of the Rock is not the actual place of the former temples, saying instead that the temples once stood just north or south of the Dome of the Rock. However, if the theory is true that the Dome of the Rock is the actual place of the First and Second Temples, the rebuilding of the temples would likely have to take place in that exact location in alignment with scripture. For example, the book of Leviticus details to the cubit how the temple was supposed to be constructed.

Evidently, either a divine act of God, or an act of man (a peace treaty or war et. al.) would have to occur for the Temple Mount and the Dome of the rock to be conceded to the Jews by the Muslims. It should suffice to say that the Dome of the Rock, which is considered to be the third holiest place in the world in Islam, will not be just given to the Jewish people for the sake of building a Third Temple. The only foreseeable way for control of the Temple Mount to be relinquished to the Jews is through a miracle from God, or some sort of spiritual war. Just as a reminder, the Temple Mount is one of the most revered spiritual places in the world, for the Jews, and for the Muslims.

PREPARATION UNDERWAY

A commonly held belief is that the temple must be rebuilt first to prepare the way for the return of the Messiah, who is expected to walk through the temple doors when He comes back to earth and touches down in Jerusalem.

Interestingly, The Temple Institute has already begun the preparation for the building of the Third Temple. For example, things like the ancient vessels of gold have already begun to be made, if not being completed already. Additionally, the Levite line of priests have been identified, and many can trace their blood lines back to Aaron and the ancient Levites.

Further, the priestly garments worn by the Levites, the menorah, table for the shewbread, altar, incense, laver, and other things are either already created, or in planning, by supporters of a Third Temple.

It's said of the sages, that when the Holy Temple stood, humanity was blessed in a way that corresponded with the temple service, according to the Temple Institute:

> ➢ The produce of the fields were blessed on account of the showbread and the omer offering;
> ➢ The yearly rainfall, on account of the water libations during the Holiday of Sukkot;
> ➢ Clothing kept one warm in the merit of the priestly garments;
> ➢ The economy prospered because of the daily sacrifices

ARK OF THE COVENANT

Various theories exist in terms of the location of the *ark of the covenant*. Some say it's been taken to Rome to the Vatican, like many of the other holy vessels such as those on the Arch of Titus in Rome. According to Jewish tradition, the ark is not lost, but hidden, and hidden very well.

Temple Institute, along with many of the Jewish people in Israel, believe that the ark is actually hidden in the secret chamber of Solomon. Here is a description of that chamber, as provided by TI:

> Tradition records that even as King Solomon built the First Temple, he already knew, through Divine inspiration, that eventually it would be destroyed. Thus Solomon, the wisest

of all men, oversaw the construction of a vast system of labyrinths, mazes, chambers and corridors underneath the Temple Mount complex. He commanded that a special place be built in the bowels of the earth, where the sacred vessels of the Temple could be hidden in case of approaching danger. Midrashic tradition teaches that King Josiah of Israel, who lived about forty years before the destruction of the First Temple, commanded the Levites to hide the Ark, together with the original menorah and several other items [the staff of Aaron that budded, the jar of manna placed in the Holy of holies as testimony, and the jar of anointing oil], in this secret hiding place which Solomon had prepared. This location is recorded in our sources, and today, there are those who know exactly where this chamber is. And we know that the ark is still there, undisturbed, and waiting for the day when it will be revealed.

That day when the ark will be revealed is perhaps the day when the temple is rebuilt and ready for the return of the Messiah.

THE RED HEIFER

One of the few remaining things that are needed for the temple is the *red heifer*. According to Wikipedia, the red heifer, "also known as the red cow, was a cow brought to the priests as a sacrifice according to the Hebrew Bible, and its ashes were used for the ritual purification of a Tumat HaMet ("the impurity of death"), that is, an Israelite who had come into contact with a corpse." The red heifer is essential to temple service. The red heifer is so important to the Divine Service because God ordained that the ashes of the red heifer are the single ingredient necessary for the return to Biblical purity and the subsequent rebuilding of the Holy Temple. The ashes of the heifer are said to rectify the human flaw of despair that brought about by the loss of the temple and the presence of God among us (Source: Temple Institute).

The true mystery of the red heifer and its requirement for the temple service cannot be explained by human reasoning. Jewish tradition holds that King Solomon in all his wisdom, even in having the ability to understand the language of animals, was perplexed when it came down to understanding the mystery of the red heifer. He purportedly declared Ecclesiastes 7:23 in response:

I said, 'I will become wise, but it is far from me'.

Certain ordinances belong in the category of *chukim*, according to Jewish tradition. That is, as opposed to being understood by humans, we are simply to do them out of love and fear of God. There is something bigger behind the requirements of the red heifer for temple service. But only God knows. The depth of the mystery is beyond human intellectual ability.

The red heifer though, is said to atone for the 'spiritual chaos' brought into the world by the *golden calf*, that idol set up by the *Mixed Multitude* when Moses went up to Mt. Sinai to receive the Ten Commandments (See Exodus 12:38).

Here's how the red heifer allegorically corrects the wrongs of the golden calf:

> ➢ The heifer must not have harnessed a yoke, for it reminds us that at the fiasco of the golden calf, Israel threw off the yoke of Heaven.

- It must be red, on account of the verse which promises "If your sins will be red as scarlet, they shall whiten as snow" for sin is alluded to as red.
- But it must be "perfect" in its redness, for Israel was faultless in her devotion to G-d before she sinned" (Source: Temple Institute).

However, these are only assumptions. The true meaning behind the red heifer is too deep for our understanding.

WORLD EVENTS

The wars, natural disasters, civil unrest, and other negative events of the 21st century are signs of the end times. They are precursors to judgment that are warning us to turn back to God. Our Father has been speaking to us in stones, allowing certain things to happen, to awaken us. Soon, He will speak in bricks, then boulders, then mountains, until the whole world falls on us if we don't get right.

Wars

A number of wars broke out in the 21st century. Here are some of the most notable ones:

- Second Congo War (1998-2002)
- U.S. War on Terrorism against Al-Quaeda, the Taliban, and ISIS (2001 to present)
- Civil war in Sudan (2003 to present)
- U.S. invasion of Iraq and overthrow of Saddam Hussein (2003-2010)
- Hezbollah/Israel conflict (2006) caused by the capture of two Israeli soldiers by Hezbollah

- Civil war on the Gaza strip between the Hamas and Fatah-loyal forces (2007)
- Conflict between Georgia and Russian Federation (2008)
- France and Islamists conflict in Mali (2013)
- Ukraine civil war begins (2014)
- Syria civil war leads to capture of territories in Northern Iraq and Syria by terrorist Islamic state (2014)
- Israel conducts airstrikes on Gaza strip for more than a month (2014)
- Mexican drug war (2006 to present)

Terrorism

The world has been fighting against terrorist organizations like al-Qaeda, the Taliban, and ISIS (Islamic State of Iraq and the Levant) since as early as the late 1980s to early 1990s. A number of terrorist attacks remain etched in our minds. One of the most memorable is the U.S. World Trade Center collapse of 2001, where two commercial jets were hijacked by al-Qaeda extremists and crashed into both towers in lower Manhattan, NY, killing thousands. "Major events after the September 11 attacks in 2001 include the Moscow Theatre Siege, the 2003 Istanbul bombings, the Madrid train bombings, the Beslan school hostage crisis, the 2005 London bombings, the October 2005 New Delhi bombings, the 2008 Mumbai Hotel Siege, and the 2011 Norway attacks" according to Wikipedia. Also, the Boston Bombing of 2013 during the Boston Marathon in Boston, MA resulted in the deaths of 3 people, injuring about 264. Then, on November 2015, a terrorist attack occurred in Paris, France, where over 129 people were killed by armed terrorists and suicide bombers. The terrorists attacked a concert hall, restaurants, bars, and a major stadium almost simultaneously, according to BBC News (2015). About a month later, another terrorist attack took place in San Bernardino, California on December 2, 2015 in the United States. A married couple, Syed Rizwan Farook and Tashfeen Malik, possibly having ties to ISIS, killed 14 people by opening fire on a crowded holiday party. We have also seen countries like Nigeria plagued by terrorism, for example, from the Islamist group, Boko Haram. Unfortunately, such countries get less media coverage than places like the U.S. Still, other lesser known incidents of terror continue to occur around the world but may not be classified as terrorism by the media.

Civil Unrest

Civil unrest has occurred all throughout the 21st century. The world has witnessed some of the most tumultuous events between 2004 and present. For example, there was the G-20 summit protests (2009), Iranian election protests (2009-2010), Greek protests over 'plans to cut public spending and raise taxes' (2010-2011), Tunisian revolution which led to Tunisia becoming a democracy, Egyptian revolution to overthrow Egyptian President Hosni Mubarak (2011), Libyan civil war (2011), Syrian Revolution (2001 to present), Occupy Wall Street (2011), Ferguson protests on behalf of Mike Brown who was killed by police officers (2014), Baltimore City protests as a result of the death of Freddie Gray (2015), and the NYC protests over the death of Eric Garner at the hands of the police (2015). Other instances of civil unrest in the past couple of years are outlined below:

> ➤ 2014–15 Venezuelan protests over high levels of urban violence, inflation, and chronic shortages of basic goods

- 2015 Lebanese protests over government's failure to dispose of accumulated waste
- 2015 protests in Brazil against political corruption
- 2016 U.S. presidential election

Natural Disasters

The Bible speaks of earthquakes in *divers* places during the time before the Lord returns. Natural disasters, including earthquakes, can be seen all across the globe. Here are a few of the more significant ones since the beginning of the 21st century:

- 2001 Gujarat Earthquake in India killed 20,000
- 2004 Hurricane Jeanne killed over 3,000 people in Haiti
- 2004 Asian Tsunami killed more than 230,000
- 2005 Hurricane Katrina cost U.S. citizens more than $81.5 billion and killed 1,836 people in southeast Louisiana
- 2009 flu pandemic with the H1N1 influenza subtype
- 2010 Haiti earthquake kills 230,000 or more
- 2011 Tohoku earthquake and tsunami in Japan
- April 25–28, 2011 tornado outbreak in southern U.S.
- 2015 earthquake in Nepal which killed 8964 people
- 2015 Hindu Kush earthquake, where 398 died
- 40 avalanches in Afghanistan from February 24-28 2015, which killed 310 people
- 2014–15 Malaysia floods that killed 21 people

- ➤ 2015 Myanmar floods which killed 103 people from July 2015 to September
- ➤ 2015 South Indian floods that killed over 400 people
- ➤ 2015 Southeast Africa floods, resulting in 176 deaths
- ➤ 2015 Tanzania flood that killed 38 people
- ➤ October 2015 North American storm complex which killed at least 25 people
- ➤ 2015 Texas–Oklahoma flood and tornado outbreak, killing 46
- ➤ Typhoon Chan-hom (2015) in the Philippines killed 6
- ➤ 2015 Colombian landslide which killed at least 78 people
- ➤ 2015 Guatemala landslide that killed 280 people
- ➤ 2015 Indian heat wave that caused over 2500 deaths

Here is a list of all the major natural disasters that have occurred just in 2015 alone:

https://en.wikipedia.org/wiki/Category:2015_natural_disasters

Global Concerns

Some of the most important global concerns include globalization, which is causing economic and cultural shifts, overpopulation, abortion, poverty, disease, war and terrorism, international relations, and the water crisis as the human population increases.

Works of the Flesh

You need not look any further than the local or national news to see how wayward man has become. The 21st century has given way to some of the most heinous crimes against humanity, including terrorist attacks, sex-murders, school shootings, public murders and beheadings by drug cartels, and others: 'Now the works of the flesh are manifest, which are these; Adultery, fornication, uncleanness, lasciviousness, Idolatry, witchcraft, hatred, variance, emulations, wrath, strife, seditions, heresies, Envyings, murders, drunkenness, revellings, and such like:' (See Galatians 5:19-21).

Based on the signs of the end times I described above, we have to be in a state of readiness. We have to know that the Lord has been gracious to us in giving us time. He has sent us revelation through His servants. He told us in His Word. He is most certainly coming back. It's only a matter of time. And only He knows what time that is.

CHAPTER 7: SPIRITUAL REALITY

I beheld Satan as lightning fall from heaven. Behold, I give unto you power to tread on serpents and scorpions, and over all the power of the enemy: and nothing shall by any means hurt you. Notwithstanding in this rejoice not, that the spirits are subject unto you; but rather rejoice, because your names are written in heaven. Luke 10:18-20

In his book, *Baptize By Blazing Fire: Divine Exposé of Heaven and Hell* (2009), Pastor Yong-Doo Kim discusses the reality of the spiritual world. Kim, pastor of The Lord's Church in Seo Incheon, South Korea, led his small congregation to engage in all night prayer from the late evening until the very next morning for 30 consecutive days. During that time, their spiritual eyes were opened, causing them to take frequent trips to Heaven and hell. They saw and spoke with Jesus face to face on many occasions. They even saw Satan and many demons that were sent out by the devil to attack the Church. The Lord's Church was deeply involved in such high levels of spiritual warfare that their story is almost hard to believe. The church has not only ousted demonic forces, but has also seen demons manifesting themselves in different forms, shapes, and colors, from vampires, dragons, and false Christs to other demonic spirits. They have even been able to witness the activities of demons as well as hear their screams of torment with their physical ears as they were attacking the demons with spiritual weapons (sword of the Spirit, etc.).

I was shocked by what I read. There were a lot of things occurring in the spiritual realm, that even in all my battles with Satan, I never experienced. For example, Pastor Kim explained how gruesome the tortures of hell were. He mentioned how devils often took turns torturing the damned. This passage talks about the devil's *weapons of death*.

> There was a table in front of Satan. The table was covered with various weapons of death. In fact, there were so many, it looked like mountains. The weapons included old time, worn farm equipment, conventional weapons, and armaments. Other various weapons were also included. Satan's subordinates would take a weapon from the table to stab, lacerate, and spear at their victims. However, the evil spirits were not satisfied. They would go to another place in hell to bring more and different types of death weapons. I was in an enormous room with many dividing walls. There were various, brutal weapons hanging on the wall. Such weapons were weapons one can only see in movies, books, Sci-Fi, and fiction stories. They were weapons of imagination from the earth. As I observed the variety of weapons hanging on the wall, I felt as though I was looking at some tool exhibition. As the evil spirits grabbed a death weapon to chop off the legs of people, it reminded me when my friends and I had casually torment[ed] insects and ants. The evil spirits found it joyous and entertaining as they chopped the legs off people to watch them in torment (p. 40).

The demons in hell are ruthless. They take great pleasure in causing excruciating pain to the lost souls that end up there.

In addition, I was amazed by one woman in The Lord's Church, Sister Baek Bong Nyu , who had a personal encounter with Satan in

State of the Kingdom Address

hell. While she was visiting hell in the spirit, she saw her mother there being tortured by devils. She was angry that Satan was causing demons to torture her mother. So she sought out the "king of the devils", Satan, in all of hell so she could fight with him. She searched high and low, asking the demons where their leader was. She eventually found him sitting upon a throne. He was big, as if he tried to imitate the throne of God. The LORD is high and lifted up (See Isaiah 6:1). Satan tried to make himself as one that was also high and lifted up, as God. So he placed himself on a big throne.

The woman eventually found Satan. Since he was big, she had to climb his body to get to his chest, face, and upper body as to have a face to face confrontation:

> Jesus, I'm not able to see you, but I believe you're always with me. Jesus, I want to give Satan a beating. However, he is too big for me. I'm not able to give him a beating! Please grant me a ladder so I can climb to the top of his head and attack him!" With the Lord's command, Archangel Michael immediately brought a large tall ladder from Heaven. The ladder was so.large it reached the confines of Hell from the ground.

> With the help of Archangel Michael, I placed the ladder on Satan's back and we began to climb the ladder. It was very high and dangerous. I couldn't make it to the top without the help of Archangel Michael. It was strange that Satan didn't move a muscle as we climbed up the ladder. When we reached the top of the ladder, I jumped off the ladder onto his shoulder. I tore into his skin with my fingernails, but it had no effect. Satan didn't move a muscle. He was ignoring me, as though I was nothing to him. The skin on

Satan's back was as hard as a rock. No matter how hard I attempted to tear into his skin using my fingernails, it was useless. I shouted with all my strength as I continued to scratch into him. "You filthy devil, take this!" I prayed in tongues to myself, saying, "Trinity God, please grant me strength! Grant me power!" Then, as I continued to scratch, I was finally able to make a mark.

I tore intensely into the scratch, but Satan's skin was very thick and I was only able to tear into it a little bit at a time. I thought to myself, 'Why is this so difficult?

'In that moment, wisdom came to me and I cried out to the Holy Spirit, "Holy Spirit, please grant me the Holy Sword! Please grant it to me now!" As I cried out, a huge golden sword descended. When the sword came close to me, I grabbed it and pierced the back of Satan. I jabbed into his back repeatedly. I used all my strength to randomly stab all over his back. As I sliced into his back, pieces of his skin fell to the ground.

Next, I climbed up Satan's head and I mercilessly stabbed into one of the eyes. Satan had eyes within his eyes. I returned to his back once more and I chopped off one of the wings. He jumped off his throne and screamed out loud. I shouted, "Devil, open your mouth! I'll go into your stomach and finish you up! I'll slice your intestines and burn them!"

Just when I was about to attack Satan again, a bright light poured down from above and the Lord appeared. He said,

State of the Kingdom Address

> "Bong Nyu, you've done a great job! Now, come down. It is enough for today. Let's go now (Book 1, Day 26).

Baptized By Blazing Fire goes on to chronicle the many trips to Heaven and hell experienced by the small Korean church pastored by Pastor Kim. One thing is for certain. Those same events that took place in the book are currently able to be experienced by faith-filled believers. If God were to open your eyes, imagine what you would experience. A whole new world exists, and most of us are unaware of it.

Not long after reading *Baptized By Blazing Fire*, and, if I can recall, praying for deeper spiritual insight, I began seeing deeper into the spiritual world. I started seeing devils in forms I had never seen before. I saw more types and shadows. I had a stronger sense of spiritual awareness, being able to discern spirits upon people, or spirits in certain places. I even began to see angels and feel their presence more keenly. At least on one occasion I saw the glory of the LORD shine in the room, as a very bright, almost blinding white light. And on another occasion, I saw Satan portray himself as Jesus. I had called on the Lord to help me out in a spiritual battle with the devil one night. And he came; only it wasn't him. It was the devil. Talk about being on edge. There's nothing like calling on Jesus and having the devil show up and try to deceive you by passing himself off as Jesus. Soon after, the Holy Spirit revealed to me that the devil tricked me. He wasn't able to deceive me long because he did not display the fruit of the Spirit—love, faith, peace, and others. However, Jesus will always display them. Always test the spirits! You will know them by their fruit (See Matthew 7:16).

THE SPIRITUAL REALITY

I'll tell you from first-hand experience, it's in the spiritual world that our lives are lived and victory over our circumstances is gained: "Whatsoever you bind on earth shall be bound in heaven, and whatsoever you loose on earth shall be loosed in heaven" (See Matthew 16:19). The battle, the life, the world is spiritual!

Elisha Sees Heavenly Army

There is a story in the Bible where the prophet Elisha is encompassed by a host of the army of the enemies of Israel (See 2Kings 6:17). His servant saw the army that was against them, and he began to panic. However, what Elisha saw, his servant did not see. That was a heavenly army up in the sky, 'horses and chariots of fire round about Elisha'. You see, there are forces at work in the spiritual world that affects how you live on earth. Those breakthroughs that you receive as a believer are first received in the spirit. Then, they transcend to the real world where you can practically experience them as a victory over your problems.

David Sees Angel

Then, I go to the story of David, where he saw an angel face to face. In 2Samuel 24:16-17, King David saw the angel of the LORD in plain sight as the angel sent a pestilence upon Israel. David had committed a sin against God by numbering Israel when God told him not to do so. The angel poured out God's wrath upon Israel, and right when the angel was about to destroy Jerusalem, the LORD repented himself of His thoughts against Jerusalem. King David, just like many of the patriarchs of old, was given the grace by God to see into the spiritual world. God may have given you the exact same grace, to see into the invisible world.

State of the Kingdom Address

We have gotten it all wrong. We have lost track of the fact that we are spirits, encased in a body. God made you in His image, and He made you up *there*. In short, you were a spirit first, and the LORD sent you down to earth as flesh. If being a spirit initially, it naturally makes sense that the life you live both now and eternally, is a spiritual life. You have to get back to the spiritual world because that's the reality of life, not just the physical world.

If you consider your work, business, family, houses, property, and so forth you will see just how temporary the things of earth are. People grow, change, or diminish those things all the time. But the spiritual world is eternal. It's the place in which we meet with God, talk to Jesus, get direction from the Holy Spirit, sit with angels, and assault Satan. The spiritual life reigns supreme. If you ever expect to live the powerfully productive, fruitful, and blessed life that God always intended you to live, you have to be *spiritually leveraged*. It's not just how you live on earth that matters. It's about how good you are at living from the foundation of God. And that is a spiritual thing—to flow from the Word of God, the power of the Holy Ghost, and the victory that is in the name of Jesus, namely spiritual. Live in the 4th *dimension!* You must live spiritually, first and foremost, to efficiently live your purpose.

Reality of Prayer

I watched a YouTube video not long ago that explained how our prayers reach up to Heaven. As you pray there is an invisible line of devils that form a canopy in the Second Heaven. They stand between you and the throne of God. Their mission is to stop your prayers from reaching Heaven. So with every prayer that you speak out, there is an assault against those prayers by those warring devils. Daniel 10:13 details the battle in the 2nd Heaven that occurs between angels and devils when the saints of God pray. Faithless prayers stand the least chance to break through the line of devils in the air. Faith-filled prayers, on the other hand, reach the throne of God. They result in an answer from God through ministering angels. You can find out more about how Satan stops your prayers by visiting http://bit.ly/1CBNbBS. In sum, you have to pray with faith if you expect to get your prayers to Heaven, and get answers from God. That's not just a scripture. It's literal.

Armed Angels

In addition, when you pray with faith, your prayers empower angels to act on your behalf and bring you an immediate answer. In the same way that the devils try to stop your prayers from reaching God, they try to stop the angels from reaching you with an answer. Take another look at the book of Daniel. Daniel had to wait for 21 days for an angel to bring him an answer to his prayer. The angel had to battle against devils in the 2nd heaven.

As you pray with faith, you give the angels power to fight devils. You also give them full body armor and weapons of warfare to go up effectively against the forces of darkness. In laymen terms, "Angels fight better when you pray better!" Here is a great video that explains more http://bit.ly/1khudbK.

The result of weak prayers means that your angels have less weapons to fight with, less power, and less body armor to protect them from the attacks of demons. You stand a much better chance of getting the victory you want when you pray with faith.

State of the Kingdom Address

The 4th Dimension

Are you living from the 4th dimension, the spiritual realm? If not, here is a reason to make a change: All spiritual victories manifest in the flesh! Satan works from, and hides in the spiritual world. If you live powerfully spiritually, imagine how much success you will have in reality. For example, you would have dealt with the most important things first such as principalities, spiritual blockages, strongholds, and sin, which makes you vulnerable to Satan's fiery darts. Additionally, you would battle the devil directly, who is responsible for stirring up the evildoers against you. Why not go to the source of the problems rather than deal with the problem itself? A wise man scaleth the city of the mighty, and casteth down the strength of the confidence thereof (See Proverbs 21:22). Next, the difficulties you may have encountered, like financial lack, bad health, and addictions would be resolved by the application of your faith through prayer, declarations, rebukes, and works. By living from the 4th dimension, that is, spiritually, you would be getting to the root of your battles as opposed to dealing with life issues on the surface level. That means they would always return. As you uproot the weeds, they are sure to be destroyed once and for all: 'For the weapons of our warfare are not carnal, but mighty through God to the pulling down of strong holds' (See 2Corinthians 10:4).

The battle is spiritual. And if you don't fight from a spiritual position, you have no chance of winning...ever.

MY SPIRITUAL ENCOUNTERS

I'm going to briefly give you several examples, of the many in my life, of the deep spiritual experiences I've had. I was still living on earth and totally cognizant of my earthly surroundings. However, I was taken *away*, living in the 4th dimension, either in real-time, in dreams, or in visions.

The Goat-Man

I was staying at an investment property my mother purchased a few years ago. It was a dark and dismal place, no electricity, no water, no plumbing. And it was from late summer to early winter (around October – November 2012). To say that was one of the toughest times of my life would be the ultimate understatement. I was not prepared for where God had me at that point in my life. I was down on my knees, beaten down to a pulp by life, and just trying to make it day by day—barely eating, barely able to keep clean, and hardly keeping warm, cool, and encouraged at the same time. I experienced the many severities that the apostle Paul probably faced when he said he could abase or abound (See Philippians 4:12-13). Many of us read the Bible and make light of it; but when Paul said he could abase or abound, he meant it. That was literal, and based on his experiences. He was fresh off of, and fresh into the abasing and abounding aspects of his ministry.

During my bout with the trials of life throughout that period (around late 2012), I was learning humility. I had nothing, no money, no clothes, hardly any food or water, and very little dignity. I was a shame and a reproach. In any event, I learned at that time that Satan often attacks you the most when you're down and out. You know, when you're an outcast, separated from your family and friends, all alone, reprehensible to those around you, and a castaway by society. He works best when you're in isolation: "Separate them from all support, then go in on them for the kill.", the devil thinks. So at that point in my spiritual journey, I had some of the most difficult spiritual battles

State of the Kingdom Address

of my life. I'd seen devils, heard devils, felt devils, smelled devils, tasted devils, and more. And during at least one stretch of a few weeks at my mother's house, I saw a manifestation of the devil—Satan himself—face to face.

I was casually spending time thinking and meditating on my life while I was in my bedroom. That house, itself, was evil by the way. I just felt an eerie feeling all over the house, as if it was a stronghold of the forces of darkness, and I was an unwelcome intruder. I felt like I was *Public Enemy #1* to Satan. The home was in Northeast Baltimore, one of the most dangerous neighborhoods in the country, let alone the city. It was one of those rehab homes. You know, the kind you purchase for a low amount since a lot of repairs are needed to make it livable? Those types. I take it the previous owners or tenants, who knows how far back, may have been into a lot of negative things. The reason is because you could immediately sense the thick cloud of darkness when you walked into the house. It seemed evil and overrun by devils. There could have been anything in there before my mother bought the house—drugs, murders, suicides, anything. So here's a lesson for you: Always check the history of any house or property you purchase if you can. You never know what could be there once you move in or buy it.

Everywhere I went in the house, I felt uneasy. One day I was sitting in my reclining chair in the master bedroom as it was getting dark outside. The room began to get darker as a result of the loss of daylight. Remember, I had no electricity at the time. Shortly thereafter, the devil began to taunt me, as if he wanted me to be overcome by fear and anxiety. I felt his presence coming very strongly from the window on the other side of the bedroom. The window was covered by plastic since I had no curtains. I was just trying to make due. It was the only way to keep the draft from coming inside the house and making it colder than necessary. Again, the house was in the process of being renovated, and was in no shape for a person to live there. According to many organizations, for a person not to have plumbing and electricity, especially in an unfinished house, they can be classified as homeless. So in a sense, I guess I was homeless based on that definition. In any case, as I felt the eyes of the devil peering at me from across the room, I could also hear him in the spirit mocking me. It was as if Satan wanted to make me abandon my mission of serving God. If you are ever facing taunting or torment from the devil and he is trying to make you afraid, never run. Stand your ground. Apply the weapons of warfare to your situation. Satan is like a loose pit bull that is after you. You may think you're doing yourself justice by running, but he will more than likely chase you. You're better off staying put and fighting—with a *stick*, *bat*, *pole*, or something else rather than to run. Besides, if you run once from Satan, you might as well get ready to run 1000 times, or even 1 million. Again, you must stand your ground against the devil.

Anyhow, I was not new to spiritual warfare. I was quite seasoned actually, because I had just come from other battlefields with the devil, at very intense levels of war. God taught my hands to fight and I was a master swordsman by the grace of God. Naturally, when I felt the devil looking at me, mocking me, and filling my room, I immediately got angry. At first a bit of fear came over me. It honestly felt like anxiety more than fear. It felt like I was preparing for a fight. But quickly that fear or anxiety turned to anger and courage. Consequently, as soon as I felt the assault and harassment from the devil, I rose up in the power of God. I had an expression of angry defiance on my face. I rebuked Satan. I literally taunted him back. I told him, "You don't scare me, devil!"

State of the Kingdom Address

Next, I stood up and walked toward the plastic-covered window where I heard and felt Satan the strongest. I spoke back to him in bold authority in the LORD:

> I ain't scared of you, devil. You got the right one this time. If you thought I was the least bit scared of you, you're dead wrong. Not only am I not afraid of you, I'm glad that you're here. Let's get reacquainted with one another. I tortured you much the last time you were here. Yet, in all the pain you received then, that still wasn't enough for you. So you came again. Therefore, the pain I inflict upon you this time, will be far worse than any pain you ever felt from me. Hear now, Oh Satan! Since you appear from my window, I immediately make that window a torture chamber. As God is my witness, I will hold you in that window as a prisoner of war. You will not run; you will not get away. As a matter of fact, I command in Jesus' name that you cannot go. I do not rebuke you away. I rebuke you here. Don't run. You ain't going nowhere!
>
> Now, I instantly command every rebuke upon you that I ever created, from now until eternity—torturous rebukes, pain and agony, humiliation, punishment, torment and defeat. I command right now that the *swords of the spirit* appear in my hands. [I closed my eyes as I was rebuking him, and saw two swords appear in the spirit]. And I thrust these into your chest, you dirty rotten dog. Be cursed, and injured by the power and holiness in these swords, which is the Word of God.

I thrust the swords into his chest as if I stood with one leg bent in front and the other leg stretched out behind me. My fists seemed to be down facing, as if I was trying to stab the devil in the chest in an upward motion (bringing the swords up from a low position). I had the swords fully lodged in the devil's chest. He screamed in agony. I had his entire body lifted up onto the swords, and sliding down to the base of the swords—totally at the swords' mercy.

I didn't know where to put the devil from that point. I wanted to put him in the Lake of Fire, but then I thought he would only be put in the Lake of Fire during his final judgment. So there's no way I can do it now. God immediately corrected me. The LORD said, "He has visitation rights." Then, to add insult to injury, I poked the swords—with the devil attached—to the bottom of the Lake of Fire. I stabbed the bottom of the lake with the swords in order to give the devil fiery torment. As I did that, Satan was pinned between the ground and the base of the swords as he felt the flames from the lake.

I lifted him up—still on the swords—and his body began to slide down the tip of the swords. So I lifted the swords upright, as not to lose Satan, so that he would slide back down to the base. I then stabbed the bottom of the Lake of Fire again with the swords, and pinned the devil between the swords and the ground once again. I lifted him back up and slid him back to the base of the swords as before. I repeated the same thing, stabbing the lake with the devil attached to the swords, and pulling him back out. However, the final time I pulled him out of the lake and slid him down the base of the swords, I twisted my wrists as in a 180 degree angle. I proceeded to walk over to the window which was covered with plastic. And I told the devil,

> Be tortured for evermore in this torture chamber. In this chamber lies the pain of these holy swords and the Lake of Fire. It also holds every single rebuke that will ever be put

State of the Kingdom Address

upon you and that ever was put upon you by the hand of God, and by the faith of man.

The devil screamed and pleaded with me not to put him in my torture chamber. I then, as if knowing the pressure point of Satan, and wanting to inflict as much pain upon him as humanly possible, pinned him to the wall on the two swords. I said,

> May you forever feel the pain of this torture and be reminded of who you're up against as you attempt to torment and afflict me. May every devil in hell feel the pain of this torture due to your resistance against me. May you be a reproach and a shame to all your subjects who viewed you as a king, only to see you be defeated by the faith of man. I continued my chastisement of Satan:

May the pain and torture upon you this moment be increased and intensified one *googol-fold* per millisecond from now until eternity. May this pain go with you into my afterlife. May you forever be reminded of the power bore by the saints of God who walk in the power and authority of the blood of Jesus and His name. And may every devil in hell revolt against you, their leader, for the pain and agony you caused them as a result of you contending with me, a man of God. I declare intense torture and pain upon you, Oh Satan, and every devil and foul spirit that is with you, just for coming against the people of God and disrupting their peace. May the inhabitants of Heaven and hell look upon you and wag their heads for the foolishness in you that still persists, ever since the day you revolted against God Almighty and got kicked out of Heaven. Shame, reproach, pain, punishment, judgment, humiliation, and defeat I declare upon you, devil.

May this torture chamber forever exist, and not be removed, but by the hand of God, or by the declaration of me reversing the curse. May any inhabitant of this house from henceforth live in peace. And may they not perceive the reality of this spiritual world and battle, lest God Almighty opens their eyes for them to see you on the wall [I didn't want the weaker spiritually to be tormented by the demonic forces]. Cursing upon you forever and ever, in Jesus' name, Oh devil. Be rebuked! And from now on when I rain a rebuke upon you, may you still feel it on this wall, no matter where you are in the world and no matter what disruption you cause upon the inhabitants of the earth. Just as a spirit can be many places at once, you can be in the world, in hell, in the heavens, all while you're simultaneously feeling the agony of this torture chamber. In Jesus' name I so command it. Amen.

I was mad.

As God is my witness, when I began to walk away from that wall to sit back down in my chair, I heard laughter. I heard uncontrollable chuckling. It was not coming from the devil, nor from hell. It was coming from Heaven. I heard the laughter from the Lord, Jesus Christ. I didn't know why He was laughing so hard. I saw in the spirit the Lord laughing. He was literally turning red in the face, and He could not stop laughing. I also felt the angels laughing, and the great cloud of witnesses laughing and mocking the devil.

State of the Kingdom Address

The more the Lord laughed, the more irritated I became. I was still infuriated with the devil. I was in battle-mode, and just got finished one of the most intense rounds I had ever faced against Satan. I was fuming. Nonetheless, Jesus kept laughing. And the more He laughed, the more I struggled to control my laughter. I cracked a slight smile. But I was sort of reprimanding Jesus about laughing, as if His laughter was making me lose my anger against the devil.

I asked Jesus to please stop laughing because I'm mad and this is not funny. The Lord then spoke to me. He said,

> David. I'm sorry to be laughing so hard. But this is so funny. This is so amusing to me. Never before has the devil ever been rebuked so. Most people rebuke him away. You accosted him. You rebuked him to you in order to torture him and post him to the wall of your torture chamber. My child, this is the manner of faith that my saints should be walking in! This is the power that I bestowed upon *you*. And this is the victory that I gave you at the Cross. I want you to tell my people—tell the Church—that this is how they should be walking on earth as *End-Time Warriors* of God! They have all the power over the enemy, if they would just exercise their faith!

I began to take it all in, like I could not believe I did the right thing, and the Lord was pleased with me. He then told me "Heaven, and God Almighty, the Holy Spirit, the angels, the great cloud of witnesses rejoices with me. There is great joy in Heaven." Jesus also went on to tell me that He has made me a spectacle, an end-time warrior, and that my forefathers of the faith, namely David, were looking down upon me. They were exceedingly glad because I picked up the torch where they left off. I was walking in their spirit of faith and assaults against the enemies of God.

Jesus told me to go in peace—to sit back down on my chair and to enjoy my night. He told me that the devil is in a holding pin, being tortured, and that He is with me (that I need not fear reprisal). I briefly looked at the wall, and lo and behold, I saw the face of the devil appear on the plastic bag which covered the window. It was really distinct. I could see his eyes, his nose, his mouth, his cheeks, all of his face. It even got so pronounced at some points of me staring at him that I could see his horns—two horns protruding up out of his head, and curving under like a ram's horn.

Although, he was like a *goat-man*, for lack of a better term—half man, half goat. According to scripture, sheep are kept by Jesus, but goats are cast away from Him during His Judgment (See Matthew 25:31-33). The devil appeared as a goat, a detestable animal, at least in terms of God's judgment. And forget about beauty and symmetry. Satan's face on the wall was absolutely hideous! It was totally deformed and disfigured. I immediately knew that face was Satan's because I had seen the same face previously in dreams I had of the devil as well as on YouTube videos and in spiritual warfare books depicting Satan. It was a split image of the face I had seen so many times before. Sure, there were times where I've seen the devil's face in perfect symmetry. But the reality is, as a result of his rebellion against God, he is super ugly. That's possibly because God removed His grace and glory from him after Satan's rebellion. Yet, the devil is always trying to get his former glory back; and it deeply pangs him that he can never be where he once was, with God, and in beauty and splendor.

I walked over to my chair to sit back down, and looked back at the window to see if I was just imagining things. "Is that face really on the

State of the Kingdom Address

wall?" I thought. "Is that really Satan? Is he really being tortured?" God confirmed to me that all of the above was true. As I looked at the window the face became even more defined from afar. The devil was repugnant! And he fussed and cursed me still from the wall, expressing his anger toward me, promising revenge. I was not afraid. I maintained my peace. Day by day, morning by morning, night by night, I saw Satan's face and was reminded of the deep levels of spiritual warfare in which I was now engaged. There was no turning back now.

It's one thing to fight a demon. It's an entirely different ball game to fight the devil. Satan rarely gets off his throne to battle a saint personally. He sees himself as a king, and it's much more honorable for him to send his subordinate devils out to attack us rather than for him to do it. The few times that he does leave his throne to fight us personally are a result of several things:

> ➢ You have a very high calling
> ➢ You are very strong spiritually
> ➢ His subordinate devils have failed time and time again to defeat you

And if he does battle us one-on-one, it's the highest level of spiritual warfare that you will ever face.

Anyway, the devil cursed me daily from that window. He still tried to mock me and instill fear in me. He still tried to turn me off of God's work from that position, the torture chamber, but all to no avail. I was dead set on completing my purpose and walking in God.

Days later I found it hard to sleep next to that image on the window since my bed was right next to it. Let's face it. That's not exactly what you want to go to sleep next to—Satan's face. I mean, it's not like having a little bug behind you. It's the devil—the ruler of the evil powers of the earth, the king of hell, the adversary of the saints of God, the accuser of the brethren, the evil serpent that caused man to fall, and our #1 enemy. So…hard to sleep? Absolutely.

I can't count the number of nights that I had to wake up several times to rebuke the devil in the middle of the night. I constantly felt an evil feeling over me as I slept on my bed, which was near the window. And when I turned my back to the devil, sleeping on my side, I felt really vulnerable. I heard footsteps on the ceiling for many nights, and there was no one living above me! There was only ceiling tile there. There were times I even felt piercing stabs, as if Satan poked me with a spiritual knife or sword. I heard whispers from the window where I posted him. I felt demonic presences from other devils that tried to come to Satan's rescue. I take it Satan must have commissioned them to remove him from captivity, at least by trying to bargain with me, if they couldn't altogether remove him.

I had experiences of demons coming from hell to me in the middle of the night with peace treaties, speaking in an evil Satanic language trying to form a truce with me. It honestly felt like they were speaking in Latin. The Holy Spirit revealed to me what they were saying: They wanted me to let the devil go and to quit fighting them and torturing them in exchange for them leaving me alone. But I never gave in. To think that they would ever leave me alone was absurd. Besides, I enjoyed inflicting pain upon the devil. So instead of accepting the peace accord, I intensified my onslaught. I was very unyielding to those negotiating demons. I was offended that they even had the audacity to try to make peace with me. I found myself constantly fighting them, rebuking them, praying for Jesus to come, calling on angelic backup, and calling for *holy missiles* to fall from Heaven and clear the premises of evil. I was in the midst of the spiritual world's

State of the Kingdom Address

version of the Vietnam War. And I was in the middle of enemy fire, needing some help. To make matters worse, I had Satan plastered to my window. I thought to myself on several occasions whether I should let him go. However, I decided against it because I knew that he would instantly be back to seek revenge against me. By God's grace, I held him as a *prisoner of war*. And I didn't believe in dealing kindly with prisoners–Holy water-borging. I tortured him. The devil became increasingly enraged the longer he stayed in the torture chamber. I didn't just leave him there to rest. I commanded daily torture on him. Every time I saw his ugly face or heard him taunting me, I commanded a new punishment upon him. It was my version of an electric chair for those accused of heinous crimes. In this case, it was Satan. And his crimes were the continuous harassment that he brought against me and the people of God, since the beginning of our existence.

One day as I slept on my side I was awakened out of the blue. I'm a light sleeper. I heard a strong, raspy voice coming from the wall where Satan was posted. It was evil. It seemed like whatever spiritual energy was necessary to muster out a sound from the wall, Satan used every last ounce of it to be able to get out a sound from the window. It was like the spiritual world meshed with the physical world. It was as if he strained to get the words out, but when they came out they were distinct and malicious: "LOOOK AAAAT MEEEE!", the devil spoke. Apparently, he tried to make me afraid and show me that he was really there in my room with me. He was trying to show me that he wasn't just the devil we read about, or see depicted in movies or in plays, or the one we see as kids dressed up in costumes on Halloween. He wanted to show me that he was a living, breathing, real evil being; and he was trying to make me afraid and pay for what I had done to him. Satan is real. He is not only real, but he spoke right from the same wall in which I—the defiant, disrespectful, God-serving, devil-defying saint—had posted him.

"Where is Jesus now?" I felt like the devil was saying. I stood my ground. I didn't budge or show any fear. I was on edge and on the defensive immediately, yes. But I didn't show fear. I more or less displayed anger. I was incensed that Satan had the nerve to continue on with his assault against me, even though I had just declared all of that torture over him. I resorted back to my *spiritual warfare arsenal*.

I kept a list of Satanic rebukes on my cell phone and in my mind, that I call my spiritual warfare arsenal. I literally created the rebukes and named them anything under the sun, so long as they resulted in severe punishment to the devil. For example, I have one rebuke called *The Big Bang Theory*. During that rebuke, I place Satan at the epicenter of what I call a *holy explosion*. All things holy, righteous, and of God, the Creator, comes from that epicenter—power, truth, mercy, love, righteousness, light, Jesus, the *blood*, peace, and more. The rebuke causes Satan to be tortured from now until eternity, second by second, feeling the big explosion every moment of his existence.

I call my rebukes out like football plays. All together I have about 75 to 80 of them at the time of this writing. Nevertheless, the list is constantly growing. I even have one rebuke called *Jesus Come*. I'm sure you can guess what that means. If not, it means "Jesus, come!" That rebuke causes the Lord Jesus to come to my situation with me and to ward off the devils. And let me tell you, when Jesus comes, devils scatter like roaches when you turn on the lights! They don't want to be anywhere near His light. I also have a satanic rebuke called *Rebuke #50*. That entails every single rebuke that I have ever given Satan, ever declared, ever created, ever put on my list or that I will put on my list, in addition to every rebuke and judgment that God has ever given

State of the Kingdom Address

Satan since the beginning of time until the end, including every rebuke ever declared by any saint of God since the beginning of time until the end to be placed upon the devil simultaneously, and recurring every second. It is an excruciatingly painful rebuke, and I try to use it sparingly. But when I do use it, it's extremely powerful and causes the devil immense torture.

In going back to the "Look at me" words by the devil, who was posted to my window, I decided to put those words into my rebuke arsenal. As the devil spoke those words to me that night from the wall, I instantly leaned up in my bed in sheer anger, faced the wall, told the devil I wasn't afraid of him, and rebuked him once more. I said,

> You don't scare me, devil. Not only will I look at you. I will gaze at you. I will cause pain upon you just by me looking at you, and by you having the audacity to look at me.

> In addition, I create a rebuke called Look At Me. Whenever you hear those words from me, or whenever you speak those words, or whenever my eyes meet your eyes, be it in this place, in the spirit, or somewhere else, I cause instant pain upon you. I cause the truth of God's words to pierce you. I cause the light of my eyes which bare the power of God to burn through you. I cause holy pain upon you from your head to your feet and all over. From now until eternity this rebuke shall stand, and it shall increase in power millisecond by millisecond. No matter if I ever declare this rebuke upon you again, it shall increase exponentially by itself.

After that rebuke, Satan was once again in agony. I found myself shooting random rebukes at him every day and night as he stood there in my torture chamber, posted to my wall by the holy swords. To this day, I have no doubt he is still there in the spirit.

I took pictures and recorded videos of the wall back when I stayed at that house. I knew people would need to see it to believe it. In fact, I recorded a YouTube video of my bout with the devil that day. I have unlisted the video so it would not be public. I didn't think it was reasonable for me to reveal my story to the general public, many of whom may be skeptical and insincere about serving God and learning about spiritual things. I didn't want the comments to get out of hand, nor for the things of God and spiritual battle to be mocked. Nonetheless, I will consider sending you the direct link if I find that you are genuinely interested. Just check out my YouTube Channel at dnvm22 and send me a message requesting access to the Satan on the Wall video. I may decide to make it public again if enough people request it. But for now, I will keep it unlisted for the reasons I mentioned already.

A few weeks later, I called in my younger brother to see the devil on my wall (just to increase his faith, and desire to walk in the power of God). It took him some time to come into my room and look at the devil on my wall. He was a bit afraid at first. He often brought me over food and water to help sustain me during that difficult time in my life.

One day, I called him into my room and told him I wanted to show him the face of the devil—the one I described to him so many times before on the phone. I told him to sit down in my reclining chair, where he could see the image the best. He sat down, and reluctantly looked at the window. It took him a few minutes to build up the courage to look at the wall without being afraid. It was as if he was a little kid, hiding under the covers from the *Boogeyman*. He slowly peeked up to see the devil's face on the wall after he meditated and prayed to God for a few seconds.

He looked up and did not see the image at first. I told him to keep looking. He looked longer, for like a minute or two. He still didn't see it. Without pointing the outline of the face out, I told him to keep staring and to not be afraid. He slowly began to see what I saw. He began pointing out each feature of the face, the eyes, nose, mouth of the devil. He could not believe what he saw. The devil really was posted to my wall.

A couple years after that, I showed my cousin the picture of the devil on my wall. He could not believe what he saw. Like my brother, he pointed out the image himself. He said he would not have believed me if I had not shown him the actual pictures. Months later, I showed the picture to a brother in Christ, he was also shocked to see what he saw. Spiritual warfare is real. The part of faith and the power of God that works for you is the part that you believe.

You have at least that same amount of power over the devil that I had. You just have to tap into your faith and live completely by it!

Strong Man of the House

I remember a spiritual situation I had a few years back. I was in the kitchen cooking. My mind was everywhere. I was hungry, thinking about business, thinking about life, and the like. I was at the stove boiling rice in a pot, and I walked over to the kitchen sink to rinse off a spoon. All of a sudden, as I turned around to go back to the pot of rice, I jumped and gasped. I was startled.

What stood in front of me was what I would call an *iron man*. He was made of some sort of metallic substance. It appeared as though he was of the material that you would see on one of those futuristic cartoon shows. His body armor was metal, but also mixed with some sort of plastic or vinyl. It was like he was snatched right from the TV, as if you could touch the cartoon with your physical hands. He was made of cartoon-material in real-life form, for lack of a better description. He seemed to be out of this world—maybe he was from outer space. His body armor was red and black (mostly red with black detail). He had a black sash in the shape of an "X" going across his chest, only it was a part of his uniform. He was built and in shape. It was as if his armor was painted onto him to reveal his definition and size. The man had a helmet on, with a sort of metal shield on his face, which was also apparently built into the uniform.

As I turned from the running water I looked at him face to face, eye to eye. His face was literally just a few inches from mine. He was a supernatural being, there with me live in the kitchen, brought from his world to mine. I froze. I was immediately in defense mode. I had to protect myself from the threat. He was an intruder in my space, and he looked to be a formidable opponent. I then recognized that he was none other than the *strong man of the house*. That's another alias of the devil: 'No man can enter into a strong man's house, and spoil his goods, except he will first bind the strong man; and then he will spoil his house' (See Mark 3:27).

Satan came in another form this time. He wasn't a spirit. He wasn't a serpent or a dragon. He wasn't manifested as an earthly man. He was a strong man from another world. And he was in my domain, though he felt quite the contrary. He felt like I was in his domain. Suffice it to say, I had to get rid of him. Otherwise, he would overthrow me and *spoil* my house.

State of the Kingdom Address

On a side note, I knew Satan was there in the house to defy me. I was actually staying with a relative at the time, and months earlier I had blessed that house. My relative told me that they had experienced a demonic attack, where something attacked them in the night while they were asleep. They said whatever it was tried to pull them into, what they called a 'mouse hole'. They said their body kept getting hot as they were being pulled, and they felt whatever it was that was pulling them, and scratching them on their neck and back. I didn't realize how serious of a satanic attack that was upon them until I saw the visible scratches on their neck days after their encounter. I told them that what was happening is that their house was being overrun by devils. Satan was attempting to kill them through sin, and drag them to hell. And that was no 'mouse hole' that they were being pulled down. That was the portal to hell. I told them that they needed to get their life right with God, and that God was warning them against their way of living. Next, I told them that I would bless their house if they wanted me to; they obliged. I eventually went over their house prior to me moving in with them, with Bible in hand, clearing everybody out of the house except me. I blessed the house, and felt the evil that they described. The devil hated the fact that I was there to send him packing. I blessed the house from wall to wall, ceiling to floor, corner to corner, and everywhere in between. I declared blessings over the house and everyone in it, and curses over the devil and anything evil in the house. To make a long story short, the devil was mad that I was in the house as God's spiritual warrior. He was mad that I blessed the house. And he was mad that I came to take spiritual territory from him. Note, as a saint of God, wherever you go in the world, you should go with the intent of taking spiritual territory from the devil, and bringing it into the treasury of God. That's what God has called you to do as an End-Time Warrior.

Anyway, picking up where I left off with the strong man of the house, within a second or two of me staring into the strong man's face, I girded my loins with strength. I defied him. My face and demeanor changed. I went from being startled to courageous and confident. I took one step back as if to protect myself. I then regained control of the situation. I aggressively charged toward him in that small space (1 to 2 feet between us), as a bull would charge at a red cape. I guess the red in his uniform reminded me of a cape that a bull would charge. I lifted my finger to his face, and rebuked him as I charged forward: "You don't scare me, devil. I ain't afraid of you. In the name of Jesus, be cursed, you wretched fool!" He immediately faded away.

I looked around the kitchen to make sure he was really gone. He was. I finished cooking my rice. And from that day forward I always expected that at any moment in time the devil could appear in my face in plain sight. He could catch me by surprise in any place, be it in the kitchen, bathroom, shower, bedroom, at the foot of my bed, in a public restroom, in the dressing room of a department store, anywhere he wanted. And I would see him, so long as God opened my eyes.

That's how Jesus must have felt when the devil tempted him in the wilderness, or when He saw Satan fall from Heaven as a bolt of lightning. Satan was real to him, and so was the spiritual world—the *double* life. That's to say you live a full life in the world, but you also live a full life spiritually; it's like you're living two lives. The Lord had plain sight vision (able to see spiritual beings), and so do you if God opens your eyes to see into the spiritual world.

After a while of battling Satan and seeing him face to face, it's no longer a thing of fear, but it becomes a thing of familiarity. You're like,

"Ok. The last time I kicked your butt in the bathroom. This time I will beat you up in my car. I fought you in my bedroom yesterday. Cool, you showed your ugly face up at my business meeting in the back of the room. I will fight you here too, devil." At some point you feel like Mohammad Ali must have felt that time that he was about to fight Joe Frazier: "I'll fight that chump in a telephone booth."

After a while you get so used to spiritual warfare that you can almost feel what Jesus must've felt when Satan tempted him in the wilderness. I doubt that the Lord had any fear of the devil. He was probably more irritated by him than anything. Lastly, beware that sometimes Satan defeats you in spiritual battle too, namely by you being in sin and disobedient to God.

Vampire Devil with Fangs

A couple of years ago, I was at home in the kitchen cooking. I was at the sink running water and I just happened to look up and toward the living room, which was adjacent to the kitchen. I saw a black (brown-skinned) man, who instantly put me on edge. He appeared out of nowhere—in the flesh. He was a devil. I got a glance at him before he disappeared. He wore a long black gown. He hissed at me with his fangs showing, sort of like a cat would hiss at a person if he was cornered. However, I knew he was upset I was there. I was immediately on the defensive, and I rebuked that devil in the name of Jesus. He was there to oppose me, the spiritual leader of the house, who was there to lead my family to salvation and the blessings of God. I resisted the devil daily. And Satan wanted me out. Any light that I brought to that house was met with the forces of darkness. That hissing devil, that resembled a vampire almost, was one of Satan's subordinates that was appointed by the devil to hinder my work and to attack me. I just happened to see him face to face in plain sight.

This is just one more example of the countless times I have seen into the spiritual realm. My life has become spiritual, and I have to accept that. Once you see into another world, you can't undo it. You can't play ignorant to what really is out there. You have to deal with the fact that you live a double life. You have tapped into the mysteries of the *real world*.

Since those experiences, I've seen Jesus, angels, devils, human spirits in the flesh, animal spirits, dog spirits, like the Doberman Pinscher that was running toward me and my brother as we walked from a local university one night. I jumped and put my laptop bag in front of me for protection. I saw a dog that my brother clearly didn't see. It was a spirit, a devil that was attacking me.

If you have not yet experienced living in the 4th dimension, but you find yourself growing closer to God, wait for it. The LORD is opening the eyes of the saints as He spoke of in Joel 2:28. You may see dreams and visions in these last days. God is providing you with operating leverage by allowing you to take your victory from the spiritual world. Devils are exposed, angels are revealed, and the hidden mysteries of Heaven, the universe, and the earth are opened up to you. Your new life may just have begun today!

WARNING AGAINST FALSE SPIRITS

By the way, many of the spiritual experiences that you hear people having today are not the type that draws them closer to God or gets them the victory in the spirit world. For example, some people are experimenting with the occult. Others deal with psychics, astrology, and ghost hunting. If you pursue any of these activities, you're only inviting evil into your life. Conversely, spiritual experiences you get from God are good by nature.

Many people have gotten sidetracked from God's will and ended up dealing with the dark side of the spiritual realm. In essence, they are worshiping Satan, or summoning him into their lives. That's not what you want. You do that and you'll be dealing with Satan all alone, and not with the help of God. You invited him, you worshiped the things of the devil, and you got the full reward, or costs of doing so. What you need to be doing is seeking God and the ability to live in the spiritual world without sacrificing your soul as a result. Godly experiences lead to Heaven; satanic experiences, such as the occult, can very well lead you to hell.

God uses the spiritual experiences to empower, teach, guide, strengthen, inform, and prepare you for what lies ahead in your life and in the Kingdom as well as what you're going through now. God will use your experiences to have you foiling the devil's plans, defeating Satan in one-on-one clashes, and achieving your breakthrough in the spiritual world.

I pray that you live the right way in the deep spiritual world, and not the wrong way (following the occult). The right way leads to victory over the devil, and closer interactions and revelation from God, whereas the wrong way leads to torment and control from Satan.

You shouldn't so much try to tap into your *6th sense* (seeing human spirits, etc.) but to tap into what I call your *7th sense*—the ability to see, hear, feel, smell, taste even deeper supernatural things:

- Seeing Jesus
- Talking with Him face to face
- Being endowed with power from the Holy Spirit and defeating Satan in that power
- Seeing angels and having them minister to you
- Seeing Satan fall before you when you're walking in the Holy Ghost
- Seeing manifestations of devils in flesh-form

Why not leverage the spiritual world to receive your victory here on earth? The earlier you do it the better results you will have in making progress in life. There may be spiritual blockages holding you up. And you have no choice but to remove them. Remove them spiritually and you will remove them in the flesh also.

REVELATIONS OF HELL

People have been walking in darkness as far as knowing about hell is concerned. They have developed a misleading picture of who the devil is and what it means to be cast into hell. It's a game to many. However, in these last days God will reveal to us who Satan really is in many ways:

Dreams and Visions

God will give believers deeper more profound dreams and visions about the devil. They will see themselves fighting Satan in one-on-one duels. They will see themselves prevail at times. They will see him prevail against them at other times. They will see the devil speaking with them, taunting them, negotiating with them, smirking at them, and otherwise.

They will see his appearance in detail, even the skin on his face and the color of his clothing. They will see his facial features and be able to describe the size and shape of them. They will see the devil in many forms, be it as a man, woman, snake, dragon, blob, shadow, spirit, beast, goat, angel of light, or even as Jesus. He is a deceiver, and God will expose him to the world.

The saints will know exactly who their adversary is, what he looks like, what he's capable of doing, what he has done, and what he plans to do against them and against the Kingdom of God. Any good champion will know his greatest challenger. God will reveal the devil, your biggest competition, to you, that you may be able to battle him effectively.

As you see him, you will be able to see and know his agenda. High levels of spiritual warfare nearly always involve a personal confrontation with Satan. He usually sends his subordinates, but for the mightiest soldiers of God, Satan will come himself. He does so to try and make sure that his work will get done. His subjects have often failed their assignment.

Portal to hell

Back in June 2010, I had been involved in very high levels of spiritual warfare over the course of several months. I was consistently hearing voices, seeing things, seeing orbs of light floating around the house, feeling demonic presences, and similar things. I had been staying in East Baltimore at the time at the former house of a relative.

That was probably one of the toughest years of my life. I lost about 7 family members and friends, one to suicide. I was going through financial troubles, emotional pain, and harassment from people in the neighborhood, just to name a few things. I was barely eating, had no running water, and was all alone.

I had gang members outside that didn't like me. So I always felt uneasy walking in and out of the house. This was in a bad neighborhood by the way. I had the SWAT team come to my house at least two to three times with guns drawn, looking for someone that lived there long before me. Life was hell.

It was even worse in the spiritual world. Satan felt he had the perfect opportunity to harass me since I was so miserable. And that's what he did. I would have to walk around with Bibles, casting devils out sporadically all day, leading up to the following situation.

Somewhere around June 9, 2010, I was in the basement of the home. I slept down the basement on a couch. It was a finished basement for the most part, and had an entertainment center with a TV built into the wall. I had a couple of cats and one dog living there as well. I should have known that there was really something wrong when I noticed the animals would never want to stay in the basement with me. They seemed scared. Every time I would have them down there, they would cry to get out. I ended up letting them out, and typically slept in the basement by myself.

It was always extremely dark. I had a TV and lights, but I am one to sleep better with the lights out. Later on I figured out why my pets were so afraid. They were trying to escape from the 'hot spot', or the most evil place in the house, which was the basement. I don't know what happened in that house prior to me living there, but I don't think there was a lot of godliness there. Then, a part of the basement had what I call 'the portal to hell', that was the laundry room, which was deep in the back near the back door. It had its own separate

State of the Kingdom Address

room and was partitioned from the other living areas by a door, or in this case a curtain, as the door was removed. The laundry room had stone walls that reminded me of an old prison or cave. It had an old oil tank sitting there. And it had old-looking windows with bars on them. It just felt like the most evil part of the house, and every time I went in there I got the chills.

One evening as I was about to go to sleep, I did my customary blessing of the house. Earlier that evening I had heard a pastor mention Isaiah 41:10, which talks about overcoming fear. I needed that scripture because I was often afraid to go to sleep at night due to the evil all around me inside the house. As I was about to lay down and turn out the lights, I felt something taunting me and peering at me from the laundry room. I slept about two rooms away from the small laundry room. However, I could see into the laundry room from the part of the basement where I was. The laundry room had a white curtain as a door. Above the curtain there were a couple of small gaps that allowed me to see into the laundry room. I saw two white eyes looking at me. At the same time I felt an evil presence and heard someone call me and taunt me. I immediately got in battle-mode. I ran to the laundry room quickly and aggressively with Bible in hand, as my sword. I quickly pulled open the curtain and looked at where the white eyes were. I defied the devil. I said "You don't scare me. I rebuke you devil. To hell with you. You can call my name 'David' all you want. I know what it means. It means 'Beloved'— Beloved of God. Be rebuked you dirty dog."

Next, in anger I walked away, closed the curtain, and proceeded to turn out the light and go to sleep. You can imagine how uneasy I must've felt, having to sleep in that old, pitch black, evil basement all by myself, where my pets didn't even want to stay, especially after just rebuking Satan. Nonetheless, I headed for bed.

I laid down on the couch with the Bible on my chest. I slept like that, with the Bible, mainly out of apprehension. I needed some extra protection and comfort. Within a few minutes I was asleep—at least in my dream. I found myself in my dream, in the exact same basement where I slept. I also found myself staring into the laundry room. I was in a duel. Before me was none other than Satan, himself. I stood about 20-30 feet away from my adversary, the devil...in the flesh.

I was tense to say the least. Then, the unthinkable happened. As I faced the devil, something lifted me off the ground and held me in the air for a second or two. I was scared, because I knew what was about to happen next. That invisible force was about to lunge me right toward Satan. It was going to make me fight him, and I couldn't stop it. That's exactly what happened. I felt like I was on the most frightening, thrilling roller-coaster ride of all time. I soon began flying fast and angrily toward Satan. I was trying to 'pump the brakes', so to speak. But I couldn't. It was as if something came over me, and whatever that something was, it was so powerful that I couldn't rebuke it in Jesus' name, although I tried. [Note: You can't rebuke *Jesus* with the name of Jesus]. Trust me, if I was never scared in my life, I was scared then. I did not want to go anywhere near the devil. I felt he would kill me, destroy me, or do whatever the devil did to people if he could get his hands on them.

Nonetheless, I kept flying toward Satan, with my arms out stretched as if I was going to choke him with both hands. I was going fast and powerfully toward him. I felt like something came inside of my back like I was a puppet. I felt the hand of God in me, and I was being used to fight Satan. While I zeroed in on Satan, he stood there cold, defiant, and emotionless. He looked like death.

State of the Kingdom Address

He was good looking in appearance, very tall, statuesque, handsome, muscular, and strong. He had black hair, and a black robe on. Yet, his face was pale as death. He looked like death. As good looking as he was, he was ugly. It's like his character, spirit, represented ugliness, especially in God's eyes. He was the epitome of evil and ungodliness. I take it this must've been Satan before the fall from Heaven, that former beautiful cherub in charge of worship. Now, he was ugly, and wanted to maintain a part of his former self. Nevertheless, all the beauty he had was gone due to the curse from God for his rebellion.

I got closer to him as I flew toward him in the power of the Holy Ghost. I had a terrible, menacing, war-face on, as if I hated evil; I wanted to inflict as much pain upon Satan as possible. While I was about 5 to 6 feet away from him about to grab his neck in the power of the Holy Spirit, he dropped to his knees. He fell down flat on both knees before the power of the Most High God within me. I couldn't even touch him. That reminds me of Psalms 16:10: 'For thou wilt not leave my soul in hell; neither wilt thou suffer thine Holy One to see corruption.'

I'm not sure why I couldn't touch him in that dream but I had in others, such as the one where I body-slammed the devil. But in either case, the devil had to submit to the authority of the Most High God, the Holy Spirit, Jesus Christ in me. Every knee must bow. Hallelujah!

I took that dream to mean that we do not understand the power that is resident in us as born-again believers. We have God Almighty, Jesus Christ, the Holy Ghost inside of us. And the devil is no match for Him. Why do we take that power, that privilege for granted? Satan can do nothing against us when we are walking in the Spirit. It's when we walk in the flesh that he prevails. Here's an example...

For several days after that dream, I had seen Satan in other dreams in the same battle arena, the basement. He had on the same black robe. He was hovering over me as I slept on the couch in the basement. I got up to fight him and overtake him like I did in the first dream. Only this time I was in the flesh. I had been committing sin that week, and it weakened my spiritual state; the anointing upon me was gone. I felt like Samson when God had left him. The Holy Spirit wasn't upon me as powerfully as before; yet I still persisted to pursue Satan. I had enough power to overcome the trance that he put me in while I was sleeping on the couch. However, in the dream, as I was endowed with some power, it wasn't enough to defeat Satan. Sin had weakened me, and given him the victory over me. I found myself pushing against an invisible force to get to Satan, yet I fell before his feet. I was pushing towards him to grab his legs, but I couldn't. I was defeated.

Here's a lesson from these two stories: If you walk in righteousness and in the power of the Holy Spirit, you win against Satan. You are serving God. Therefore, Satan will fall down at your feet during a battle. He will bow down before you. Alternately, if you are caught up in sin, you will lose against Satan. You will be serving him when you serve sin. You will bow down before him.

Serve God and win, serve the devil (sin) and lose

Shortly after those dreams, I told a sister in Christ about them. She has an incredible prophetic gift. She told me that God was raising me up as an apostle, and I was being prepared for it through all my challenges, battles, and discomforts. That was long before I knew about the Five-Fold Ministry (apostle, prophets, pastors, evangelists, and teachers). All I knew was that I was engaged in extremely high-levels of spiritual warfare. The only way out was to go through it.

State of the Kingdom Address

Plain sight appearances

People will not only see the devil in dreams and visions, but also face-to-face. And that's not just entailing some type of mirage, or spirit, that many people currently see today. They will actually see the devil face-to-face in the flesh. Hypothetically speaking, he will be so real to them that if they touched him, they would probably feel the heat on his arm burn their hand. It would be as if they touched their own arm—that's the level of plain-sight appearances that some faithful servants of God will have of the devil. It is a gift from God to be able to see these things; and what once was deemed a curse, seeing the devil, will be seen as a blessing by God's true servants. What you can see you can attack. You can know his exact position, armor, strengths, weaknesses, and so forth. No more guerrilla warfare, where the devil attacks you and runs off. If God allows you to see the devil, you will engage in spiritual battle much more efficiently, as a trained and deadly warrior of God.

Movies and television documentaries

Movies will begin to popularize Satan. That's typical Hollywood, and it will continue to be done there. Only, those movies in Hollywood undermine who Satan really is. So the general public will be misled by the false sense of reality in the movies.

Nonetheless, real Christians with genuine spiritual experiences will arise and begin to produce movies that depict who Satan really is. They will show the truth about Satan, and detail spiritual encounters and battles that saints have had with him. Those movies may be produced independently, as big production companies may be reluctant to play them. Still, Christian producers will put them out, especially by way of Christian media channels and partnerships with other believers in Hollywood—some with big names and popularity.

The mainstream public will gain more and more interest in these types of movies, whereby they will even consider it as the occult. However, the new interest in spiritual experiences will gain popularity like never before as the movie-goers become intrigued by such movies that will be deemed horror. The movies will be more scary than some of the most popular scary movies of all time. The reason is because most people are unaware of spiritual battle. They have become tone deaf by Hollywood and the fictitious portrayal of evil and the devil. The reality of the devil will not only wake them up, but keep them awake, since they may be scared in real life after the movie. Although, for faithful Christians, the movies will not scare them. In contrast, they will empower them to share more of their stories, fight valiantly against the devil, and anchor in on God, who is their Deliverer from the devil.

Church services and sermons

Preachers will feel a strong mandate from the LORD to preach about Satan and the reality of hell and evil. They will share their own personal testimonies, and teach Christians how to ward off devils, and engage in battle. That will be a requirement from those on the platform. Apostles, prophets, and people in high-level church leadership will start to inform pastors of the new directive of God. God wants them to preach more on Satan and how to fight with him. He wants his saints to know how to battle because He wants His army to finally advance. The Church will be equipped to defeat the enemy.

State of the Kingdom Address

Radio programs

Radio programs are not currently doing much with regard to discussing the devil and hell. Listeners have enjoyed positive music. They have become numb to the truth about hell. God wants the radio DJs and producers to share more with the people about hell and the devil. He wants people to know that the devil is real, and hell really is a scary, gruesome, miserable place. He wants them to tell their audience that Satan is coming out more and more to attack them because he knows his time is limited. He knows that the Church is sent forth by God, and that now is the time for God's army to advance. The devil is prepared, and so are his troops. The Church must be prepared. Radio will be another outlet that God uses to inform His Body about the times and the looming spiritual battles with Satan.

Conferences and meetings

More and more Spiritual Battle conferences will arise and will occur all over the globe. The Korean church that I discussed earlier in this chapter has gained attention recently due to its members' high-levels of spiritual warfare. I first heard about the church of Pastor Kim about a year ago. I found out about him on a site called spiritlessons.com. The Korean church fights with many spirits and often sees them face to face. Such are the ways of true spiritual battle. The church holds meetings throughout the world to expose the devil, and defeat him in spiritual battle.

Pastor Kim as well as many of his church members have been taken to hell in visions to fight with Satan. They have shared their story with the world. And as soon as I read their story, I began having plain-sight spiritual battles with the devil. I believe I saw him in the kitchen that time only after I read Pastor Kim's book, *Baptize By Blazing Fire*.

The Korean church exemplifies where God is taking his Body with regard to warfare. It's a privilege to be able to see such things. God will help his children locate and attack the devil—that's why He opens their eyes.

Personally, through Jesus

As spiritual warfare increases and the pressures of life encompass the children of God, the people will have an urgent need for Jesus. They will call on Him to come. They will seek Him in business. They will want Him at times of pain and hurt. They will look for Him when they are all alone. They will call on Him, and He will come. You may be thinking, "I already call on the Lord, and He does come to comfort me." No, that's not what I mean. What I mean is that you will call on Jesus, and He will come in plain sight and in full glory. The faithful saints will have the best chance to see the Lord in person. He is faithful to those with faith. Yet, He will also appear before the unbelieving in order that they might believe, even as He did with Thomas. The Lord will show up especially in your times of great pain and discouragement, or at times of spiritual battle, when you are fighting Satan and his devils, if they are too much for you.

Ministering Angels

On one occasion, I called on angels to come to protect me during a heated battle I had with the devil. They weren't just any angels, they were Michael and Gabriel, the mighty Archangels of God. I was being tormented by devils and once again found myself constantly in battle with them. I was in my room rebuking them. The room was full of evil; it became like a battle arena between me and the devil.

State of the Kingdom Address

That night, I was having trouble sleeping. I felt apprehensive because there were many devils around me trying to assault me. I was rebuking them like normal. But the more I rebuked, the more came. I felt overwhelmed.

I called on God and told Him to dispatch angels on my behalf. I may have even used a rebuke of mine that called on angels. Either way, I know that I specifically asked for Michael and Gabriel, mighty angels of God to come warring for me. I had faith, believing that without a doubt that my prayers would be answered by God. And sure enough, they were.

Within seconds, I felt the presence of two mighty beings. They were good-natured, and powerful. It's as if they filled my entire room. Though, I didn't see them. I felt them there (I just knew they were there). Then, almost as if I felt convicted by it, I spoke to them. I said something along the lines of "Wow. How could this be, that the angels, even the Archangels Michael and Gabriel, came when I called?" I *felt* their weapons—swords. Michael was a warrior and had such a presence as a focused, mighty servant of God. Yet, he spoke nothing. He was serious. Gabriel, instead was the one that spoke. Gabriel responded to my question. He said, "You asked us to come, David. We came because you called on us in faith. Tell believers that all things are possible if they believe. Even angels will come on their behalf if they just have faith!"

The devils departed immediately, as if they knew they were up against mighty opponents and could not prevail. My room was at peace once again. The angels stayed for about a second or two, then left. I knew that my faith could dispatch angels, and so could yours. They do not just come when God tells them to come to fight. But they also come when you call on them by faith. God allows them to go—to ride on—the chariot of your faith to your situation.

"Ask Me How I Framed the World"

In these end-times, God will reveal the deep mysteries of the world to His beloved children. People will ask Him in prayer for answers, and He will give them hidden knowledge. I had a coworker many years ago tell me of how her son received revelation from God about how He made the universe. The woman was a Christian, and so was her son. Her name was Margaret, and she worked with me at this paper supply company I worked for years ago. She told me that her son, who was a teenager at the time, was growing in God. He was really committed to the LORD, and seeking more of Him and His word. One night, her son prayed to God for understanding about how He made the universe. He may have gotten the inkling to ask that of God after reading this verse: 'Thus saith the LORD, the Holy One of Israel, and his Maker, Ask me of things to come concerning my sons, and concerning the work of my hands command ye me' (See Isaiah 45:11).

Margaret's teenage son prayed for that knowledge, and God gave him a dream. The LORD began revealing to Him how He made all sorts of insects and living creatures—of how He formed them. God took her son through the process of creation, showing him how he formed certain living things from scratch! He had given Margaret's son the answers to his prayer. However, that was because her son asked God for answers, and he had faith to believe he would receive them.

God is going to do the same thing with other believers. He will open up their minds to receive hidden knowledge of God, concerning His

Kingdom, the universe, and the things of earth. God will not only show them how He created things, but He will give them unique experiences, such as giving believers more frequent trips to Heaven and hell, flying them around the universe and through the heavens, taking them to the outermost parts of the earth and showing them natural phenomenon, and teaching them about deeper aspects of life. God will even reveal information to them in business, science, medicine, health & wellness, relationships, governance, leadership, money & finance, cooking, arts, music, entertainment, fashion, and many other fields.

SUPERNATURAL POWER MANIFESTED

Increasing numbers of spiritual experiences have already begun to happen around the world. People are telling stories of seeing angels, Jesus, the devil, and demons. Aside from the visitations, saints of God will begin to exercise more of their authority on earth, and they will do it with miracles and with power. For example, some may cause tidal waves to cease. Some may even cause earthquakes to stop in the middle of a tremor. I've done that myself recently.

The earthquake

There was a minor earthquake in Baltimore about a year ago. My house began to shake, and I felt as if the ceiling was about to cave in. There was only me, my dog, and two cats living there. I was on the second floor, and I was so scared that I couldn't think straight. So I finally came to my senses and figured that I didn't have much time to stay in there. My thoughts were to round up the pets immediately and usher them downstairs and out of the house.

But I figured, "Wait. I don't even have time for that; the house is about to collapse." So I stopped. Then I rebuked the earthquake. I did it once in fear. Then I did it twice in assertion. Then the third time I did it with total faith, anger, and authority. The earth instantly stopped shaking and the house was calm. Neighbors stood outside and couldn't believe it stopped. It seemed like the earth shook for about 20 seconds, then all of a sudden, nothing.

That is the type of authority more and more believers will walk in on the earth. They will cause the supernatural to occur, not just when they are alone, but in the presence of others. They will rebuke devils. They will rebuke wind, rain, earthquakes, fires, droughts, sickness, death, and more. Some may even cause lightning and fire in the sky, or something more spectacular, just as Elijah did. This is only for the truly faithful. And all of this is done for the glory of God.

There is a spiritual reality that exists that people rarely consider. Believers must become aware of it if they are ever to get to the root of the problems they face in life: 'While we look not at the things which are seen, but at the things which are not seen: for the things which are seen are temporal; but the things which are not seen are eternal' (See 2Corinthians 4:18).

CHAPTER 8: SAGE STRATEGIES FOR SUPERLATIVE LIVING

But we all, with open face beholding as in a glass the glory of the Lord, are changed into the same image from glory to glory, even as by the Spirit of the Lord. -2Corinthians 3:18

About 10 years ago, I found myself strolling into the Mayor's Office of Minority Business Development in Baltimore City. I was bright-eyed as I walked into the meeting. Happy, and full of confidence, I went up to the receptionist in the welcome area. "Mr. Newby?" she said, before I could even get out a word. "Yes." I replied. "Hi. The Director will be right with you."

I felt so accomplished. I was a man. Weeks prior to that day, I emailed my idea to develop the Empowerment Zone in Baltimore City to the then-mayor, Martin O'Malley. He then forwarded it to the Office of Minority Business Development, and had them contact me directly to set up an appointment at City Hall with the director.

At the meeting, I was dressed up and well-rehearsed in what I was going to say to the director. "Right this way, Mr. Newby". The receptionist ushered me back through the hallways of City Hall, past the labyrinth of historical memorabilia, portraits, and documents, into the meeting room.

"He'll be here in a second" she said. I sat down nervously, waiting for him, thinking of what I was going to say. He eventually came in, introduced himself, and gave me a chance to present to him more details about the proposed project.

My plan was to revitalize the Empowerment Zone by equipping disadvantaged adults with the life skills and resources they needed to become self-sufficient, productive members of the community. For example, my program would provide them with business development training, job skills, basic math and arithmetic, leadership skills, and personal financial counseling. I had 30 minutes for the meeting, so I had to be thorough with my presentation. However, I had to be concise to leave time for us to discuss questions, concerns, and possible next steps.

I gave my presentation to the best of my ability. My nervousness was concealed by my passion and confidence in the proposal. My fear turned into faith about where we could take the city. And my inexperience was replaced by my desire to do whatever it took to see the program successful.

After my presentation, I looked to the director for his input. He considered the program carefully. I mean, I had statistics, tables, graphs, pictures, and just about everything you can think of with me. And most of it came out in a matter of about 15 minutes.

Nonetheless, the response of the director made me feel as if my efforts were in vain. "This is a great idea, David. I commend you for all that you did to pull this together and help improve the city." I listened, to see where he was going. "Do you have any type of experience in what you're trying to do? Maybe a college degree in business, or something like that?" I replied, "I completed some college, about two years in business administration."

State of the Kingdom Address

"Ok. Well, I think what you should consider is going back to college and finishing up with your degree. That way, you can gain some more experience in business and help your program be successful."

I was disappointed. I just knew I would somehow partner with the city and bring about a change that would be publicized all over the news. Wishful thinking, perhaps. But I was young and naive. I learned from that meeting that it takes more than a simple idea and passion to make something successful. It takes more than drive. You have to be willing to go the extra mile—gain the experience, become educated, develop spiritually, personally, and professionally.

In the same light, it takes more than a simple idea or vision of success to become successful in life. There are specific things you must do, habits you must develop, mindsets you must take on, paradigm shifts in your feelings you must have, changes you have to implement in order to go from where you are to where you want to be.

Soon after the director suggested that I go back to school to get my degree, I was enrolled full-time in school. A couple of years later, I got my BS in Business/Public Administration. A couple years after that I got my MBA in Global Management in 2009. And even to this day I will outwork just about anybody in developing myself. I put the time in daily, improving myself, spiritually, mentally, physically, and otherwise. I read the Bible to start each day. I pray daily, and praise God when I wake up. I talk to coaches and consultants, mentors, and others. I read books, listen to empowering audios, watch uplifting videos. I attend seminars, workshops, and more. I exercise early in the morning. I do whatever it takes to be successful, so long as it's ethical, lawful, and profitable. And with every activity, project, or opportunity I take on, especially those that come directly from God, I do my absolute best to make sure it's successful.

There are so many things wrong with the world economy that the need for this chapter on strategies for superlative living was apparent. The Church is broke. And many of the world's financial problems could be fixed if the people of God were more wealthy, spiritually and materially. Consider these examples from Statistic Brain (2016):

"Living below poverty":

> - Total Percentage of World Population that lives on less than $2.50 a day is 50%.
> - Total number of people that live on less than $2.50 a day is 3 billion.
> - Total Percentage of People that live on less than $10 a day is 80%.
> - Total Number of children that die each day due to Poverty is 22000.
> - Total Number of People in Developing Countries with Inadequate Access to Water is 1.1 billion.
> - 25 million middle-class people in America live paycheck to paycheck (Source: Black Christian News Network, 2016)
> - The poorest 40 percent of the world's population accounts for 5 percent of global income (Shah, 2013)
> - The richest 20 percent accounts for three-quarters of world income (Source: Shah, 2013)

If we want to revitalize the world, spread the gospel, and minister to those in need, we need the money to do it: 'A feast is made for laughter, and wine maketh merry: but money answereth all things' (See Ecclesiastes 10:19).

State of the Kingdom Address

GIVE MORE TO GET MORE

The reason I opened up with the story about City Hall is because I want to encourage you that in order to get more out of life, you have to give more. Develop yourself spiritually. Read and apply the Bible. Go to school. Get some training. Take a class. Talk to a consultant; hire one. Get a personal coach. Get some exercise. Eat better. Enjoy life. Give more of yourself to God, first and foremost. But also, give more of yourself to yourself. Do what you can do to develop spiritually and personally. As you do, you will find your life taking on a new meaning. You will have a greater sense of fulfillment, purpose, and direction. You will feel more accomplished and prosperous in everything you lay your hands to. You will feel more effective and efficient at making the types of progress, or getting the types of breakthroughs you want in life—not just one every now and then, but all the time, with everything you do. Imagine that, everything you do prospers. Well, that's a promise of God. And that's exactly where you should be; everything you touch should prosper!

Over the past 10 years of my life, I've learned what it takes to achieve the results I want. I have faced my own pitfalls and have learned from my own mistakes. I have watched others, both succeed wildly in the marketplace or in life; and I have watched them fail horribly. I identified what made them successful and what made them fail. I have read the Bible countless times, studying how a person can be blessed and what leads to curses. I have benchmarked great Biblical fathers, such as Jesus Christ [no pun intended], Abraham, Job, Joseph, David, Solomon, and others. I have read a number of the most notable personal development books of all time: *Think and Grow Rich*, *The Success Principles*, *7 Habits of Highly Effective People*, *Rich Dad Poor Dad*, and *How To Win Friends and Influence People* as examples.

In addition, I continue to train and develop all types of people around the world as a Life Strategist. And as an *End-Time Revivalist*, my goal is to equip, empower, and enrich the Body of Christ with the resources it needs to be more effective at reaching the world with the Gospel. Besides, I live by 1Corinthians 10:24: 'Let no man seek his own, but every man another's wealth.' All this to say, it's a part of my purpose to develop people for the sake of advancing the Kingdom on earth.

The things you do day in and day out, whether in business, leadership, as a professional, a skilled laborer, an entry level employee, a student, or whether you're between jobs and looking for work, could help position you for unimaginable levels of success. Only, you have to do more of the right things and much less of the wrong ones. Many of the following principles of success are tried and true. They are passed down from generation to generation, person to person, situation to situation. And many of them are linked to Biblical scripture. Yet, many are based on fresh revelation I receive from the Holy Spirit. All in all, all of the principles are more than likely related to God's divine laws of success (Ex. Faith, giving, hard work, walking in virtue, etc).

Granted, you may or may not be at the same place in life as another person reading this, so I decided to break the strategies up in stages. For example, you may want to launch a new business, whereas they may already be in business and want to double their income. So, this section is more like a reference list of what you need to do to go higher in the Kingdom and in the world. At the crux of each stage of success is a pure, solid relationship with God. I will discuss that aspect of life first. I will follow that up with recommendations in other stages in life. Once you are certain you placed your relationship with God first and foremost, review the other suggestions depending on where you are in life right now, be it in starting a new business, launching a new project, seeking a promotion, becoming more healthy or losing weight, finishing school, becoming a better leader, or else. I hope that you find these life development strategies helpful in getting you to reach the pinnacle of success in any area.

PRACTICE THE SPIRITUAL FUNDAMENTALS

It would be pointless to try and develop your life without having a real connection with God. That true connection gives you *spiritual leverage*. Spiritual leverage will help you deepen your connection with God and operate from a position of spiritual power, which far surpasses worldly power. Here are some things you can do to help you grow spiritually.

Put God first in everything you do

God is the foundation of your life. Keep Him there. Put Him first in all things. Repent of any sin. Read, meditate, and apply His Word. Also, God should be the first person you talk to in the morning. Start each day with a praise of thanksgiving, a prayer, or meditation. I don't talk to anyone before I talk to God. I don't have coffee in the morning before I talk to God. Imagine how triumphant you will be in all things when you have God with you.

Make God your Strategic Partner

God has everything you could ever need. Make Him your strategic partner in all that you do. He wants you successful. So, naturally He will help you, giving you wisdom and guidance in every area of life. You strategic partnership with God will give you a sustainable competitive advantage over all your competition. I don't care what they know, who they have as a consultant, who they're connected to, or how deep their pockets are, if you have God you will win. He has more wisdom, power, provision than your enemies could ever muster up. And He gives them to you to help you win in life.

Follow God's direction

If you want to get better results, listen to God. Jesus has been where you are, is where you are, and is where you're going. He covers the past, present, and future. I think He knows how to get you from where you are to where you want to be. Follow His lead. He will never lead you astray.

Start everyday with favor, here's how:

> ➤ Praise and worship—Praise and worship God for all your specific blessings, like the children of Israel did in Exodus 15:1 when they came out of Egypt.
> ➤ Pray—Pray for forgiveness of your sins. Then, pray for what you need and want in life, according to God's will.
> ➤ Rebuke—Rebuke the devil and make a declaration of faith over your life. He *shoots* at you every chance he gets. Why not shoot a dart at him first? Get offensive minded, and rebuke the devil. Think, outgoing missiles.
> ➤ Read—Read at least a chapter of the Bible. Take something from what you read and apply it immediately to your life.
> ➤ Request—Ask God specifically for more of His presence and direction. He will be your *great coach in Heaven*, if you ask Him for guidance.

State of the Kingdom Address

Read and obey the Word

I mentioned above that you should read the Word every day. I reiterate that here. Such value did the ancient Israelites place on the Word of God. They knew that all their victories, blessings, and protection came from adhering to the Word:

> The Levites literally had to walk around the Temple on guard, defending the Ark of the Covenant, and the Temple from its enemies (See 1Chronicles 26). Also, think of how many times the ark of the covenant (which contained the Ten Commandments inside it) accompanied Israel in battle and helped them in war:

> And when the people were come into the camp, the elders of Israel said, Wherefore hath the LORD smitten us to day before the Philistines? Let us fetch the ark of the covenant of the LORD out of Shiloh unto us, that, when it cometh among us, it may save us out of the hand of our enemies. (See 1Samuel 4:3).

> And how great was Israel blessed as a result of following the word? For example, Obededom, of the Levite lineage, had his house blessed greatly as a result of simply having the ark of the covenant inside it: 'And the ark of the LORD continued in the house of Obededom the Gittite three months: and the LORD blessed Obededom, and all his household' (See 2Samuel 6:11).

> Moses was given the Ten Commandments from God on a mountain; that's how important it is, that God *hand-delivered* the Word to Moses (See Exodus 34:27-28).

As Joshua led the children of Israel into the Promised Land, God instructed him to always meditate on the word day and night:

> This book of the law shall not depart out of thy mouth; but thou shalt meditate therein day and night, that thou mayest observe to do according to all that is written therein: for then thou shalt make thy way prosperous, and then thou shalt have good success (See Joshua 1:8).

- David went to get the Ark of the Covenant from the Philistines when they took it from Israel (See 2Samuel 6).
- David even took the ark from Obededdom's house and brought it to Israel so Israel would be blessed (2Samuel 6:12).
- And think of how many times the Book of Psalms mentions meditating on the word of God.
- Above all, John calls *the Word*, God: 'In the beginning was the Word, and the Word was with God, and the Word was God' (See John 1:1).

God's Word is your blueprint for success in life. It covers all areas. You should thirst for it. Don't just stop at reading it. To be successful, you have to live it: 'that thou mayest observe to do according to all that is written therein: for then thou shalt make thy way prosperous, and then thou shalt have good success' (See Joshua 1:8).

Serve others

Want more out of life? Then, you must do more to serve others.

State of the Kingdom Address

'Our rewards in life will always be in exact proportion to our contribution...our service.'

-Earl Nightingale

'You can have anything in life you want if you are willing to help enough other people get what they want.' –Zig Ziglar

Operate in the law of faith

Everything you do should be done in faith. According to mid-1900's writer, Dorothea Brande, as quoted from American inventor, Charles Kettering, you should 'Believe and act as if it were impossible to fail.'

Fight from a spiritual position

Your battles are not fleshly battles. Realize that you deal with deeper enemies, in the spiritual realm. Fight them with your faith. Bring down the powers, principalities, high places, and rulers of darkness by battling spiritually. It's only after the spiritual forces of darkness are dealt with that you can effectively deal with things in the real world. Also, it doesn't matter how much you deal with a problem or situation in the physical, if the spiritual enemies are still free to roam around, they will forever wreak havoc on your situation. It makes no sense to bind the problem in earthly terms, but leave the devil free to roam. If you bind the devil, you bind the problem. Nip the problem in the bud—spiritual first, then physical. Bind and loose things in heaven, and they will be bound and loosed on earth (See Matthew 16:19). We have to learn how to flow from the spiritual realm to the natural.

Follow the FOG

Have you noticed how fog always leads to water? Try it someday. Follow some fog and I guarantee you it will lead you to a body of water, somewhere. That's how my F.O.G formula works. FOG—faith, obedience, and *glory* (i.e. the glory of God, and giving God the glory)—always leads to water (i.e. provision, breakthrough). Fog also represents a low-hanging cloud. As the children of Israel came out of Egypt with Moses, they were led by a cloud by day and fire by night (See Exodus 13:21).

Submit your work to God

People in God's Kingdom aren't blessed because they aren't submitting their work to God. They want to do things their way, and in their timing. Give God your labor. Let Him direct your paths, or the activities you need to be doing, and He will prosper them. I've wasted a lot of time in life doing things my way, when God told me years before exactly what He wanted me to do and how to do it. 'Commit thy works unto the LORD, and thy thoughts shall be established' (See Proverbs 16:3).

Vessels of glory VS. vehicles of glory

As a child of God, you are a *vessel of glory* (See Romans 9:21-23). God is inside of you. He uses your body as His vessel. He does His work on earth through you. Alternately, everything about you, including your education, experience, personality, connections, finances, property, and so on, are *vehicles of glory*. In short, God uses those things in your life as vehicles, from which He obtains glory, to help you achieve your purpose. You as well as your life accomplishments are supposed to glorify God. If not, rededicate yourself to Him and see how far and how fast He takes you in His Kingdom.

State of the Kingdom Address

Don't escape the spiritual development process

God builds you up from glory to glory. His spiritual development process results in blessings. Escaping it delays your progress or success because it brings you right back to it over and over again. Be humble, and let God take you from glory to glory in His image (See 2Corinthians 3:18). Then, let Him do it again, and again, and again. You are forever growing spiritually and learning new lessons as long as you are alive.

Conform to the word of God

God is the same yesterday, today, and tomorrow: 'Jesus Christ the same yesterday, and to day, and for ever' (See Hebrews 13:8). He doesn't change, neither does His word. I see people all the time trying to make God conform to them and their thoughts and beliefs. The quicker you conform to God's word, the quicker you will get to where He wants you to be.

Implement the 7 Infallible Secrets of Success

After grappling with my own struggles to develop my life several years ago, I have developed what I deemed the *7 Infallible Secrets of Success*. I wanted to account for the spiritual blockages as well as the worldly blockages of life progress. I came up with this list:

> Put God first—Your life decisions should always center on God.

Attack the *world* in the same way you would attack the devil—Go after the world, in other words, your goals and desires with the same zeal that you would attack the devil if he came in your house to kill, steal, and destroy. Well, the world won't just give you what you want. You have to take it. Attack it. Go after what you want.

Learn the success networks—

> ➢ *ABC* (Always Be Challenging yourself)
> ➢ *NBC* (Never Be Comfortable where you are; push for more)
> ➢ *CBS* (Change Before Success: the wrong friends, environments, habits, thoughts, feelings, actions, etc.)

Faith overcomes fear—Jump out in faith and your fear will be suppressed.

Establish Godly goals and objectives—Stay aligned with God. Then, set some incredible goals. Be sure to stretch them out because all things are possible with God on your side.

Fail forward and fail fast—Get your failure out of the way quick. Learn your lessons. Jot down ideas for improvement. Then go at it again…and again. Never give up.

Benchmark the best—Find out whoever did, or are doing what you want to do, and learn from them. Don't just learn from their successes; learn from their failures too. If there is no benchmark in your industry, follow God's lead. Then, become the benchmark for the world to follow if what you're attempting is something new.

Follow these steps to bigger breakthroughs

> *Know God's Will*—You must know God's will. You can't do anything that God doesn't want you to do, and expect to succeed. You also can't avoid the things He wants you to

do, and expect to succeed. Why? It's because God is the Supreme Ruler. As we operate according to His will, we are in alignment with His rulership, His laws.

Have faith —You need supernatural faith to get supernatural blessings. Most people are trotting along through life in the same level of blessings that they've had for the past 10 years. They simply fail to believe for more from God. You get out of God what you put into God through faith. Incredible trust in God results in incredible breakthroughs.

Make daily declarations and decrees—Death and life are in the power of the tongue. Christians get this verse misconstrued at times. It doesn't say life and death are in the power of the tongue. It says death and life are in the power of the tongue. In other words, people are killing themselves before they've even had a chance to live. They are speaking negative things all the time, and have a negative, losing, defeated type of mindset:

- ➢ "I am sick."
- ➢ "I am broke."
- ➢ "I only have $5 to my name."
- ➢ "I am about to get evicted."
- ➢ "I am going to lose my house."

Speak positive and positive will come. Speak negative and negative will come. In short, if you can't speak positive about your situation, shut up!

Powerful works—Want better results? You need bigger, badder, bolder actions to get them. And that's what God will most certainly lead you to because He likes to be glorified by all that you do. Big breakthroughs require big action...consistently.

Now that you have the foundation of God down, let's discuss other practical areas of life development.

VISION, VALUES, MISSION

I once heard an analogy of your vision, values, and mission statements being likened to building a house. The values act as a foundation of the house. They are what the house is built on, for example, integrity. In contrast, your mission is the structure of your house. It's sort of like the walls and the roof, what holds the house together, and helps you reach your vision. Finally, the vision is the completed house, or how the house would look to you if you were to stand across the street from it and look at it. These three elements are incredibly important in helping you live your purpose, or live it more effectively. Here is what you can do to make sure you have optimized each of them.

Create the right values

Build your house, your business, your dream, your goals, or whatever else on the right foundation of values. Things like virtue, integrity, honesty, and selflessness go a long way in life. Don't neglect them.

Develop a life mission

What's your purpose? Keep it simple and memorable. Remind yourself of it when you have new challenges or opportunities. Make sure that everything you do in life aligns with your mission.

Be sure it's aligned with God's will

Always make sure that your mission aligns with God's will. The last thing you want is for His hand to be against it; it won't prosper that way.

Never forget your mission

Put it at the top of your mind, and persevere through all difficulties. Jesus' mission was the Cross, and to save humanity though his death and resurrection. That got him through the difficult times He faced. It even got Him past the negative opinions of others, like Peter, for example, who tried to talk Jesus out of going to the Cross.

Just say 'No'

Learn when to say 'No' to things that don't match your mission or help you achieve it. Opportunities abound in life. Still, you don't have to take on all of them. Focus only on those that are right for you. In a recent speech uploaded to YouTube, Darren Hardy, former publisher of *SUCCESS* magazine, reported that Warren Buffet says 'No' to 99% of the opportunities that come his way (Source: Hardy, 2015).

Sell your vision

Get others to buy-in to your vision. You don't always have to use your own resources to become successful. Use the skills, minds, finances, time, work, and resources of others if at all possible. And be sure to reward them accordingly. That increases your chance of reaching your vision in many cases. "Teamwork makes the dream work", according to leadership expert, John Maxwell (Source: Maxwell, 2016).

David Newby

STRATEGY, PLANNING, AND GOAL-SETTING

Focus mostly on strategy

Strategy should be the primary area of focus for a leader, and dare I say, for you also, even if you're not a leader. For example, Matt Barrett, as cited in the *Harvard Business Review* article, "Stop Wasting Valuable Time" (Mankins, 2004), states that, "80% of the EXCO's [Executive Committee's] time is now focused on strategic decision making". You can see the full article here https://hbr.org/2004/09/stop-wasting-valuable-time. Be sure to hone in on your strategy so that you move ahead with the right plans, goals, and objectives in whatever it is you want to accomplish.

Develop a plan

Transform your strategy into a tangible, workable plan. "Write the vision, and make it plain" (See Habakkuk 2:2). Have some goals and objectives in place. Create some targets. Identify your resource needs. Establish a budget for achieving your plan. Have a timeline in place. Also, develop some controls and ways to monitor your progress. Perform a SWOT (Strengths, weaknesses, opportunities, and threats) analysis before launching out into the deep. Notate the internal and external variables that could derail you. Create a *mindmap* with a tool like XMind at https://www.xmind.net/. Have faith in your plan. It's the blueprint to your success. Far too often, people have faith to start out on a mission, but somewhere along the line they deviate from their plan of action. If that sounds like you, don't deviate from the plan that God gives you to achieve your vision. The LORD is very faithful and gracious towards us. Not only will He give you the promise, He will give you the vision, the plan to achieve that vision, and the exact steps along the way to achieve it because your steps are ordered. To add to that, He even gives you Himself along the way to achieve the vision; He walks with you. Again, your plan for success, if it's divinely prescribed, is the way to reach your goals. Never abandon it. If you do, you'll end up coming right back to it because it's the pathway to victory.

Don't just create SMART goals, create STRETCH goals

- SMART (Simple, Measurable, Attainable, Realistic, Timely)—Smart goals get you the basic, status quo results
- STRETCH (Supersede Those Reasonable Expectations and Thoughts, then Champion Hope)—Stretch goals help you accomplish the miraculous

All your goals should align with God's will, whether SMART or STRETCH goals. Another thing is that SMART goals help you reach realistic levels of success. But STRETCH goals require faith and courage, and take you beyond the ordinary. It's important to have both sets. However, shoot for the stretch goals, but settle for achieving nothing less than the smart ones. Shoot for the stars, but at least land on the moon, so to speak.

Review your goals each day

Write your goals down and be very specific. Moreover, refer to them each and every day, preferably in the morning and evening. That way, you start your day with direction, focus, and purpose, and end the day meditating on ways to achieve your goals. Also, check off an item when you complete it. I learned from Jack Canfield's best-selling book, *The Success Principles*, to make a list of all your life goals—at least about 100 or more—and review them each day (Source: Canfield,

2004). There's something about writing down your goals and reviewing them, actually seeing them on paper, a computer, tablet, cell phone, or other place, that makes you feel accountable for achieving them. As you write down your goals and look at them, you are telling your subconscious mind, "I have to do this. There are no excuses." Then, eventually you will do it. By the way, I would highly recommend you get a copy of *The Success Principles*. Though, it's not really a spiritual book, there is a lot of practical advice in the book that will help you achieve much more in life. You can watch the success principles in action, live on DVD at http://bit.ly/4moresuccess. If you prefer to read about them, check out Jack's *The Success Principles 10th Anniversary Edition* at http://bit.ly/10yearsofsuccess.

Think and act BIG

You only get one chance at life. Make it count. Leave nothing on the table or in the tank. Live full, die empty! Take massive action with every endeavor you partake in. Below are some keys I use to have a great impact with my work in the Kingdom. Some or all of these pointers may be helpful to you. Launch projects with…

- ➢ Big, colossal moves…
- ➢ Ubiquitous impact…
- ➢ Profitably…
- ➢ Expediently…
- ➢ Fast and furious…
- ➢ Decisively…
- ➢ Unregrettably…
- ➢ Boldly…
- ➢ In full faith…
- ➢ Calculated risks…

State of the Kingdom Address

- ➢ Incredible returns...
- ➢ Shockingly...
- ➢ Repeatedly and consistently...
- ➢ All the time...
- ➢ Live the lifestyle...

Excellence

Do everything with excellence. If you only had one chance to do something, how would you do it? How would you want the world to remember you? What type of mark would you leave on the world? Whether you're writing a book, launching a new business, giving a speech or presentation, or managing an event, work with excellence. Excellent work often leads to outstanding results.

Be somewhat flexible

Be flexible enough to deal with and respond to unforeseen situations and opportunities. They may not be a part of your plan, but they could be a part of God's plan. Sometimes things come up to redirect you, send you on a detour. Fret not. God, who gave you the vision, is well able to put you back on course, without missing a beat.

Be generous

Have a plan to give back to others through charity, help, encouragement, exercising social responsibility, etc. The reason God enables you to achieve your goals is so you can be a good steward of what He gives you.

EXECUTE THE PLAN

Now that your strategies, plans, and goals have been devised, let's move onto the execution. Here's how you can become better at executing.

Start each day empowered

Start each day positive-minded and empowered. Use affirmations, audios, or other resources to inspire you. One of my favorite motivators is ET the Hip Hop Preacher. This man just knows how to rev people up in the morning, or anytime for that matter. You can watch some of his material on YouTube, hire him as a speaker, purchase some of his products, or enroll in one of his coaching programs. Find out more about ET (Eric Thomas) here.

Get organized

Gather the resources and people you need to get the results you want.

Be efficient at project management

Learn to manage your goals and resources effectively to achieve your desired results.

Practice good team management

Find the best people first, find a place for them later. If you work alone, be the absolute best you can be. Develop yourself, and encourage your team to do the same, if applicable.

Develop a good production plan

Focus on the 4% of all the activities that you can do. Get the other 96% off of your plate and onto somebody else's.

MANAGING AND MONITORING RESULTS

Prepare for contingencies

Contingencies may come up on occasion. That's life. Think of it like this: Famous athletes spend hours upon hours preparing for a major championship or playoff game. They study film, workout, practice, and more. They develop the perfect plan to beat their opponent. However, the plan is rarely executed perfectly to a tee. They would be lucky to get 90% of the stuff to go right. Yet, they still planned, correct? If they could get just 80% of their victory plan executed, there's a really good chance that they will win the game. Stuff simply comes up when the game is on. The situation doesn't work out perfectly. Distractions arise. Fatigue sets in. They forget plays, moves, or tactics, and so on. Still, if they could just get about an 80% effective rate for achieving their plan, chances are they will defeat their opponent. Life is the same way. You should always plan to win, and know that your plan is the blueprint for winning whatever it is you're doing. However, you should still give way for contingencies, for example, a 20% margin of error in executing your plan. The unexpected things in life do occur. Work your plan, but don't be set back by the circumstances that arise.

Track your progress with milestones and controls

You should always have ways to track your results, be it analytics, direct feedback from others, or otherwise.

Minimize your risks

Find ways to reduce your risks. Examples include diversifying your portfolio or investments, pooling resources with other people to accomplish a project, or dumping anything or anyone that poses too big of a risk to you.

Maximize your rewards

Make sure anything you do or take on in life is something that will get you an invaluable benefit, whether that be money, position, peace of mind, or some other opportunity. Don't waste time doing the wrong things in life. Your time is limited on earth. So make it count.

Consider all stakeholders

Put the needs of others above your own. If you help to prosper other people, you will prosper in turn yourself.

MAKE CONTINUAL IMPROVEMENTS

Improve yourself

Develop your character, experience, and skills. Never stop growing. Find ways to do and be better.

Be objective

Don't be defensive. Seek constructive criticism. Listen to sound advice from people who have been where you are, or who may know something you don't.

Learn from the best

Find the absolute best people who have done what you're trying to do. Copy their strategies. Don't reinvent the wheel; roll with it!

Test and improve

Administer surveys. Analyze data. Talk to stakeholders and get their input. Do what you have to do to improve yourself or your performance.

Seek outside coaching or consulting

Consider getting coaching or consulting in your problem areas. Be sure that person has a good track record in getting you the results you want.

Implement ideas for improvement

Implement everything you learned above. Seek to continually improve.

CREATE BIGGER PLANS AND GOALS

Think even bigger than before

Outperform what you previously did. Think of ways to get a bigger return on investment (ROI), whether you invested money, time, work, or other resources on your goals.

Start movements not projects

Movements lead to a greater impact on the world and more benefits to you. Think ubiquitous. How does your movement affect the entire world?

RINSE AND REPEAT THE SYSTEM

Your success system is flawless

Apply it time and time again until it becomes routine in everything you do.

SELF-MANAGEMENT

The more you improve yourself, the better your work and performance will be. Here are some things about yourself that you may want to improve.

> ➢ *Self-confidence:* Believe that you're the best in everything you do. Noone can do your work better than you.
> ➢ *Commitment:* Give everything to live the life you know you deserve to live.
> ➢ *Determination:* Never give up on your dreams.
> ➢ *Organization:* Establish some order if you have any chaos in your life.
> ➢ *Focus:* Get laser focused on all your goals; burn right through them.
> ➢ *Be strong and diligent:* Don't back down from pressure, setbacks, or disappointments.

State of the Kingdom Address

- *Persevere through pain:* You are built to endure challenges; you have to go *through* to get *to* your destination.
- *Think positive:* Positive thinking, more often than not, leads to positive outcomes. Do away with negativity.
- *Speak positive:* Say something positive, or say nothing at all.
- *Treat people fairly and with respect:* Relationships will invariably be a part of most things you do in life. Learn to deal with people and treat them how they deserve to be treated.
- Find courage and harness it to bust down walls: Be as bold as a lion.
- *Walk in your inherent power:* You are fearfully and wonderfully made (See Psalms 139:14); act like it.
- *Don't make excuses, make solutions:* Excuses are a well-planned lie, according to Dani Johnson at danijohnson.com. According to Leadership Expert, John Maxwell, at johnmaxwell.com, "It's easier to get from failure to success than it is to get from excuses to success"

SUCCESSION PLANNING

It's one thing for you to become more successful in life. What's more important is to help make future generations successful. The goal here is to pass the baton to leaders of tomorrow so that they can effectively carry on the work of God on earth long after we're gone.

Accordingly, the two principles I focus on here is leaving a legacy and succession planning. Here are some great ways to do both.

Create the archetype, model, for future leaders to follow

Prepare your *blueprint for success* for the next generation. Moses gave Joshua the Ten Commandments to follow. David gave Solomon the plans for the Holy Temple. Paul gave Timothy instructions. Jesus gave us salvation through Him. Pass something useful down to your successors.

Think of how you want to be best remembered

Ensure your descendants know what's most important to you, for instance, supporting certain social causes like world hunger. Choose trusted people to carry on your work and legacy.

Prepare for the long haul

In regard to your work, business, organization, or movement, plan for it to be around long after you're gone. Implement values, principles, or systems that can stand the test of time.

Identify potential heirs

Find potential heirs early. Start molding them as soon as possible. Entrust them with more and more responsibility as they prove themselves to get them prepared to lead. Train a child in the way he should go and he will not depart from it when he is old (See Proverbs 22:6).

State of the Kingdom Address

FOLLOW THE STRATEGIES

By following the success strategies outlined in this chapter, you will greatly increase your chances of getting to where you want to be in life much faster. Whether you are running an organization, trying to grow a relationship, or seeking a new job, you can at least glean something from the information above to push past any plateaus you face in life.

They have greatly enhanced my life, and have even helped me write, market, and publish this book. I have no doubt that they will be a tremendous advantage to you moving forward with your work, goals, dreams, and aspirations.

ABOUT MY TRAINING AND SPEAKING

I teach many of these success strategies, and others, in depth through my training business. I am also available for speaking engagements. To inquire about my training business, programs, products, services, or public speaking, please visit me at **http://belovedhq.com** or connect with me on LinkedIn at https://www.linkedin.com/in/davidgnewby.

CHAPTER 9: A CLARION CALL TO LEADERS

For the time is come that judgment must begin at the house of God: and if it first begin at us, what shall the end be of them that obey not the gospel of God? -1Peter 4:17

I read an interesting article the other day from Apostolic Movement International, a ministry that I attribute to helping me develop spiritually over the last few years. In the article, AMI discusses what it means to carry out each particular office of the Five-Fold ministry, whether apostle, prophet, pastor, evangelist, or teacher.

If you're called to the five-fold, check out the article when you have a chance to learn more about what you should be doing, or could be doing better to fulfill the duties of your position of leadership in the Church: http://bit.ly/22ZgetN (Source: Apostolic Movement International, 2016).

That article as well as many of the wrongs I see in the Church compels me to address the Church, and world leadership. Judgment starts at the house of God (1Peter 4:17); and as the *head* goes the body follows. So, I will start with church leadership in the beginning of this chapter. Then I will follow up with world leadership inclusive of government officials, corporate CEOs, and others. First, let me paint a picture of how God sees leadership.

State of the Kingdom Address

LEADERSHIP IN GOD'S EYES

The fancy titles you see on earth, *CEO*, *President*, *Vice President*, *Chairman*, *Director*, *Commissioner*, and others, only come into play after leadership from God's eyes is considered. So what's leadership from God's eyes? It's spiritual. God looks at the heart, and not so much the achievements and capabilities of man. Ask yourself…

- ➢ Is my heart pure?
- ➢ Do I walk in love?
- ➢ Am I harboring unforgiveness?
- ➢ Will I obey God in everything He instructs me to do?
- ➢ Do I have faith?
- ➢ Will I trust the LORD?
- ➢ Will I be a giver?
- ➢ Will I hear the cry of the hungry?
- ➢ Will I serve others?
- ➢ Am I humble?

These are things that are necessary for God to propel you into greater levels of leadership. The LORD is looking to exalt people into leadership who have the right spirit upon them. Alternately, He will cast down people who have the wrong spirit.

With God, people can literally be the most inexperienced, uneducated, unskilled person in the world, yet have a right spirit within them, and God will take them up past today's highly regarded leaders in the world. In addition, you can have the most achieved, experienced, professional Christian leader, and have them either brought down low, or stagnant with regard to their ministry, due to a poor spirit. They are spiritually impoverished, therefore their impact follows. For example, they may be a pastor of their church, yet lack humility, and won't do everything God wants them to do. So they may tarry in their present position for years, or decades, while novice leaders will shoot past them in no time because they have a better spirit than them. It's been said that God is no respecter of persons. I say, God is a respecter of persons in a sense, in that He respects those that love Him and do His will. And He favors them as a result.

I love the story of David, of when God replaced King Saul with him. The LORD told Saul, he found someone better than him. Imagine that: you're a king, decked out with all the royal apparel, all the big titles, with all the power, all the honor, all the riches, and so forth. Nonetheless, God looks at you and says, "You're not good enough. I found somebody better (See 1Samuel 15:28)." The LORD was clearly looking at the heart of David, especially after the fact that Saul disobeyed God in refusing to utterly destroy all the enemies of Israel and their stuff.

We see how the heart of David led him to exaltation in the case of Goliath as well. All of David's brothers, and the army of Israel were decorated war veterans. They had all the apparel and the armor. They were dressed to the tee, adorned in shiny helmets, breastplates, and so forth. You know, they had the credentials, college degrees, connections, familiarity with the system that made them appear to be great leaders. However, they lacked the heart—the right spirit. Then, in comes David with almost none of that stuff. He had a simple slingshot, faith, and a genuine heart for God. He wanted to defeat the enemies of Israel, and those that defied the living God. David had the right spirit. He had a heart for God; he had a heart for the people. Accordingly, David defeated Goliath and was lifted up in leadership, and that's without all that pretty armor that his brothers had. He had no real experience, no degrees, no major connections, or bank accounts. Nonetheless, he proved that stuff like that doesn't make you a leader in God's eyes. The LORD looks at the spirit, first and foremost. And if God has selected you to be a leader in His Kingdom, either you have the right spirit to lead others and do His will, or you are in a fast track program to learning how to walk in the right spirit. What am I saying? If you want to be a leader, or a better leader in God's Kingdom, work on your spirit! Ask the Holy Spirit to search you. Ask Him to remove anything from you that's not right with Him—unforgiveness, pride, lust, disobedience, guilt, fear, lack of faith, hate, bitterness and others. Work on developing your spirit because that's what develops you into God's type of leader.

Another thing I want to mention is that by and large, Christian leaders, especially Fivefold ministers, have more authority on earth to God than worldly leaders that may not be in God. That's because they are leading as unto God, with God, and from God. Spiritually, a divine order is in place. God operates His Kingdom through this order. He implements His plans on earth through them. He gives them new strategies and directives for the world to follow. Where the Church goes, the world follows. In other words, God has made His people the head and not the tail of any major movement He does on earth (See Deuteronomy 28:13). Why do I say this? If you want to reach higher levels of authority, or you want to maintain your position of leadership, you have to make sure you lead from God, even moreso now than ever. A change is coming to earth; the world system is going to be completely obliterated. And you need to make sure you're in proper position to walk in end-time authority. In summary, lead better, as unto God.

God is calling all five-fold ministers to step up in their leadership. He wants them to lead more effectively, work with a greater level of responsibility, and demonstrate more personal sacrifice for the

Kingdom's sake. The LORD wants leaders of the Church to know that their work is more important than ever, and that they are the ones responsible, moreso than anybody else, for preparing Jesus' Bride, the Church, for His return. What a calling! What responsibility! What honor! What a gap between where they are and where they need to be as leaders!

If you are a leader outside of the church, your work in the Kingdom of God and on earth is very important as well. However, it must be done in alignment with God's will and His Word. Outside of reading the Bible on your own, and hearing from God yourself, God's Fivefold ministers are typically the ones that lead people to God's will: How then shall they call on him in whom they have not believed? and how shall they believe in him of whom they have not heard? and how shall they hear without a preacher? (See Romans 10:14).

In the old days, kings in the Bible had prophets and high priests to lead them to God's will. They also or corrected them if they were living contrary to the word of God. It's the same today. Leaders must always follow God's plan, either through divine revelation of the Holy Spirit, or as administered by His appointed leaders in the church. Put simply, if you are a leader and you aren't saved, there is no way for you to clearly hear from the Holy Ghost. Therefore, you may be being led by the devil. Naturally, if you have trouble hearing from God, the next best option is to listen to someone who can hear Him, and who has been anointed and appointed to give you a word. They have been selected to guide you back to God and where He wants you. Let's not disregard God's elect. Rather, let's understand that they are the ones that lead the world back to God and His plan on earth.

State of the Kingdom Address

In accordance with God's divine order (Church before the world), here is what needs to be changed in leadership, both in the Fivefold ministry, and in the rest of the world.

LEADERSHIP IN THE CHURCH

Grim Statistics: Headed To Hell in a Hand-Basket

Before I delve into the condition of the Fivefold ministry, if you are a part of the Fivefold, I want you to look at a few startling statistics. The majority of the world is well-positioned for hell:

> - 185 million people in China practice Buddhism, whereas Christianity only accounts for about 33 million; Confucianism, Islam, and Taosim are the other major religions in China (Source: Travel China Guide, 2016)
> - 1.6 billion Muslims worldwide serve Allah (Source: Pew Research Center, 2015)
> - There are about 1.2 billion Catholics around the world, according to BBC News (2013). Many of them probably worship Mary, and try to earn their way to Heaven by keeping the *Seven Sacraments* or through good works: 'Not of works, lest any many should boast' (See Ephesians 2:9).
> - 1.1 billion atheists, agnostics and people who do not identify with any particular religion (Source: Pew Research Center, 2015)
> - There is an innumerable amount of backslidden believers

> It's estimated that only 1 in 1000 people are born-again believers and make it to Heaven, which is less than 1% of the world population. And that's a favorable estimate, as others have predicted that far less people make it into Heaven. Considering the average church size doesn't even have 1000 members, but more like under 200, 3 people in church out of every 200 that show up for a Sunday morning service, are saved. Based on those stats, nearly the entire congregation is positioned for hell if things don't change, possibly even the pastor
> 33% of Americans don't consider themselves religious (Source: Pew Research Center, 2015)
> The 2014 General Social Survey reported that 21% of American had no religion with 3% being atheist and 5% being agnostic (Wikipedia).
> Atheism around the world: 47% of China claimed to be Atheist, 31% of Japan, 30% of Czech Republic, 29% of France, and 15% of South Korea to name a few (Source: Gallup, 2016)

In our present state, people are headed to hell in a hand-basket. We have to get things right to get more people into the Kingdom of Heaven. And revival starts with church leadership, as discussed below.

A FIVE-FOLD CALL TO ACTION

What can be done to get God's elected leaders where they're supposed to be? Here are a few suggestions. This is not an exhaustive list of all things that we need to fix in church leadership, as it's coming only from my perspective and what God gives me. However, it's at least something to get us moving in the right direction. Hopefully other leaders in the Body of Christ will step up, pray to the Holy Ghost to reveal anything in us separating us from Him, identify some other wrongs in the Body, their congregation or in those congregations they witness firsthand, and work diligently to fix them as soon as possible. Jesus is on His way. And judgment, again, starts from the house of God. If you're a Church leader, you will be held accountable by Jesus for what you allow or support, if it's not right with God.

Apostles—

As leaders of the Fivefold Ministry, apostles are the great builders of the new movements of God on earth. If you are an apostle, you have a great deal of responsibility on you. That's to say, you receive the *blueprint* from God. You give the same to the Church, ensuring that it all gets constructed, or operates, according to the plan that God gave you.

You were set apart from birth, and have always been different from everybody else. That difference in you is what God needs to usher in His revival on earth. You have sacrificed it all for the calling, going up against great pain, struggles, and persecution for the sake of doing God's will and achieving His mandate. Your work is not in vain. God sees your labor, and has great rewards for you, both in Heaven and on earth.

Still, burn out to do better. Serve better. Give more. Take your work more seriously. Be ever diligent; now is the time that God needs you most. The Church will be revived, refreshed through you, saith the

LORD. You are a leader in God's end-time revival that will pave the way for the Lord Jesus.

Dare to be different, bold, and an example for others to follow. You are a sign and an ensign. You are a *sign*, a symbol of God's grace, mercy, love, and demonstrative power through faith. You are a representative of God on earth, and should be walking around, giving others the desire to serve God. They should see who you are, and what you have (peace, wisdom, self-control, love, power, etc.) and want to have the same.

You are also an *ensign, a* standard. Jesus is our standard. But He set you up on high to make you a standard, a representation of Him on earth, for the Church to follow to Him. You are God's highest representative on earth in terms of the Fivefold: 'And God hath set some in the church, first apostles, secondarily prophets, thirdly teachers' (See 1Corinthians 12:28). You must be in alignment with God. Otherwise, you will teach people to do the wrong things, think the wrong things, say the wrong things. Think and act like God. You ought to be thinking like and acting like Jesus would think and act if He were on earth living your calling. The fact is, He is living your calling through you! And it's an urgent calling.

Apostle, it's time for you to raise the standard. The world is but a step away from eternity. Everybody carries the title, *apostle,* these days. However, you are more than a title. You are more than someone who has been given a high calling.

You are one that has been broken down to a worm: 'But I am a worm, and no man; a reproach of men, and despised of the people' (Psalms 22:6). You have been through battle after battle, spiritual trial after trial, loss after loss, victory after victory, situation after situation—

State of the Kingdom Address

all done to teach you humility, build your faith, strength, commitment, and love necessary to do the work ahead. You have been processed for the process.

Your title as an apostle is not one that you strive for, but one that was bestowed upon you from the Almighty God since birth: 'But when it pleased God, who separated me from my mother's womb, and called me by his grace' (See Galatians 1:15). He raised you up in your calling, and you are one to bear that title in word and deed.

However, to do your work more effectively, you must consider these things.

Commit to the call:

You will encounter a great deal of challenges as a result of your high-calling as an apostle. Your office is still alive today, and is as strong as it's ever been. You are an end-time leader, selected by God to get the world ready for the return of Jesus. And you will do that in whatever way God wants you to, and in what it is specifically that He called you to do. Come hunger, thirst, abasing, abounding, or even death, you should be totally sold out for your call. You will invariably go through the ups and downs of leadership. Jesus, Moses, Paul, Peter, David, and others have gone through the same thing. You will too. Be prepared.

Endure toughness like a soldier of Jesus Christ (2Timothy 2:3):

Your road is not for everybody. Otherwise, everybody would be walking it. It's a path that most people would turn away from instantly. It's humiliating at times, inconvenient, and uncomfortable. You may have to go through crucibles that those you are ministering to do not have to go through: 'We are fools for Christ's sake, but ye are wise in Christ; we are weak, but ye are strong; ye are honourable, but we are despised' (See 1Corinthians 4:10).

It's a part of your preparation. You should be able to abase or abound, knowing that God has you covered and protected in all things. He will bring you down low, to set you on high. Endure the process like a soldier. Every great soldier goes through boot camp. You, as a mighty warrior of God, must go through even more intense training—perhaps moments of lack, affliction, persecution, extreme poverty, or even isolation and mockery. Everything works together for your good. God will use it to build you up spiritually and increase your faith and power in Him.

See the big vision and don't let anyone take it from you:

Hold onto your vision. And don't let anyone take it from you. Think of how Noah had to build the ark, when there was no rain, only a word from God to build it. Think of how Abraham had to leave his family and go to a place that God would show him, despite his family not having that word (See Genesis 12:1). They must have been confused. Think of how Jesus was going to the cross and even Peter tried to talk him out of it. Apostle, the vision is for you to see and you to know, and you to hang onto, come hell or high-water. Look from God's eyes and see the success at the end of the road. Let His mind be in you (See Philippians 2:5). Never let anyone, anything, or any situation take your vision—the one that God gave you for His Church.

Sacrifice everything for your work:

Be a faithful workman for the LORD. Be willing to work late, go in early, put in extra time, skip lunch, skip dinner, wear yourself out, be paid, be unpaid, and more for your work. Your work is an invaluable work—it's God's work. What a calling!

Serve God with all you have:

Burn out for the LORD. Give Him everything you have. Why would you want to leave the earth with fuel left in your tank? That wouldn't do anybody any good. Instead, build up treasures in Heaven by your service to God on earth. Every single task that God gives you, whether big or small, should be done with excellence, to the best of your ability. You are an example for others to follow. Live full, die empty.

Serve the people out of love:

Make a love sacrifice for the people, as unto God. Serve them with a pure heart, and not to be greedy of gain. Do not manipulate, use, abuse, mistreat, cheat, or take advantage of the people you serve. The gospel is free to all those who will receive it. Serve freely. Know that it's God who meets your need, not the people. If God leads you to earn money through your work, in whatever endeavor that may be, then so be it. But do not get focused on making the money. Serve first, and the God of all creation will meet your need. As you pour out into them, God will pour out into you. I like to say it like this: 'There's profit in the purpose, but there ain't no purpose in the profit.' In other words, you don't have to chase money. Chase God and His will, and the money will come: 'But seek ye first the kingdom of God, and his righteousness; and all these things shall be added unto you' (See Matthew 6:33).

God is your supply:

Never forget that with your calling you depend solely on the hand of God for your survival. You are literally eating from His hand, day by day, hour by hour, second by second. He is your source. You have a greater dependency upon Him than most anybody in ministry. Learn to live by His grace, mercy, and divine provision. In short, live completely by faith.

Teach the truth:

No matter who you offend, speak the word of God. God doesn't have to conform to the people; the people have to conform to Him and His word. Speak the truth of God's word, and the people will eventually line up with it. You don't have to change to match the people's beliefs; they have to change to match God's will. You are already aligned. Help align the people you serve also by speaking and teaching the truth of the gospel.

Understand that you are in very high-levels of spiritual battle:

You are in a deep spiritual battle with wickedness in high-places, and with the ruler of this world. Satan will continually be on your back trying to thwart everything you do for the Kingdom. Learn to fight with faith. Do not run away from battle and contention with the devil. But be bold, and strong, willing to fight him anywhere, anytime.

To whom much is given much is required:

God has no desire to keep you where you are. No matter what you accomplished in life so far, God wants to give you more and entrust you with more of His gifts and resources (power, wisdom, provision, etc.). You have already gone through much for that sole purpose, to prepare you to execute your office the right way.

State of the Kingdom Address

Equip the saints:

Give the five-fold ministry and lay believers what they need to effectively live their calling (edification, empowerment, information, spiritual warfare training, revelation about Satan, etc.). Everything you learned in ministry and coming up into your calling you should be sharing with the people, unless God forbade you to share it. If you learned how to get blessed from God, share it. If you learned what you did that caused you to go through trials, share it. It's one body, one army. *Generals* should impart their spirit and experiences onto soldiers that are coming up under their leadership. Build up the present, and next generation of leaders. Your job is to equip the Church with new revelation, insight, information, and so on. Everyone you serve should be able to effectively do their work for the Kingdom and live their purpose as a result of your love, support, and guidance.

Lead others by example:

Teach people to be doers of the word and not hearers only. Also teach them how to walk by faith, hear from God, tear down strongholds, pray, fast, raise up other leaders, and the like.

It's necessary for you to be different:

God called you to be a strange, peculiar people (See Deuteronomy 14:2). The LORD is ushering in a new movement through you. Old stuff just won't do it. He needs you to stand out. Your life should be a spectacle for the whole world to see. You should be doing something to shock people, and wake them up out of their stupor. Exercise the power of God that is in you. Make a big, bad, bold move. Implement a new system, movement, blueprint, or whatever God will have you do.

Be unafraid about achieving God's will:

You should want to achieve the LORD's purpose more than you want your next breath. The apostle Paul said "death, where is thy sting?" (See 1Corinthians 15:5). Be willing to take the gospel to the grave with you, unwavering on anything God calls you to do.

Build something new:

You are called to lay a new foundation, not to build on an already existing one (except that of Jesus). Give the Church something to carry on with them into the future. You should be laying the foundation of a big, important, glorious work that will stand the test of time. Don't be afraid of the vision!

Build up other Five-Fold Ministers:

Help them live their calling the right way, according to the direction that God gives you. Help them be the best that they can be at their particular calling. Also, help them to operate freely as the Holy Spirit leads them. Help them gain more of God and give more of it to the people.

Prophets—

Prophets of God offer suffer a great deal of affliction, and with patience, in order to bring a word of God to the people and set them free: 'Take, my brethren, the prophets, who have spoken in the name of the Lord, for an example of suffering affliction, and of patience' (See James 5:10).

If you're a prophet, you're a straight to the point type of person who doesn't sugarcoat things. You give it to the people exactly the way that God gave it to you. Sometimes you offend people. In fact, it's more

State of the Kingdom Address

than likely that most of the time you offend people. You speak the word, and the word offends. It's sharper than a two-edged sword, not you. Consequently, since you may offend a lot of people, you are often rejected, as if you find it hard to fit in anywhere.

Also, chances are you may have had a difficult life and upbringing. Satan probably sends a lot of attacks your way, being that you have a word for the Body that will transform it into what God wants it to be. Likewise, you identify wrongs and you speak on them, don't you? That's the life of a prophet. And one of the most important aspects of your calling is to find people in the Body of Christ and place them where they belong, and release them into their ministry, whether as an evangelist, pastor, or someone else.

Your unique voice, mannerisms, and approach are critical to the success and advancement of the Kingdom. God needs true prophets now more than ever to speak to His people, that which He wants them to speak, totally unwavering. And if you won't step up and do God's will, He has 7000 other prophets that have not bowed down to Baal (See 1Kings 19:18).

Here are some things that will make you more effective in your ministry.

Hear God, not the devil:

Establish a clear line of communication between you and God. Do not let Satan deceive you and portray himself as God, or give you a word. Test the spirits. Be absolutely sure you are hearing from God before you pay a word forward to God's people. Pray and repent of any sin if you are ever in doubt. Reestablish your connection with God.

Speak the truth:

Speak God's word no matter what the circumstances or fears or doubts you may have. Speak prophetically only what the LORD tells you to speak. Don't speak prophetically if you are not led by the Holy Spirit to speak. Heed the warning from the book of Jeremiah: 'Therefore thus saith the LORD concerning the prophets that prophesy in my name, and I sent them not, yet they say, Sword and famine shall not be in this land; By sword and famine shall those prophets be consumed' (See Jeremiah 14:15).

Trust the vision:

God's vision is true. Even if it seems to tarry, wait for it. It will surely come to pass: 'For the vision is yet for an appointed time, but at the end it shall speak, and not lie: though it tarry, wait for it; because it will surely come, it will not tarry' (See Habakkuk 2:3). Your life should be lived as though that vision is certain. Prepare for it to come to pass. You validate the prophecy by doing so. It speaks volumes when it occurs: "God's word is true; and this is a real prophet."

Trust God:

If God gave you a word, is He not capable of twisting things around and manipulating the world to align it with His word? Believe that God can and will make it happen if it's His will.

Pastors—

Pastors are God's shepherds: 'And I will set up shepherds over them which shall feed them: and they shall fear no more, nor be dismayed, neither shall they be lacking, saith the LORD' (See Jeremiah 23:4). They are compassionate ministers who have a heart for the people, protecting them, encouraging them, teaching them, and building them up.

A true pastor that cares for Jesus' sheep will give his life for the sheep. He will sacrifice his very wellbeing to make sure they're alright. He nurtures them up, as a father to his child. And each child is special to him because he sees their potential. His goal is to help them live up to their potential by equipping them with all the spiritual guidance and support they need.

The sad thing is I have witnessed first-hand, and have even encountered myself, some pastors out there attacking the sheep, the same ones they're supposed to be defending. Attacks have occurred on many levels—verbal abuse, slander, manipulation, unjust financial gain, sexual molestation and advances, and others. Now, this is not always the case obviously, but when it does occur, it is very unpleasing to the LORD. Pastors, you must once again care for the sheep as if you were Jesus caring for them. He is living in you and vicariously through you. As you spend more time caring for them and nurturing them, the spiritual transformation in them that God needs to happen will take place. That, will, in turn, not only make them more successful in the Kingdom, but also a very productive, and efficient harvester of the lost souls in their communities, families, and networks. Accordingly, here are a few ways to pastor more effectively.

Prepare for the influx of churchgoers:

As the spiritual awakening, or end-time revival unfolds on earth, more and more people will flock into the church. Be prepared. Have a way to retain them, nurture them up in the faith, and lead them into a deeper relationship with God. Look at each new person that walks through your church as a jewel in the crown of Jesus. He wants them in Heaven.

Lead the sheep better:

Lead, love, and protect God's sheep, even as Jesus would Himself if He were here. He loves them with all of His heart, and so should you. Are you willing to die for the sheep? If your life is not on the line, your *life* is on the line. Are you willing to forgive them for any wrong they've done? Are you willing to accept them back into your congregation after some major conflict with them? As a pastor, and entrusted shepherd of the Lord, you should be. Otherwise, they will probably be led by the world, which is full of darkness.

Build up existing members:

Help current church members grow into greater roles of leadership, responsibility, and service, in their businesses, homes, jobs, communities, families, and church. Speak to convict them, challenge them, direct them, edify them. Do not let them become complacent and assume service is for everyone but them. Each joint supplies (See Ephesians 4:16).

You are a representative of God in your church:

You are representatives of the love of God for His flock. You must abandon all habits, beliefs, or practices that hinder your ability to lead saints to Heaven. Repent. And give more of yourself to God for His service.

You are accountable:

God holds you accountable for believers that fall out of grace due to failed guidance. There are many pastors in hell for failure to lead God's sheep the right way.

State of the Kingdom Address

Be more mature and responsible:

It's time for you to step up into greater levels of responsibility and spiritual maturity. Old ways just won't cut it anymore. A reform is in order. The devil is winning the battle for souls. It's often estimated that 1 in 1000 people make it to Heaven. Other estimates are more along the line of 1 in 7000, and in some cases 1 in 11000. Preaching is much more than a position, or a job. It's a critical part of God bringing people into His Kingdom, and delivering them from the hands of the devil, who waits in hell for the lost souls. God needs you now more than ever. Give more. Be more for Him. Your reward is great in Heaven.

Evangelists—

Evangelists, you have come to the Kingdom for such a time as this. You are naturally a person that has a passion for saving souls, though you may not be that well-versed in scripture. You are probably someone that has gone through a lot in life, lived through dark times, and was separated from God. Yet, you have a powerful story of redemption. You have a personal testimony of how Jesus saved you, and you want to share with others. However, there is still more work that needs to be done in your ministry.

You are here for a reason:

Evangelist, Jesus is prepared to come back. It's no mistake that God selected you to be the 'voice of one crying in the wilderness' (See Matthew 3:3). You are an end-time leader. Heaven rejoices for you work and commitment to the LORD. God needs someone as passionate as you and with a *voice* as strong as yours to sound the alarm. He has chosen you for this time to:

- Convict people of their sins
- Preach about holy living and sanctifying ourselves to God
- Witness to all those who have not heard about Jesus Christ
- Witness to all those who have heard of him but who have not accepted Him as their Lord and Savior
- Ignite a new fire for God into existing believers
- Inspire backsliders to return to the LORD

Burn out for the Cross:

Burn out turning people to God. Go out in flames of fire for the LORD. Let your light dim only when you leave the earth. Save souls; let nothing hinder you from grafting people into the Kingdom and telling them the truth about God's love and grace.

Your work is not futile:

Everything you do on earth is being recorded by God. According to a famous pastor, who had a near death experience and was taken to Heaven, DL Moody, one of the greatest evangelists of all time, built up one of the biggest mansions in Heaven. That's because he spent his whole life evangelizing on earth: 'But lay up for yourselves treasures in heaven, where neither moth nor rust doth corrupt, and where thieves do not break through nor steal' (See Matthew 6:20). Again, you are the voice of one crying in the wilderness, eating locusts and wild honey. That's all you really need to eat. You're more concerned with saving souls than you are with eating five-star meals at your local restaurant. You build treasures up in Heaven by getting people saved. You should look forward to your blessings up there, not down here.

Don't hold back:

Do not hold back your voice. Continue to reach people for Christ. God is exceedingly proud of you for your commitment to Him. You are His delight, and Heaven celebrates for each soul that you bring into the Kingdom. Witness from wherever you are and to whoever God leads you to, no matter the circumstances.

Keep up the work:

Continue in your good work. God has a great reward for you when you return *home*. Even if it seems like people are not getting saved, they are. The word is effectual and your voice is heard and received with fire.

Teachers—

Teachers are zealous for spiritual knowledge as attained from the Word of God. As a teacher you are forever learning and studying scripture, searching for new layers, hidden meanings, deeper revelation: 'Study to shew thyself approved unto God, a workman that needeth not to be ashamed, rightly dividing the word of truth' (See 2Timothy 2:15). You also read many other books, and tend to be very inquisitive. You are an important part of God's Body because you change people's old mindsets by giving them fresh revelation of scripture. You are totally against heresy, and you defend the Word of God faithfully, challenging any watered-down doctrines taught by people in the world. Nonetheless, teacher, God needs you to step up to a higher level. And here are a few ways you can do it starting today.

Teach the truth:

Teach people the truth about the Word of God. Make them realize it's the infallible, authentic word of God and every bit of it is true and expedient to gaining the life that God has for them. Challenge heresy and other doctrines with the word and the truth in it. Be bold in your convictions and stand up for God, especially when you hear something that goes against His Word.

You must value the Word more:

It's time for you to value the word even more than you do now. It's not a book, it's God: 'In the beginning was the Word, and the Word was with God, and the Word was God' (See John 1:1). It's also your pathway to Heaven and all the blessings of God. I literally have an old, beat-down Bible laying around in my house—beat-down from the countless nights of tears and sweat that dripped onto it. I was in daily battles with Satan. I literally slept on the word, rolling over onto it, having it on my chest at night, crying on it with tears pouring out as I used it to rebuke Satan during a period I faced intense torment from the devil. I used to keep it, *my sword*, open to my favorite scriptures during my personal bouts with Satan. One of my favorite scriptures is Revelation 20:10: 'And the devil that deceived them was cast into the lake of fire and brimstone, where the beast and the false prophet are, and shall be tormented day and night for ever and ever' (See Revelation 20:10). He hates that one. Such value I placed on the Word of God because it was all I had to live. You should value the word even more than that! And teach others to do the same. One day it will be *gone*: 'Behold, the days come, saith the Lord GOD, that I will send a famine in the land, not a famine of bread, nor a thirst for water, but of hearing the words of the LORD' (See Amos 8:11).

State of the Kingdom Address

Worship those red letters:

Those red words in the Bible, the words of Jesus, are exceedingly important. David L. Johnston (2016), of Redletterliving.org agrees. In this video, Johnston lists at least 20 reasons why the words spoken by Jesus in the gospel must be worshipped: http://bit.ly/1Kg7dkp They are not merely the words of a writer. They are the words of God.

The Lord is so strong that in the beginning He said "Let there be light" and there was light, and there still is light. Do you understand how powerful Jesus' words are? The Lord spoke, and the truth of what He spoke in the Bible in those red letters still resonates with us today. They will go with us into eternity. When he rebuked the devil in the Bible, the devil never stopped being rebuked, only because it was the Lord who rebuked him. In the same way that light never ceased, neither did Jesus' red words ever cease achieving what He wanted them to achieve. Value the red letters; the Lord himself spoke them. Worship the word, those red words especially, and apply them diligently and wholeheartedly to your situation and your teachings. Teach others to do the same. The Lord speaks softly, yet His words have infinite power. Again, as He spoke in the Bible, those things are still in existence, and still being done, because the Lord spoke them.

Show the Word value to the people:

Show saints how valuable the word is. They should guard it with their lives and not let anyone take it from them. They should diligently apply everything they read, being doers, and not just hearers of the word: 'But be ye doers of the word, and not hearers only, deceiving your own selves' (See James 1:22). They should eat it and taste the sweetness of it, the Word being as pure as honey. This is *life* to them.

Show them how to live in accordance with the word, ever being changed from glory to glory in His image.

DEVELOPING A GLORIOUS CHURCH

What can be done to help make the Church without spot or wrinkle, and prepare it for Jesus' return? The problems of the Church go way deeper than they appear. They cannot be resolved in a single chapter of a book. It would take not only the grace of God, but a massive, united effort from all believers, especially those in leadership. However, here are some things we can do right now to start to transform the Body of Christ, which will ultimately lead the world to revival.

You Are the Revival

Revival starts with you, and personal responsibility. Know that you are the revival. What are you doing to renew your spirit, refresh your mind, and break old habits that prevent you from being who God wants you to be? What level of faith are you walking in, the one from 1995, or the new, more powerful, effectual faith of 2016 and beyond? Are you working in that faith, as in doing the work, starting the projects, launching the businesses, ministering to the people, and taking the actions that God wants you to take? Or are you just sitting around waiting for revival? Again, *you are the revival*. Be the change that you want to see in the world. As the entire Body of Christ starts to think like that, God will kindle a revival fire across the globe that the devil can't put out.

International Repentance

State of the Kingdom Address

We must repent. And it has to be done internationally, on every continent, in every country, in every city, every community, every household, and by every member of the Body of Christ. It can't just be repentance like usual. We need to practically sit down in sackcloth and ashes, shedding sincere tears of repentance, asking God to forgive us of all of our sin. You can start from where you are now by repenting right now of all the sin in your life, and ask God to renew a right spirit in you. In addition, pray for others and encourage other people around you to repent of their sins and turn back to God. Show them the benefits and blessings that result from confessing their sins, and obeying the LORD's commandments. As we repent on an international level, starting with ourselves, our families, our communities, and our network of people we know and influence, God will heal our land (See 2Chronicles 7:14).

Sanctification

We must sanctify ourselves and remove anything hindering our relationship with God. It could be illicit relationships, bad habits, buying dirty magazines, style of dress, how we speak, association with ungodly people in ungodly ways, watching the wrong things on TV, listening to the wrong things on the radio, searching the wrong things on the Internet, a foul mouth, and others. Sanctification will result in us drawing in the presence of God into our hearts and lives. As we remove the 'accursed things', we will be walking in greater fellowship with God, which leads to us having greater power, influence, and impact on the world.

Rededication to God

We have to rededicate our lives to the Most High. We have to give all of us to Him, once more, and let Him reign in us. Everything about who we are must be given to God—our thoughts, our goals, our plans, our ideas, our energy, our resources, and more. We are the Body of Christ, which means that he operates through us. The Lord operated through His own body when He was on earth, performing miracles, healing the sick, spreading the gospel and so forth. Since He has been resurrected and is seated with the Father, we are placed on earth to be who He was when He was here. Now, we are His Body. We are His hands and feet, and He wants to live vicariously through us. So that means we must die. We must die daily, in fact. Consequently, Christ will live more and more in us, until it's no longer us living, but solely Him: 'I am crucified with Christ: nevertheless I live; yet not I, but Christ liveth in me: and the life which I now live in the flesh I live by the faith of the Son of God, who loved me, and gave himself for me' (See Galatians 2:20). While we let Jesus live in us the way He wants to, He will naturally lead us to His perfect plan, which is to bring in a powerful revival which sweeps across the nations and beautifies His Church.

Leadership Training

Church leaders need to be trained, or retrained to effectively raise up the Body of Christ. For instance, they need to be taught to deliver more transformational, effectual, inspiring, revelatory, unwavering, true, church-mobilizing sermons. That will lead to the change that God wants to see in the Church. God will cause the change, but He will do it through pastors and other church leaders. Notwithstanding, church leaders need more support from church members. Everyone in the Body of Christ must support each other and work together for the common cause, which is to save as many people as possible before Jesus comes.

State of the Kingdom Address

Leaders outside of the church must also be trained in the tenets of the Christian faith. It's not just going about training as usual. It's much more prolific than that. It's about connecting them with an authentic, Holy Spirit-appointed man or woman of God that's walking in power from on high, who can nurture them up in the faith. It's about helping them understand the implications of making decisions outside of the will of God. It's about making them aware of the spiritual world in which we live. It's about teaching them about higher level leadership that is being executed from high places, seated in Heaven with God. Ultimately, we will see the spiritual development of our leaders. It will be evident in not only the fruit of the spirit that they walk in, but in the real-world application of what they learn. Their ideas, goals, plans, programs, projects, and agendas will seem as though they came from God, because in essence they did. That's leading from Heaven.

We need an overhaul in our leadership system. No longer should it be world-based. But all leaders in the Body of Christ should flow 100% from the Spirit. They must be spirit-driven in order to have the type of impact that God wants them to have in the world. Real, effectual leadership always flows from the Holy Spirit, and is aligned with the Word of God.

Here are a few other ways to train leaders:

> - Equipping them with powerful new revelation on the Kingdom or the Word of God
> - Showing them the creative capacity of faith
> - Giving them a deeper understanding of the Trinity
> - Making them more aware of the spiritual reality
> - Giving them breakthrough spiritual warfare strategies

> Providing them with advanced leadership skills, such as efficient time management and strategic planning
> Developing their interpersonal skills to relate better to people and influence them more
> Teaching church leaders advanced business skills to efficiently run the church

These things will help people become more productive leaders, in their local churches, in their businesses, in their government, in their families, and in their communities.

Just recently, I had a man of God, an apostle by title, tell me that we could not bind the devil. I emphatically opposed that argument, especially since I came fresh off of binding him up, and I literally live a life of binding Satan, by the grace of God. The man of God claimed, with scriptural evidence, even, that the devil could not be bound. I claimed, on the other hand, with experience, and revelation from the Holy Spirit, which kept jumping in me when the apostle made that assertion, that the devil could most certainly be bound. However, not being as versed in scripture as the apostle was, I did not have in mind all the exact verses I needed to prove that. I had only a couple of scriptural references, and the physical experiential evidence from my own life (a picture of Satan being *bound*, which I could not and would not present to him at the time). Nonetheless, I stood my ground. And although the timing may have been inappropriate—we were on a business call talking about how we could work together to advance the Kingdom—I could not let what he said about not being able to bind the devil slide. I had to speak up. Perhaps that was my protective nature, and my calling to the apostolic stepping up. I was not going to let some other leader mislead God's sheep into thinking they have to live a life of defeat and oppression from the devil. I felt uneasy about the thousands of other people he may have been telling the same thing. Later that day I felt bad that I, in my mind, disrespected the man of God. However, God felt otherwise; He felt it was much needed correction. The LORD, that same day, gave me scripture after scripture, example after example in the Bible and in my own life, that proved we can bind the devil. I later presented the same scriptures to a colleague, who, in turn, presented them to the apostle via text. He eventually conceded to my argument. I am glad I stood my ground. Now, he has better insight as to what power we walk in, the Holy Ghost. God can bind and loose the devil anytime He wants. And if we're walking in the LORD, so can we.

It was the faulty thinking, maybe attributed to the institutionalized, restricted way he may have come up in his calling that caused the apostle to assert that Satan could not be bound. But it was my God-given duty to correct him, as it is his God-given duty to correct me if I'm out of line. That situation is a prime example of why we need to train or retrain Christian leaders, with fresh, God-inspired revelation. Otherwise, they will keep spreading fallacies to their followers, and the Church will be living far beneath our potential as people of God.

Singleness of Focus

I see so many people in the Body of Christ talking about their ministries. "My ministry this", and "My ministry that". Who cares about your ministry, unless your ministry supports His ministry. There are so many hidden agendas and selfish motives out there that causes division among God's people. The problem is too many people are focused on their needs and desires and not on God. We have to turn back to God. All that we do must be for Him and His glory, no matter what the assignment is. That's *singleness of focus*, putting our concentration on the Father, and pleasing Him, while paying less attention to ourselves. When the Church unites like that, under the common goal, of Jesus, we will cut through the devil's army like a hot knife through butter. There will be an exponential increase in the number of lost souls being brought to the Kingdom and receiving salvation. And we will see revival on earth.

Global Revival Coalition

I am in the process of developing a *Global Revival Coalition*™. This Coalition will be comprised of Christian Revivalists (leaders), and organizations wholly dedicated to revival on earth, and who are doing everything they know to do to make it happen. In short, members of the revival understand that revival starts with us, and we must be proactively doing our part to usher in the revival, this great spiritual awakening, on earth. "God, bring us a revival", I so often hear churchgoers say. Beloved, you *are* the revival. We don't need to wait on God; God is waiting on us, to step up and get out there and change this world.

Furthermore, the sole purpose of the GRC is to empower churches, Christian leaders, *revivalists*, and every day people all over the world to become actively involved with the end-time revival. That's to say, they are not just complacently going about church business, ministry, and life as usual to pass time. Instead, they are deliberately, passionately, aggressively bringing revival to their community and transforming the lives of everyone that comes in contact with them, whether through a sermon, community program, meeting, speech, book, audio lesson, face to face encounter, social media update, or via a phone conversation.

The Global Revival Coalition will be involved with things like:

- ➢ Recruiting people and organizations to join the coalition
- ➢ Bringing fresh revelation from God to the people
- ➢ Setting the operating rules of the coalition
- ➢ Overseeing members of the coalition
- ➢ Developing new leaders
- ➢ Providing inspiration, encouragement, and support to all members and constituents
- ➢ Providing the necessary resources for members to be proficient at their work

Leaders of the coalition will work with members to give them principles and procedures to incorporate at their local churches and in their ministry. Coalition members can then reach out to the community. The coalition will have a manual, such as a corporation's bylaws, to help each individual member or organization operate in accordance with the mission of the coalition.

Finally, the GRC will be very well organized. It will have a strict chain-of-command flowing from the top down. Yet, it will be decentralized, in that it will allow members to flow freely in their spiritual gifts or ministry, while allowing them to also make important decisions (recruitment, training, etc.) at the local level, without getting senior coalition officers involved.

Surveying churchgoers

There is no better way to get the truth about the impact of your ministry than asking believers directly how they feel. If you're a church leader, you should make it a habit, if you're not already doing so, of surveying believers. Try to find out about their church experiences or how your messages impact them and how much it helped improve their life. A good question to ask is whether each person feels they are becoming more closely connected to God, and whether they feel they are getting out of your service what they hoped to get. Ask them, "On a scale of 1 to 10, how would you rate the quality of my service to you [or 'the sermon' or whatever it is]?" For anything less than a 10, ask them "What can we do to make it a 10?" Surveys should be administered often, and changes made to your ministry as necessary to connect better with your audience. Always put God first, but you should also know the type of affect you are having on people that seek your guidance.

Grassroots Organizations

More grassroots organizations need to be used to spread the Word to those outside church walls. We need to encourage the Body of Christ to continue to reach out to people who aren't in church. Leaders need to empower them to start and grow businesses, ministries, programs, projects, services, communities, and other things that can reach people who don't attend Sunday morning service. We need to encourage the Body to meet people where they are. A drug addict will more than likely need to meet you in drug addict territory, a prostitute, in an area known for prostitution, a drug dealer, in an area known for drugs and crime, or a gang member, in gang infested territory. Many of these areas run together. In other words, where crime is, there is a good chance that drugs may be there as well. Nonetheless, we must be ready, willing, and able to go to where the people are and where they need us most.

Also, we must use content as a means of reaching people outside of church. For instance, social media, the Internet, blogs, articles, videos, online radio programs, streaming TV services, podcasts, teleconferences, webinars, books, ebooks, online programs, ecourses, seminars, workshops, conferences, Bible Study, home fellowships, and public meetups are a great way to connect with the people who may want God, but don't regularly attend church.

Business Benchmarks

Christian leaders need to be trained in practical, hands on, business management. The secular world is light years ahead of the Church in terms of basic business measures, such as profitability, website optimization, Internet marketing, productivity, efficiency, customer service, sales, and the like. There are so many secular books out there, that if the Church read and benchmarked, would bring us up to speed in no time. Examples include *Think and Grow Rich*, *The Success Principles*, *Rich Dad, Poor Dad*, *Titan*, and many more. The Body of Christ often feels the Bible is the only book they need to read. The Word of God is the most important, yes. We should, therefore, look first to the Word for answers in business, especially by doing what our successful forefathers did. Following that, we want to take a look at very successful Christians and Christian companies. Examples include John Rockefeller, Henry Ford, and Sam Walton. However, we can't skimp on learning from successful secular people, past and present, including Andrew Carnegie, Bill Gates, and Warren Buffet to name a few. We have to see how they did it. For the most part, they operated in integrity, and God blessed them as a result. For instance, they are known as being generous givers. As a result, God continues to prosper them because they are functioning in accordance with His law of sowing and reaping. In large part, they have also invented and mastered the wheel. At least from a business perspective, the Church can now step in and apply what those business leaders have learned in order to make our organizations more profitable. In terms of learning business from non-Christians, my rule of thumb is if what you learn from them is legal, ethical, and profitable, do it.

Business Support from Successful Christian Businessmen

It's time for the Church to begin generating more wealth. Church leaders not only need to embrace additional training in business, they need to be supported by Christian business men and women in the marketplace who have established successful businesses. These individuals can serve as coaches and consultants to Christian ministers to help them improve their organization, marketing tactics, fundraising methods, websites, and similar things. Better business, which your ministry can be considered as, leads to a greater influx of people to your organization. Whether a for-profit organization or a nonprofit church, business doesn't change: Better business practices lead to better results, and more often than not, better income. Obviously, the growth in income can be used to advance the Kingdom.

OTHER CHRISTIAN LEADERS

You may not be called to the Five-Fold ministry, but you are a very important part of God's Kingdom and His end-time revival on earth. The LORD has a plan for you in your specific area of work. He has placed you in a position of leadership because He wants to use you for His glory.

God has picked you up and set you on high. You are chosen of God to help prepare the world for Jesus' return. God wants to give you more authority, provision, guidance, and wisdom so that you may execute your office in accordance with His will.

It's only by your obedience to Him that He will entrust you with more of the blessings He has planned for you. God wants to take you higher, and use you in more mighty ways than you could ever imagine. However, He will not force His will upon you. You must come to Him, and be desirous of helping Him achieve His plan for the world—which is to lead people to Christ.

Consider God's calls to action to leaders in the areas of government, business, families, and communities below.

DEVELOPING A BETTER GOVERNMENT

Government upon His shoulders

I was at Living Faith Christian Center church, just outside of Camden, New Jersey, about a week before Christmas 2014, where the pastor delivered an incredible sermon. He discussed how the nation is so out of order in many ways because the government is not on the shoulders of Christ. The pastor pointed to the Book of Isaiah, which states that Jesus is the head of Government: 'For unto us a child is born, unto us a son is given: and the government shall be upon his shoulder' (See Isaiah 9:6). According to the scripture, the government is supposed to be on the Lord's shoulder. "Things are messed up in the country because the government is not on His shoulder", according to the pastor at LFCC.

Last Great Revival – Your Responsibility as the King Josiah of Your Day

In 2Kings, Chapters 22 and 23, the Bible describes the life of who I refer to as the last righteous king of Judah before Jesus came to earth. That king was King Josiah, who began to reign in Jerusalem at the tender age of eight. I find an interesting parallel between Josiah's responsibility as a king and your responsibility as a leader in the government. Josiah came into leadership to be a person that would turn the hearts of the people back to God. As Reverend Robert Evans so eloquently explains, revivals come and go throughout time. But each generation encounters its own unique spiritual move of God on earth:

> As we have found on the other occasions, devotion to God rises and falls. There is very little steady growth. Not only can individuals grow cold, so that a new surge of revival is needed within a generation. But, when one generation experiences revival, the next generation cannot live long, living on the spiritual credit account of the previous generation. Each new generation needs to experience the deep things of God for itself. (Source: Evans, 2016, Study Seven).

We see the righteousness of Josiah exhibited in one of his first acts as king–repairing the breaches of the house of God:

> And it came to pass in the eighteenth year of king Josiah, that the king sent Shaphan the son of Azaliah, the son of Meshullam, the scribe, to the house of the LORD, saying, Go up to Hilkiah the high priest, that he may sum the silver which is brought into the house of the LORD, which the keepers of the door have gathered of the people: And let them deliver it into the hand of the doers of the work, that have the oversight of the house of the LORD: and let them give it to the doers of the work which is in the house of the LORD, to repair the breaches of the house, Unto carpenters, and builders, and masons, and to buy timber and hewn stone to repair the house (See 2Kings 22:3-6).

State of the Kingdom Address

Of course, in the context of this scripture, breaches of the house of God refer to the temple of God in a literal sense. However, they refer to the Body of Christ, the people, and their worship of God, in a literal sense. There are breaches, or *gaps*, in between how you are leading the people through government, and how God wants you to lead them.

For example, do you lead from the guidance of the Holy Ghost? Do you meditate and apply God's Word, the Bible, in the decisions you make? Do you put the things of God before the things of man? Do you implement executive orders that bring your country and citizens closer to God or are you establishing orders that lead the people away from God? Are you helping to lead your people to blessings or cursing? Those things are examples of breaches, gaps, between man and the Most High. Are you repairing the breaches like King Josiah, or are you continuing in the practices of the previous administration, which may have perpetuated that breach between your people and the LORD? You must help to repair spiritual breaches in order to bring forth a revival in your country and on earth.

Later in 2Kings 22, Josiah received the book of the law from Shaphan, a scribe, who received it from Hilkiah the high priest. Afterwards, Josiah rent his clothes when he heard the book of the law. Then, the king sent to Hilkiah to inquire of the LORD concerning the book, saying, "

for great is the wrath of the LORD that is kindled against us, because our fathers have not hearkened unto the words of this book, to do according unto all that which is written concerning us" (v. 13). Hilkiah did as Josiah commanded; and the LORD responded accordingly:

> Thus saith the LORD, Behold, I will bring evil upon this place, and upon the inhabitants thereof, even all the words of the book which the king of Judah hath read: Because they have forsaken me, and have burned incense unto other gods, that they might provoke me to anger with all the works of their hands; therefore my wrath shall be kindled against this place, and shall not be quenched. But to the king of Judah which sent you to enquire of the LORD, thus shall ye say to him, Thus saith the LORD God of Israel, As touching the words which thou hast heard; Because thine heart was tender, and thou hast humbled thyself before the LORD, when thou heardest what I spake against this place, and against the inhabitants thereof, that they should become a desolation and a curse, and hast rent thy clothes, and wept before me; I also have heard thee, saith the LORD. Behold therefore, I will gather thee unto thy fathers, and thou shalt be gathered into thy grave in peace; and thine eyes shall not see all the evil which I will bring upon this place. And they brought the king word again (See 2Kings 22:16-20).

King Josiah then went into the house of the LORD with the people of Judah and the inhabitants of Jerusalem with him. He subsequently read the book of the covenant to the people, great and small. Josiah then made it his purpose to make a covenant with God to follow His commandments with all his heart:

> And the king stood by a pillar, and made a covenant before the LORD, to walk after the LORD, and to keep his commandments and his testimonies and his statutes with all their heart and all their soul, to perform the words of this

State of the Kingdom Address

covenant that were written in this book. And all the people stood to the covenant (See 2Kings 23:3).

Josiah ultimately went on a conquest of tearing down all the high places, idols, and idolatrous priests that served other gods. He took away...

- the vessels that were made for Baal (v. 4)
- the incense that was burned in high places in the cities of Judah (v. 5)
- the grove in the house of the LORD (v. 6)
- houses of sodomites (v. 7)
- horses that the kings of Judah had given to the sun (v. 11)
- chariots of the sun (v. 11)
- altars of the upper chamber of King Ahaz who, was an idolatrous king of Judah (v. 12)
- images, or columns, of other gods (v. 14)

He also...

- spied out the sepulchers of the priests of the high places, and he burned their bones upon the altar, in accordance with prophesy from 1Kings 13:2 (v. 16)
- took away all the houses of the high places which the kings of Israel had made (v. 19)
- slew all the priests of the high places (v. 20)
- put away workers with familiar spirits, and the wizards...and all abominations in Judah (v. 24)

According to 2Kings 23:25, there was never a king like Josiah that turned to God with all his heart and soul:

> And like unto him was there no king before him, that turned to the LORD with all his heart, and with all his soul, and with all his might, according to all the law of Moses; neither after him arose there any like him (See 2Kings 23:25).

As a result of Josiah's faithfulness, God decided to spare Josiah from the wrath to come on the nation (See 2Kings 22:18-20). Nevertheless, God promised judgment on Judah due to their transgressions:

> Notwithstanding the LORD turned not from the fierceness of his great wrath, wherewith his anger was kindled against Judah, because of all the provocations that Manasseh had provoked him withal. And the LORD said, I will remove Judah also out of my sight, as I have removed Israel, and will cast off this city Jerusalem which I have chosen, and the house of which I said, My name shall be there (See 2Kings 23:26-27).

It's essential that as a political leader, you help turn your country back to God by the reading of, and the application of the Word of God, in the same way that King Josiah did. As Reverend Robert Evans points out...

> This story also provides us with a major lesson in what happens when people cannot read for themselves, and the Scriptures are not readily available. It is hard for people living in Western countries at the end of the Twentieth Century to reali[z]e what it can be like if people cannot read, and if the

Bible is not available. Such a shortcoming has an enormous negative impact upon the possibilities for people to grow in personal spiritual maturity. The struggle to encourage good teaching and doctrinal knowledge is much harder under these restrictions, and people are much more prone to adopt strange doctrines derived from ignorance and a vivid imagination (Source: Evans, 2016).

What are some key takeaways from King Josiah's story? Well, if you expect to live in a blessed land, and avoid the wrath of God, here are things you must consider:

The responsibilities of a leader:

There is tremendous pressure on a leader. The lives of the people are in your hands. In the same light, so is their blood if you help lead them away from God and into darkness. God holds you accountable for the things He's entrusted to you, including men's souls. Sure, everyone makes their own decisions concerning obeying God, but if you are a partaker in leading them away from the LORD through the laws you pass, or the agendas you set forth, or the ungodly practices you accept and promote, you are held accountable. To whom much is given much is required, especially in terms of the souls the LORD has given you:

> And like unto him was there no king before him, that turned to the LORD with all his heart, and with all his soul, and with all his might, according to all the law of Moses; neither after him arose there any like him (See 2Kings 23:25).

I find it interesting that Josiah was so committed to the things of God that he even tore down the high places erected by King Solomon, such as those dedicated to Ashtoreth, the god of the Zidonians, Chemosh, the god of the Moabites, and Milcom, the god of the Ammonites.

Josiah was diligent in returning the people back to God:

You must be diligent and zealous in returning to the law, which is the Word of God. Josiah, just like many of the righteous leaders of ancient Israel, was a respecter of the law. He knew that obeying it would lead to divine covering and favor. Disobeying it would lead to curses. So immediately, upon learning that his forefathers had gotten away from the law, he repented, and made efforts to ensure the entire nation adhered to it:

> And the king stood by a pillar, and made a covenant before the LORD, to walk after the LORD, and to keep his commandments and his testimonies and his statutes with all their heart and all their soul, to perform the words of this covenant that were written in this book. And all the people stood to the covenant (See 2Kings 23:3).

Tearing down the high places:

One of Josiah's primary objectives was to tear down every high place that exalted itself against the knowledge of God. Idols, images, groves, wicked priests, and others. Ask yourself today:

> - "What high places am I allowing to exist?"
> - "What things am I promoting or endorsing that are not consistent with the Word of God?"

> "What people am I putting into office who don't belong there due to their negative, sinful ways?"

> "What worldly principles am I adopting and adapting that are contrary to the Bible, and what impact are they having on my office and my leadership?"

> "What people am I idolizing and exalting above the LORD? Do I cherish them more than I cherish God?"

Those things are considered high places, and they will inevitably lead to judgment from the LORD on you and the nation.

Instant judgment on the entire nation:

God will instantly judge our nations for forsaking Him and worshipping other *gods*. His judgment leads to macro problems, such as economic declines, terrorist attacks, pandemics, civil unrest, political instability, collapse of the government, and more:

> Because they have forsaken me, and have burned incense unto other gods, that they might provoke me to anger with all the works of their hands; therefore my wrath shall be kindled against this place, and shall not be quenched (See 2Kings 22:17).

Generational curses:

Generational curses will proceed us, making it harder for our children and future generations to live in the blessings of God. Instead, they will be plagued by difficulties, such as hunger, poverty, attacks from their enemies, and more. What we do today affects our descendants:

'[F]or great is the wrath of the LORD that is kindled against us, because our fathers have not hearkened unto the words of this book, to do according unto all that which is written concerning us' (See 2Kings 22:13).

Josiah spared, then dies:

If you obey the Word of God and seek to turn your country back to the LORD, He will bless you and your household, no matter what judgment the world around you may face. In the same way that He spared Josiah (See 2Kings 22:19-20), He will spare you for being a righteous, God-fearing leader:

> Because thine heart was tender, and thou hast humbled thyself before the LORD, when thou heardest what I spake against this place, and against the inhabitants thereof, that they should become a desolation and a curse, and hast rent thy clothes, and wept before me; I also have heard thee, saith the LORD. Behold therefore, I will gather thee unto thy fathers, and thou shalt be gathered into thy grave in peace; and thine eyes shall not see all the evil which I will bring upon this place. And they brought the king word again (See 2Kings 22:19-20).

Alternately, we see in 2Chronicles 35:20-24 that even righteous King Josiah died as a result of not hearkening entirely to the word of the LORD. In all his obedience, one simple act of disobedience, one moment of misalignment with the will of God, one episode of doing what he wanted to do and not doing what God wanted him to, going out to battle another king when he wasn't supposed to, cost him his life. God expects much from a king. One wrong decision from a king could result in dire consequences for them and the people they lead, even if that action seems small.

Pass laws in accordance with the Bible:

A recent survey to find out what should determine the laws of a country, was conducted in the book, *UnChristian: What a New Generation Thinks About Christianity…and Why It Matters*. Overall, 22% of those ages 18-29, 33% of those ages 30-49, 32% of those ages 50-64, and 44% of those over age 64 felt that the Bible, not the will of the people, should drive the laws of the country. That leaves the vast majority of the people across each age category feeling like the will of the people is more important than the Bible with regard to driving the laws of the country.

No wonder why the world is full of problems. We have put man before God! It's time to change that. And if we don't, God will—and we will not like the way that He does it.

Create a blessed country:

Pat Robertson (as cited in Shea, 2010), of CBN (Christian Broadcasting Network) made an interesting point several years ago during the earthquake that caused all of the devastation across the small country of Haiti. Robertson compared Haiti to the Dominican Republic, which is on the same small island of *Hispaniola* as Haiti. While Haiti suffered a severe earthquake, the Dominican Republic did not. While Haiti suffers from extreme poverty, the Dominican Republic is in a relatively better position financially. Additionally, although Haiti, when viewed from a satellite seemed to be dry and dusty, with little vegetation, the Dominican Republic, on the other hand was a lush country, full of trees and vegetation. They are two adjacent countries on one small island, yet with two different results.

Robertson concluded that Haiti practices witchcraft and voodoo, and was being judged by God for turning away from Him. The Dominican Republic, though, being a Catholic nation in general, was blessed by God in comparison. That same distinction in blessings and curses still exists with us today, from country to country, city to city, person to person. God knows who will be blessed and who will be cursed: 'Though hand join in hand, the wicked shall not be unpunished: but the seed of the righteous shall be delivered' (See Proverb 11:21).

Safeguard God's hedge of protection:

I go back to the deadly tsunami that killed over 200,000 people in Southeast Asia in 2004. The majority of those people were probably not Christians, and are likely to have practiced Buddhism, or some other religion outside of Christianity. The sad thing is not just that many unfortunate lives were lost, but that chances are many of them did not come to know and accept Jesus as their Lord and Savior. Granted, natural disasters and judgment can happen to any people, whether Christian or not. Nevertheless, God is only tolerant to a point. If we continue to ignore God, and live outside of His will, and even serve other gods, judgment becomes inescapable. If we don't have God in our lives, or in our countries, we open the door for a curse. However, curses cannot touch those that are covered by the blood of Jesus and who are standing pure before God. They have God's divine hedge of protection around them.

Preserve the hedge:

As a political leader, it is your responsibility to help safeguard that hedge of protection by leading people back to God. We see all throughout history, particularly in the Bible, where kings were either being brought up or cast down based on their obedience to God. You can find perfect examples in 1 and 2 Kings, and other ones in 1 and 2 Chronicles. Look at yourself in the likeness of a king. The lives of the people and the wellbeing of the nation is in your hands. Their destiny is tied to your decisions, as it pertains to obeying or disobeying God. If you obey God and follow His law, the country will be blessed and protected from their enemies. If you disobey God and turn from His commandments, the nation will be cursed and therefore vulnerable to attacks from enemies, destruction, and even total collapse.

A grave warning:

The other night, in January 2016, as I write this, I had a dream of warplanes flying into the U.S. It appeared that there was some type of war going on, perhaps even a Civil War. I know that dream was a warning by God for me to share with Americans. We must get right, or face the consequences of judgment, which in this case, might be war, either with an outside country, or internally between U.S. citizens. 'Hear, O heavens, and give ear, O earth: for the LORD hath spoken, I have nourished and brought up children, and they have rebelled against me' (See Isaiah 1:2). I issue a grave warning from the book of Isaiah: 'Your country is desolate, your cities are burned with fire: your land, strangers devour it in your presence, and it is desolate, as overthrown by strangers' (See Isaiah 1:7). It's time to turn back to God before it's too late.

As an additional point to ponder, Wikipedia reports that Since 1900, the top ten deadliest disasters occurred in countries that are known to primarily practice other religions than Christianity, for example, China, Bangladesh, Haiti, and Japan.

Consider the impact of Christianity on other nations:

Ironically, certain Eastern countries, such as China are becoming more and more Christian, and are more than likely beginning to prosper as a result. According to the Huffington Post, China is on track to becoming the world's largest Christian country by 2025. Currently, there are over 68 million Christians in China out of its 1.4 billion citizens, accounting for about 5% of the population. Sociology professor, Fenggang Yeng estimates that China will have about 160 million Christian citizens by 2025 and 247 million by 2030, 'just as America's Christian population appears to be waning' (Source: Blumberg, 2014, para. 6).

Ungodliness Growing in the U.S.:

One of the greatest examples of how God blesses those that receive Him and His Word is that of the United States. The country, for the most part, is a Christian nation, that was founded on the precepts of the Bible by its forefathers. The U.S. has been a world power, perhaps for the past 65 years (since the end of World War II). However, as the country gravitates toward more and more ungodly practices, such as homosexuality, fornication, pornography, idolatry, and so on, it's becoming more vulnerable to judgment from God. Just since the year 2000, the world has watched the U.S. deal with a number of misfortunes as a result of God's judgment. They include terrorist attacks, economic downfalls, and natural disasters. God still blesses and curses, according to Deuteronomy 28. The LORD is no respecter of persons. Anyone that turns away from Him, be it individual or nation, will suffer as a result.

Stop the wasteful spending:

State of the Kingdom Address

Just this year, 2016, Joe Biden, Vice President of the United States, suggested that the U.S. government spend $5.2 billion to find a cure for cancer (Source: Canal, 2016). That's a lot of money, and a noble cause. However, it's also a lot of waste. Cancer can be cured by simply repenting as a nation, sanctifying ourselves to God, obeying His commands, and praying. If anything else, a team of powerful, anointed men and women of God coming together in prayer, fasting, praise, worship, rebuking cancer, and applying scripture to the sickness is a much more effective solution. And it works. It just so happens that the world is so much less God-dependent, and more government-dependent that we lost track of the healing power that is inherently in the blood of Jesus.

That $5.2 billion could be spent on something else, such as feeding the hungry. And cancer could be cured for little to no money at all, but just by believers coming together as a nation and turning to God in sincere repentance. Why not create a nominal budget to coordinate such a massive spiritual event? It would turn people back to God and brings believers together in prayer, supplication, praise, and worship of God, which would not just break cancer, but eventually a lot of other yokes and bondages that destroy us. A great example of an event to support is the *National Day of Revival*™, mentioned in Chapter 3 of this book. For about $30 million annually, we can create the NDR and literally shift the spiritual atmosphere of our country. And it can be done in other nations as well.

The money spent on cancer research is only one example of the countless billions of dollars that are being wasted worldwide from country to country, trying to solve problems that faith and obedience to God would resolve in an instant. The problem is not that we have cancer. The problem is that we have a devil running loose in our backyard, and most people don't know how to get rid of him. But I assure you, he got in there due to sin. We must repent.

A few days ago there was a Powerball drawing worth about $1.6 billion, which was eventually won by John and Lisa Robinson of Munford, Tennessee, among two other winners (Source: Sickles, 2016). Prior to the winners being announced, people were all over social media sharing a meme. The meme claimed that a Powerball jackpot of $1.3 billion, divided by the U.S. population of 300 million, would give everybody $4.33 million, and solve national poverty. Discarding the poor math, I stand with the overall notion. Instead of running state lotteries and getting millions of people to lose money, why not take that money and use it for developing the country?

Senator Jeff Flake, in *Wastebook: The Farce Awakens*, details the preposterous amounts of money the U.S. government spends annually on ridiculous things (Source: Flake, 2015). *Wastebook* tracked national spending in U.S. Fiscal Year 2015, which spread from October 1, 2014 to September 30, 2015. There were a number of outlandish expenses that could have easily been eliminated; and that money could have been used somewhere else. For instance, Flake claims:

> A $2 million campaign paid for by the U.S. Agency for International Development (USAID) is encouraging tourism to Lebanon, a country the U.S. State Department is urging Americans to avoid due to the heightened risk of attacks and kidnapping by terrorists (p. 2).

Here are some other notable examples of U.S. waste, but the complete list can be viewed at http://1.usa.gov/1SYwZ3N:

State of the Kingdom Address

- In Texas/Maryland, twelve little monkeys were trained to run in a rodent ball on a treadmill in a National Institute of Health (NIH) funded study. The total cost of the study was about $1 million
- Unnecessary data centers ($5 billion)
- Bogus payments ($100 billion)
- Unused spare vehicles ($2.5 million)
- Suspicious bar coasters ($2.5 million)
- Empty buildings in Afghanistan ($110 million)
- Block party ($86,000)

As opposed to wasting taxpayer money on unnecessary things, it should be used for more life-sustaining and world improving matters, such as resolving poverty, hunger, and sickness. That brings me to my next point, which is, the government should...

Give people what they need and want:

Suffice it to say that all people deserve the basic necessities of life (food, water, shelter, clothing, safety, etc.). However, there are also other needs that people typically have, which money may be able to buy, in some instances. Examples include jobs, business capital, healthy food, clean communities, and affordable education, among others. All of the excess money left over from cutting unnecessary programs could be used to ensure all citizens of your country have their basic necessities met.

Many of these things are already afforded to people, but what about the people that may lack such pleasures in life, for example, shelter? In 2014, there was a reported 49, 933 homeless veterans in the U.S., which made up about 8.6% of the homeless population (National Alliance to End Homelessness, 2016). Some of those wasted dollars mentioned in the previous section could be set aside to build more homes for homeless veterans and others without shelter.

Godliness in leadership:

One of your first orders of business is to get yourself right with God. Then, you should create a Godly cabinet. Whoever is advising you and spending time around you or running your programs should be a spiritual equal. You can only get Godly counsel from Godly people. That's not to say that you don't hire secular people. It's to say that for the most part, you should work with people that support godliness and building your country as God wants you to build it. Your team should know that God has your nation's best interest at heart. It's only appropriate to allow Him to direct you and your cabinet to where He wants you to go and to do what He wants you to do.

Lead from God:

Separation from God destroys a nation and its people, whereas drawing close to God results in prosperity and protection. Government leaders are responsible for leading their citizens back to God, not just for passing and enforcing laws. God must once again be at the core of your nation's values, plans, and laws. That would inevitably position the country for God's favor.

As a government leader, you must take responsibility for turning your nation back to God. Build it up on the principles of the Word of God, by ensuring the laws passed are in accordance with God's will. Otherwise, your nation could just as easily become one of the less fortunate ones mentioned earlier. Economic challenges, natural disasters, social unrest, sickness, plagues, and the like are usually a result of people getting away from God: 'Righteousness exalteth a nation: but sin is a reproach to any people' (See Proverbs 14:34).

State of the Kingdom Address

A word to political leaders:

In the face of opposition, public scrutiny, the potential loss of followers, friends, influence, popularity, support, and even office, you have to do what's right. When it comes to decisions you make, you must choose in the path of righteousness, because in the end, it's God who judges a nation, not man. I encourage you to be the leader God destined you to be. Stand up for the LORD and He will stand up for you. It's time to turn your nation around, or make it better than it already is.

Return to the Word, and understand that revival starts from within. It starts from the Spirit, and as God changes the spirit—mind, will, emotions—of people, an outer change will be reflected in the flesh (the world). The onus of national revival is placed on your shoulders. How will you respond? How will you execute your office moving forward? Will it be in the same way as usual, or in a way that fully serves the LORD, blesses your nation, and brings people to Him? If you will implement changes, what will they be? How soon? What resources do you need? What challenges can you expect?

Please, write your answers to the questions down. Make a note to yourself, and refer to it often, doing exactly what it is you say you will do. Your actions from henceforth will be a destiny-defining moment for you, your country, and the people you serve. If you choose in the path of righteousness, God has you covered.

BUSINESS

God-centered business

Dani Johnson, at danijohnson.com, is well-known as a business leader that has gone from some of the most trying times in life, including a history of extreme poverty, child abuse, and drug use, to being a leader in the personal development industry. She has been featured on shows like *The Secret Millionaire* and *Oprah*. Dani mentors thousands of people around the world on how to be successful in business and in life, counseling them in areas such as sales and marketing, relationship building, and financial management and responsibility. Yet, in all her successes, Dani accredits God for changing her life. She frequently tells stories of how she made a million dollars by the time she was about 23, eventually lost it all due to a self-destructive lifestyle she was living at the time, and eventually gained it all back. The sudden turnaround in Dani's life and business occurred when she started doing things God's way and not her own. She started reading, meditating on, and applying the Bible to her life. She started putting serving others above making money. As a result, she eventually began to make more money after losing her first million. She began giving to others instead of spending all of her money on material things. It's by these principles that success in God's Kingdom is built—serving, giving, obedience, and personal responsibility.

Famous Christians and Christian businesses in the marketplace

There are innumerable others success stories in business, by which people have built their businesses on the foundation of God, and consequently prospered wildly in the marketplace. Some other notable examples include the late Zig Ziglar, John Maxwell, and Tony Robbins who all built successful businesses in the personal development industry, but also on Christian precepts. In fact, Tony Robbins' personal mission statement follows: "To humbly serve the Lord by being a loving, playful, powerful, and passionate example of the absolute joy that is available to us the moment we rejoice in God's gifts and sincerely love and serve all of his creations (Robbins, 2016)." Aside from the individuals I just mentioned, you also see some of the most successful organizations of our day built on Christianity, including Wal-Mart, Chic-fil-a, Forever21, Tyson Foods, MaryKay, In-N-Out Burger, Timberland, Alaska Air, Marriott, JetBlue, Interstate Batteries, Service Master, George Foreman Cooking, Curves, and Tom's of Maine just to name a few.

Business is important to God

In addition, it's no mistake that the word *business* is written at least 29 times in the Bible. Business is important to God, and His Kingdom is the most successful, efficient, profitable, long-lasting, sustainable business ever. If you're a business owner, it only makes sense for you to build your business on the foundation of God's business, His Kingdom. There is nothing in the world like having a *God-advantage* over your competitors. That's like having a supernatural edge that propels you ahead of your competition, which may not have God in their lives or businesses.

There are people out there in the world who say you should never mix faith and spirituality with business. I'm here to tell you you'd be foolish if you don't mix the two. As you acknowledge and exalt God, He will do the same for you. Start placing God at the head of your business and He will place you at the head of your industry.

FAMILY

Fathers and mothers, step up!

Where, oh where are the fathers? I'm not just talking about fathers of families, but spiritual fathers, who are supposed to be leading their families and their households to God. Families nowadays need leaders who are not just going to take care of their household by providing and protecting, but who are going to keep them safe from the devil. I see far too many families that are spiritually exposed to Satan.

Sure, the man of the house goes to work. Sure, he pays the bills. Sure he protects the family. But as is often the case, he is not doing those things from a spiritual standpoint. The household is left open, and all sorts of evil spirits flow in and out like customers at a Black Friday sale at the mall. Men must step up and be men once again. Lead your families spiritually and in the world. Grow up, if you find yourself falling short of God's standards for you as a man of the house. Women, I say the same thing to you: grow up if you are falling short of God's mandate to you as a woman of your house. Teach young ladies how to be women of God, full of virtue and integrity.

The sad thing today is that men are teaching women how to be women, and women are teaching men how to be men. In short, the spiritual mothers and fathers are having to step up and raise children of the opposite sex because the men and women who are supposed to be doing it are immature, irresponsible, uncommitted, ungodly, or missing.

Whether you are a man or woman head of your household, you have to lead and protect your family as Jesus would if He were on earth. Godliness starts at home. Build your family right. Keep sin out of your doors. Draw a circle around you, your household and your family. Don't let anything in the circle that's evil. Kick out everything from that circle that's evil. Bring in goodness, and don't let goodness leave that circle. That is the key to success or restoration to your family.

COMMUNITY

World Peace

I read a book recently called *World Peace: and other 4th Grade Achievements* by John Hunter (2013). It's a great book that asks the all-important question: *How can we attain world peace?* How can we make our world so every single person is prosperous, and every person is safe and protected? What an ambitious idea by the author, and one that I aspire for as well. In the book, world peace is actually a game, where 4th graders, given various fictitious countries, powers, and resources are challenged with the notion of achieving world peace. All types of situations, problems, and obstacles occur, including nuclear arms, warfare, struggling economies, political strife, environmental issues, and the like. The job of the 4th graders is to sort through all of the confusion and stresses dealt to them, and work together to achieve world peace and prosperity for every country. Ultimately, there was at least one situation, in the game, where a 4th grader helped accomplish world peace. Although *World Peace* is only a book, we need to think about what it would take to achieve world peace for the Body of Christ in reality? How could Christians around the world, in various communities, cities, states, countries, and continents reach a level of peace and prosperity unsurpassed throughout history? I'll tell you how: through God. A spiritual revival must occur before an actual revival can occur on earth. It's only after man gives himself to God that he will be able to make the decisions, in politics, business, families, relationships, economics, environment, and otherwise that benefit society as a whole. It's simply because God, in His infinite goodness, holiness, and righteousness, leads people to actions and decisions that are in their best interest.

Spiritual reformation

Communities in the world must be reformed, spiritually. There are so many community development programs and plans out there, which is good. Much attention is given to the infrastructure, economy, health of local communities and similar things. However, wouldn't it be better to start with spiritual restoration? Doesn't real reform start with the spirit? As a man is changed spiritually, he changes in other ways as well, mentally, emotionally, physically, relationally, financially, and more.

I talked previously about a global revival coming on the earth. Well, man has proven that he can only do so much by himself. He is limited, in power, resources, and wisdom. A true revival can only occur if we put spiritual things first. It has to occur within a person first, then it finds its way out of them to the world. They become more positive, encouraged, and willing to serve others. They get creative ideas to foster community development. They find Godly ways to help their fellow citizens.

As a community leader, it's time for you to put God first. Develop yourself spiritually, and encourage your followers or constituents to do the same. Once the spiritual foundation is established, you can build your community up, brick upon brick, block upon block, precept upon precept, and it will all be directed by the hand of God.

State of the Kingdom Address

OTHER ISSUES FOR CHRISTIAN LEADERS

There are a few other issues in Christian leadership that need to be addressed here. The first is spiritual weakness.

Spiritual Weakness in the Church

Church members have been receiving watered-down sermons of the word. Many preachers have not spoken with the power of God, and with truth. Many have been catering to the ears of parishioners by preaching what is generally accepted by the masses. Consequently, church attendees are often left wanting; they have not been filled off the Word.

The Body has become weak, and is unfit for battle as a result. The majority of churchgoers do not walk in the full authority of God through Jesus. The devil laughs at them because he knows that a clash with them is imminent. If we were to battle Satan right now to conquer new territory, being unprepared for battle, we would lose terribly.

The Five-Fold ministry is responsible for getting the Church strengthened and ready for battle. Do all that you can, using your gifts, knowledge, and experience to prepare the Church as an end-time army of warriors for God.

Ending Malnutrition

Hunger plagues church leaders and parishioners as well. Many church ministers have been getting full off of watered-down doctrine, such that their sermons became non-transformative. As a result, church attendees are suffering from malnutrition because they are eating the same things that their leaders are eating. Churchgoers often leave church the same way they came in—no change. No spiritual progression. No power to destroy every yoke holding them back in life. People have a real need, a real desire, for real nutrition. And they can only get that from the unaltered, authentic word of God— delivered in truth, and under the anointing of the Holy Spirit.

Many pastors are preaching for the world. The Body of Christ is about to start regurgitating all of that junk up that it has become so accustomed to eating. God is once again going to feed His flock with the truth. The children of the Kingdom will hear His truth, and He will put people in office that will deliver it effectively and without compromise. Church leaders and ministers, it's time to feed the children right. Let's teach them the truth about God, salvation, the devil, Heaven, hell, blessings, and cursing.

Deeper Levels of Spiritual Battle Must Be Taught

As you may know, Christians face a literal spiritual battle against Satan and his army. However, people somehow take that lightly. Millions of people are showing up to church week in and week out. Yet, many don't acquire the faith or understanding necessary to turn their financial situation around, or cast out devils from their home. They seem to be much more content with getting the front pew rather than engaging the devil in spiritual warfare and taking back everything he ever stole from them.

There was a service at a popular church on television not long ago where the pastor called on a woman from the audience to come to the stage. This woman was a regular churchgoer, and I often saw her in the front pew, week by week., as I watched the streaming service from home. As the pastor called her to the stage that particular day to pray for her or whatever situation she was facing and needed victory over, he told her to rebuke the devil.

Pastor: "Tell the devil to get out of your situation" the pastor encouraged her.

Woman: She said something along the lines of, "I rebuke you Satan."

Pastor: "No. That's not enough. Tell him like you mean it.", the pastor exclaimed.

Woman: The lady responded, "I rebuke you Satan, in the name of Jesus."

Pastor: The pastor railed on her, "No. You've got to say it like you want him out. Say it louder."

Woman: "Satan, I rebuke you in the name of Jesus" the woman said.

Pastor: "Louder and like you mean it", the pastor challenged her.

Woman: "I rebuke you Satan, in the name of Jesus", the woman replied.

Every time the woman rebuked the devil she seemed to get louder and louder, speaking with more strength, faith, and conviction. It's great that the lady mustered up enough faith to get the devil out of her situation. But why is it that a person that goes to church on a regular basis, and has direct access to the pastor (being the wife of an elder), and sits in the front pew week in and week out, barely had enough faith and boldness to step on the devil's throat and cast him out of her situation? It's not so much that she didn't love the LORD, or that she lacked faith. It's that she became a part of the status quo: "Go to church. Show up for fellowship. Then, go home without any real change, power, or victory in my life, and my day-to-day battle with the devil."

The devil will give you the front seat with the padded pew of any church. He will help you get to church and hear a wonderful sermon. He will even help you put gas in your car to get to church. He will do all this and more, so long as when church is over and you go home to face him in your everyday life, nothing changes for you. Satan is totally content with you showing up at your weekly services, as long as you don't walk in the faith and the power that you have through Christ. People are becoming too acquainted with church services, and less acquainted with the victory they have through Jesus.

As a church leader, you must teach your church about real spiritual battle. Tell them the truth about devils, and spiritual manifestations. Tell them about dreams and visions you may have seen or heard of someone else seeing. Encourage them to share the dreams and visions with others in the Body, especially, believers who can help discern these dreams. Teach them about principalities, names of evil spirits, and the like. Teach them about the negative impact of sin in our lives and how it gives the devil a license to kill and destroy us.

There is a term called *spiritual leverage* I've used throughout this book, and that I often use in my training business. As a Life Strategist in addition to the many other things I do in the world to develop the Kingdom, 'I raise up and develop revolutionary leaders for the Kingdom of God. I help you have a bigger impact on the world through the work you do!' You can find out more about my training at http://belovedhq.com. I operate in the principle of *spiritual leverage*. And it's that principle that needs to be applied widespread across the Church.

State of the Kingdom Address

More on Spiritual Leverage

Spiritual leverage, or the lack thereof, is the reason that the church struggles in so many areas—lack of finances, poor health, broken relationships, loss of control over children, and similar things. Most churchgoers are not spiritually leveraged. They have become victims of the mundane, monotonous, ineffective system of the same old sermons, church friends, organs, and church songs. Instead, they need to experience the real power of God through the Holy Spirit. Then, when they walk out of church they will take that victory home with them. Church should be less about the announcements, and much more about the transformative power of the Most High God. Are you teaching your people about God, the right way? If not, it's time for you to change things. Go in the way of the Holy Spirit, who will direct you to how He wants you to preach, teach, love, lead, and support other believers.

CHAPTER 10: RAISED FROM THE DEAD

Jesus said unto her, I am the resurrection, and the life: he that believeth in me, though he were dead, yet shall he live: And whosoever liveth and believeth in me shall never die. Believest thou this? -John 11:25-26

A few months ago I went into the local McDonald's to have breakfast. I was sitting not too far from a group of about five Catholic women who frequent that McDonald's, everyday around 9am or so to talk. It's usually about 4 to 5 of them that come in to chat. I usually don't pay much attention to the group of ladies, other than an occasional *hello* or *good morning*. However, on that particular morning they caught my attention. They opened up their meal by saying their grace, as is often the case. I guess I hadn't given them much notice before, but this time I just happened to catch a bit of what they prayed: "Hail Mary, mother of God…"

I had never witnessed anyone praying to Mary before in person. I was double-shocked to hear them call Mary the 'mother of God'. The mother of Jesus, according to the flesh? Yes. But, the mother of God? Clearly not. "Are they praying to Mary?" I thought to myself. "The only one anybody should be praying to or praising is God." Part of me wanted to get up and go and talk to them about their faith. The other part of me wanted to remain seated, and keep the morning peaceful. I decided to do the latter. That was extremely difficult because I knew that such beliefs—idolizing the Virgin Mary—could separate someone from God, is viewed by God as a sin, and could possibly land them in hell. Perhaps that wasn't the right time or place to address that issue—at a public restaurant, peaceful breakfast, with a bunch of innocent, elderly women. Things should be done in decency and order. So, this book is a better place to address idolatry, worshipping anyone or anything besides God. My hope is to influence the Catholic Church into praying to God, and God only.

You may or may not be Catholic, and idolizing Mary may or may not be a practice amongst all Catholics. Nevertheless, I'm here to tell you, it's absolutely wrong. God takes offense to it. The LORD is the only one you should be serving.

A WAKE-UP CALL FOR INDIVIDUALS

There are many other issues I want to bring to light in this chapter. The proceeding paragraphs serve as a wake-up call to individuals. There are some things you may or may not be doing that could separate you from God's perfect plan for you.

The Truth About Heaven and Hell

I was on a spiritual website called Divine Revelations: face to face encounters with Jesus Christ, about a year ago. You can visit it at spiritlessons.com. It's a site that describes the true nature of Heaven and hell, and the spiritual world. The site explains what you can expect to see if you die saved, and what you will see if you die unsaved. We know that the saved get to inherit the Kingdom of Heaven. The unsaved, hell.

I read of accounts of people who had near death experiences (NDEs) who were taken to hell. Some of these individuals were sinners and given a warning by God to turn their lives around, lest they should die unsaved and spend eternity in hell. Other people who had NDEs and shared their testimonies were righteous, but allowed by God to see the pains of hell so they could go back to earth and warn people about the horrors they experienced. I heard testimony after testimony of people who had been taken to hell and saw the burning, tortured souls of many Catholics, who were sentenced to hell for idolatry, more specifically for the worship of the Virgin Mary.

The Pope, in Hell?

Even the pope, the late John Paul II was depicted in some images on the site as being in hell. He was said to actually be there according to some eye witness accounts of people who were taken to hell in NDEs. Despite any good the pope was believed to have done, and despite how holy he appeared, it's a commonly held belief amongst many Christians that he often put money and power before God. He also led the Catholic Church in serving the Virgin Mary. Not to mention, he never stated publicly that he was born again, nor did he confess faith in Jesus, alone, as being the only way to salvation. As a leader in the Catholic Church, he should have led the people to worship Jesus, and not other men, women, or idols. To whom much is given, much is required (See Luke 12:48). God placed a great deal of responsibility in the hands of the pope. However, his failure to lead the Catholic Church in the way that God wanted him to lead it may have cost him his spot in Heaven, and many Catholics that followed his teachings, unless they turn to God and not idols, their spot as well.

Now, I'm not Catholic. I'm not writing to condemn Catholics. Nor do I know entirely how the Catholic Church operates. I subscribe to Jesus' saying from Mark 9:40: He that is not against us is for us. Obviously, there could be many Catholics who wholly follow God and don't get caught up in some of the ungodly practices in the

Catholic church. Just like any church, be it Baptist, Methodist, or otherwise, there could be ungodliness present in the religious practices. Some of the practices could be deemed 'tradition', and passed on from generation to generation. However, that does not excuse us from being responsible for our actions and beliefs. I focused on the Catholic Church here, because of its power, prominence, and well-known ritual of idolizing the Virgin Mary, perhaps not in every Catholic Church, but in a great majority, yes. What I do know is this: whether you are Catholic or Protestant, or anywhere in between, if you serve idols, be it statues, people, money, power, or others, you are not operating in the will of God. Let your religion be Yes to the will of God, and amen to obeying His word!

Become Unlearned

Whether you're Catholic, Baptist, nondenominational, atheist, agnostic, or practice some other doctrine, there are probably some things ingrained in you that separate you from the truth about God. It takes us years to learn the wrong things, so common sense would say that it could take an equal amount of time to learn the right things. To say it another way, it took you some time to get where you are with regard to your mindset and beliefs. It's going to take some time to undo all of that stuff and get you where you need to be. You, like many of us who come to the Cross, may have to become *unlearned*. I'm not necessarily saying that you may not know the truth. I'm just saying that you may not know all of the truth. And all of the truth sets you free; not just some of it. As we become more and more aware of the truth about God and salvation, we must inform others about it also. Souls hang in the balance, including the souls of those close to you.

Heaven Ain't a Nightclub

Isaiah 5: 14 says, 'Therefore hell hath enlarged herself, and opened her mouth without measure: and their glory, and their multitude, and their pomp, and he that rejoiceth, shall descend into it.' Hell is making more room for the lost souls that are headed there. You have to wake-up, child of God! Paul warned us well in Philippians 2:12: 'work out your own salvation with fear and trembling.' Heaven is no nightclub. You don't just walk up to God's pearly gates and stroll on in like you're going out dancing. You'd better be covered in the blood of Jesus, and be a true child of God to enter Heaven. If not, the angel that guards the gate will kick you across the universe until you land in hell.

"How many of you know that if you died today…"

It bewilders me when preachers get up on the pulpit and pose the question, "How many of you know that if you died today you would go to Heaven? Let me see your hands." Really, pastor? Since when does anyone know whether or not they will make it to Heaven? Consider this verse from when Jesus was on the Cross: 'But Jesus turning unto them said, Daughters of Jerusalem, weep not for me, but weep for yourselves, and for your children...

For if they do these things in a green tree, what shall be done in the dry?' (See Luke 23:28, 31). Also, the Apostle Peter stated that if the righteous scarcely be saved, how much less the ungodly (1Peter 4:18).

No matter where you believe you will go when you die, the only person who really knows is God (See Revelation 5). He is the one that has the *book of life*—not the Son, not the angels, not you, but God only.

State of the Kingdom Address

Jesus is the Way

Repentance for sins should be done in tears, fear, and with great remorse. It's only through Jesus Christ that we even have a chance of entering Heaven. Notice, I said 'a chance'. The *blood* is sufficient, but people must believe in it, accept it, and apply it. Likewise, you must turn away from sin, and not use the grace-card (believing that God's grace gives you a pass to live in sin) to continue doing wrong.

Also, good works are futile without salvation. You cannot earn your way to Heaven by your works: 'For by grace are ye saved through faith; and that not of yourselves: it is the gift of God: Not of works, lest any man should boast' (See Ephesians 2:9). Our righteousness is as filthy rags (See Isaiah 64:6).

More Testimonies of Heaven and Hell

I can't help but recount the near death experience of Mary Baxter, a Pentecostal minister and author of the controversial book, *A Divine Revelation of Hell* (Baxter, 1993). Mary experienced the realities of hell when she was taken there on a visit. Mary's account of hell is one of the most popular ones that I've heard of to date. Jesus took her to visit hell for 30 consecutive nights. He wanted to show her the horrors of hell in order to have her show people what happens to souls when they die unsaved, and to servants of God who don't obey their calling.

One of my favorite testimonies of the afterlife came from Reverend Park, Yong Gyu. After a near death experience, Pastor Park was taken to both Heaven and hell, as discussed in this video http://bit.ly/1ZyNIut. He was shown how our work on earth determines how we live in Heaven. For example, those that did the most work on earth for the Kingdom of God typically lived in the biggest mansions and had the best homes and rewards in Heaven. Others, especially those that barely made it to Heaven, or who did very little work for the Kingdom of God on earth, received small homes, shacks, and little rewards in Heaven. Conversely, Pastor Yong visited hell, and bear witness to some of the gruesome things that unbelievers go through. Pastor Yong's story, like so many other stories that detail the realities of hell is a clear wake-up call to individuals in the Kingdom to start living right, and be sure they repent of their sins. People have gotten so comfortable with life, that they may give no second thought to eternity. Jesus said, your treasures ought to be stored up in Heaven, not on earth (See Matthew 6:19).

Lake of Fire

I had a dream not too long ago where I was sent to hell as a witness of what occurs there. I was in what looked like a dark cave, but I was suspended in mid air, looking down on a lake. It was the *Lake of Fire*, which resembled a lake full of lava from a volcano. I was dressed up like a priest, with the Roman-collar and all. As I looked down I saw the lake swirling around the cave. It contained the bodies of people that were sent to hell, floating in the lake naked. They were screaming in pain, swirling with the lake as it twirled and swished around the bottom of the cave. Their arms were flying up, and reaching out as if they were asking for help. I looked in awe. I knew I was witnessing people in hell, being tormented for their way of life on earth.

God somehow protected me, putting me out of harm's way: 'Only with thine eyes shalt thou behold and see the reward of the wicked' (See Psalms 91:8). I assume God was warning me about the severity of hell. Maybe He was telling me to get right with Him, or calling me to tell the people what I saw. Either way, God wanted me to help people avoid that place. Unfortunately, many people are living separated from God. So souls are ending up in hell at a rapid pace: 'Hell and destruction are never full; so the eyes of man are never satisfied' (See Proverbs 27:20).

The Roman Road

Disconnection from God has led people to all sorts of doctrines that leave them in the dark. You are required to fulfill God's Great Commission, of witnessing to other people about the truth of salvation. You have to stand up for the truth even when it's not the most popular thing to do. If you don't then God will hold you accountable for any soul that is lost as a result of you withholding the truth that the Holy Spirit guides you to speak.

It's well-known amongst Christians that the *Roman Road* leads you to salvation—named such because the path to salvation is outlined in the book of Romans, namely Romans 3:23; 6:23; 6:23b; and 10:9. Gotquestions.org provides a great summary of the Roman Road here: http://www.gotquestions.org/Romans-road-salvation.html

Common Misconceptions About Spirituality

I thought about many of the common misconceptions about spirituality that leaves people living less than blessed, or even positions them for hell if they die. God said in His word, "My people are destroyed for lack of knowledge" (See Hosea 4:6). Just in the past week alone, I've heard unbelievers, or misinformed people share things about God and spirituality that made me cringe. I not only thought of how their limiting beliefs separated them from the truth about God, and possibly making it to Heaven one day.

Here are some of the many statements I hear from the secular world, and even some believers. These beliefs could very well lead a person to hell:

"Once saved always saved":

People can fall off the 'saved' bandwagon just like a dieter can fall off the diet program. Being saved is a lifestyle and not just a single act of repentance. Remember, God can put your name in the Book of Life, or He can erase it: 'Let them be blotted out of the book of the living, and not be written with the righteous' (See Psalms 69:28). We're not saved by what we know. We're saved by what He knows, and what we work out, according to what He knows. We have to work out our salvation.

"If you simply repent of your sins, you are sure to go to Heaven.":

Repentance is an ongoing thing. It means you turn back to God. If you are in Jesus, with every sin you commit, you simply repent and put it under the blood through confession and asking God for forgiveness. You are saved by grace through Christ. However, if you are not in Jesus and have not made Him your Lord, then you are operating under the law. Every new sin you commit under the law places you in danger of hell fire once again. In the law, you must be near perfect to make it to Heaven, hitting every single mark, and being in perfect obedience. In Christ we are made perfect through Him: 'I in them, and thou in me, that they may be made perfect in one; and that the world may know that thou hast sent me, and hast loved them, as thou hast loved me' (See John 17:23). Also, know this. If you have accepted Jesus, living a life of sin, and exploiting the name of Jesus just because you have a grace-card, can very well cost you your salvation. In short, don't just intentionally sin, or easily give into

State of the Kingdom Address

sin just because you can repent to God through Christ. We should be living a holy lifestyle: 'I beseech you therefore, brethren, by the mercies of God, that ye present your bodies a living sacrifice, holy, acceptable unto God, which is your reasonable service' (See Romans 12:1). Even professing Christians who carry sins like unforgiveness, though accepting Jesus, could be in danger of hellfire if they don't repent of that sin: 'Remember therefore from whence thou art fallen, and repent, and do the first works; or else I will come unto thee quickly, and will remove thy candlestick out of his place, except thou repent' (See Revelation 2:5). Accept Jesus as your Savior, live a life of holiness and righteousness, forever examine yourself and be circumspect, hearken to the voice of the Holy Spirit, always repent of sin, and you will greatly increase your chances of being with God for eternity.

"You are saved by works, and if you do good and treat people good you go to Heaven.":

You are justified by faith, not by works (See Galatians 2:16). Otherwise, you're saying that you, and not Jesus, are the path to Heaven.

"God loves everybody and everyone that accepts God makes it to Heaven":

God loves everybody, yes. That's why He sent His Son to die for everybody. But only those that accept Jesus Christ as their Lord and Savior will be saved (See John 3:16-17).

"We are all God's children.":

We are only God's children through adoption in Christ. Only those grafted into the Kingdom by believing in Jesus, and accepting Him as their Lord and Savior, are children. All others are strangers to God. There is no way to the Father, or to even call God our father, but by the Son. If we try to get to God by some way other than Jesus, we are not children of God: 'Ye are of your father the devil, and the lusts of your father ye will do. He was a murderer from the beginning, and abode not in the truth, because there is no truth in him. When he speaketh a lie, he speaketh of his own: for he is a liar, and the father of it' (See John 8:44).

"Families are saved and none of your family can end up in hell.":

Each person is judged as an individual (See Revelation 20:11-12). God has a family plan of redemption, true. However, it's up to you to see it come to pass. You must work God's harvest. You have to help get your family saved. If all families were automatically saved, how did anybody end up in hell, according to Mark 16:16: 'He that believeth and is baptized shall be saved; but he that believeth not shall be damned.'? If people in your family don't accept Jesus, they will not be saved if they die. God judges us as individuals: 'The soul that sinneth, it shall die. The son shall not bear the iniquity of the father, neither shall the father bear the iniquity of the son: the righteousness of the righteous shall be upon him, and the wickedness of the wicked shall be upon him' (See Ezekiel 18:20).

Work out your salvation

It's thinking like that that gets people on a slippery slope, placing them in danger of hellfire. If any of the above reminds you of your beliefs, you need to make some immediate changes. Below, I provide a few examples of what you can do to increase your chances of entering Heaven when you leave this earth:

State of the Kingdom Address

- Receive the free gift of salvation.
- Turn away from sin.
- Make repentance a lifestyle activity; do it daily and after every new sin.
- Live righteous and holy.
- Live unto God and not unto the world.
- Live as if Jesus could show up anytime, because He can.
- Live totally immersed in God; give Him all of you.
- Live free in the LORD by having a real, genuine relationship with Him.
- Seek to please God and not the world.
- Obey God.
- Think bigger and long-term as opposed to seeking instant gratification.
- Have a paradigm shift in your old thoughts; they may not get you to Heaven.
- Minister to everyone you know and seek to save your family and household.
- Live in the Holy Spirit.
- Meditate daily on the Word of God.
- Pray, praise, fast, and worship God often.
- Put your thoughts and mind in Heaven; act as if you're seated in high places.

The Great Awakening

There is a *Great Awakening* in the U.S. and in the world on the horizon. This awakening is much like those spiritual awakenings of the past several millennia in the U.S. For instance, Wikipedia lists some of the most popular ones: First (c. 1731–1755), Second (c.

1790–1840), Third (c. 1850–1900), Fourth (c. 1960–1980). It seems like every 50 to 60 years, these awakenings come along—at least for the past couple centuries. One of the greatest revivals, The Azusa Street Revival, occurred about 100 years ago, in Los Angeles, CA on the heels of a spiritual awakening. However, you can expect another worldwide revival to come very soon. Like Azusa Street, this revival will be preceded by a spiritual awakening. People will have a deep desire to serve God with all their heart, mind, and spirit. Consequently, I believe we will shortly experience the greatest revival of all time. It will be a powerful international revival that will prepare the way for Jesus Christ to return. It will be the End-Time Revival; and we are on the brink of that End-Time Revival, which will be spurred on by another Great Awakening.

I encourage you to not only be a part of this world-transforming awakening, but to be a leader in your particular 'movement' as it relates to it. Be it in business, politics, education, coaching, or the like, you can step up to the forefront of your field so others get attracted to the light that's in you. A spiritual transformation to the world is about to take place. However, it starts with individuals. We must change from within to see the change without.

Tithes and offerings

One of the most dismal statistics in the Kingdom of God is the lack of giving. According to *Relevant Magazine*, tithers make up only 10% to 25% of a normal congregation (Holmes, 2016). In addition, only 5 percent of the U.S. tithes, with 80 percent of Americans who tithe only giving 2 percent of their income. Also, giving these days occurs less than in the past. Christians are only giving at 2.5 percent per capita, while during the Great Depression they gave at a 3.3 percent rate.

State of the Kingdom Address

To the lay believer these statistics mean nothing. Though, to the believer who looks from a Biblical perspective, they will see the ripple effect of the reduction in tithes. Here is a perfect illustration of that ripple effect:

> - People don't give as much as they should.
> - The Word doesn't get spread around the world.
> - The less fortunate people are not able to survive due to a reduction in their basic resources, such as food, water, shelter, and clothing.
> - The unbelieving world, especially those that are traditionally non-Christian, do not get a chance to hear the word.
> - People die unsaved, not knowing God, and not accepting Jesus as their Lord and Savior.
> - Their soul ends up in hell, forever separated from God.
> - That person suffers for eternity.
> - Then, it comes back to you.

God looks at His Body to see why people are perishing, and souls which had a chance to be saved are not. He then looks at the body of believers that failed to give to His Church in tithes and offerings, time, work, food, clothing, resources, shelter, motivation, and other things, when they knew to give. He considers their inaction as sins of omission—not doing what you know you should do (tithe). The death of that lost soul is upon your head—perhaps not directly, but at least indirectly as a saint who did not give his tithes and offerings.

Do you see why giving is so important in the Body of Christ? God cannot advance His Army appropriately nor save the souls He desires to save if you do not give to His Kingdom. We need the financial resources in place in order to spread the gospel. And those resources come from tithes and offerings.

If your country's army gathers the financial support of its citizens to fund a war, how much more should the Army of God be able to garner the financial support from the Body of Christ to advance the Kingdom? You should give at least your tithes and offerings of 20% or more of your gross income. After all, it's God's stuff, not yours. He deserves the bare minimum of a tithe and offering back for what He gave you. That goes for your time and other resources as well, time, talent, and treasures.

In "What Would Happen If the Church Tithed?", Mike Holmes (2016) shows how tithing has dropped tremendously over recent years. What would the world look like if people gave regularly to the Kingdom of God? Here are some of the author's conclusions:

> - $25 billion could relieve global hunger, starvation and deaths from preventable diseases in five years.
> - $12 billion could eliminate illiteracy in five years.
> - $15 billion could solve the world's water and sanitation issues, specifically at places in the world where 1 billion people live on less than $1 per day.
> - $1 billion could fully fund all overseas mission work.
> - $100 – $110 billion would still be left over for additional ministry expansion.

The social ills in the world are not just a result of bad luck or coincidence. It's because the Church is not tithing! Many of the world problems that play out on the news could be greatly reduced if people gave what God wanted them to give. God is not going to miraculously fix all of our societal issues. The fixing of it comes from the work that people do. It also comes from tithes and offerings. And the tithes and offerings come from us.

State of the Individual Address

Now that I'm off my soapbox about the importance of tithes and offerings, let's look at a few other facts, many disconcerting, about the spiritual state of individuals around the world. I examine a number of categories that I feel are important in growing closer to God and getting where He wants you to be. See if any of the elements below apply to you.

Here are the number of people, Christians or otherwise, that...

Cannot truly hear from God and discern His voice from the devil's:

According to Tanya Marie Luhrmann (2012), psychological anthropologist and writer for CBN, "In 1999, Gallup reported that 23% of all Americans had heard a voice or seen a vision in response to prayer" (para. 7). While that number seems encouraging, I'm still concerned about the other 77%. The truth is, 100% of born-again believers should be able to clearly hear the voice of God, through the Holy Spirit, 100% of the time. If they don't hear from God all the time, the problem is either people...

> ➤ Aren't in God when they pray—They are unsaved and God doesn't hear them. So naturally, He won't respond: 'The LORD is far from the wicked: but he heareth the prayer of the righteous' (See Proverbs 15:29).
> ➤ They don't have the faith to get an answer—They believe in God, but don't believe *in* God: 'But

without faith it is impossible to please him: for he that cometh to God must believe that he is, and that he is a rewarder of them that diligently seek him' (See Hebrews 11:6).

➢ They are deceived, and get an answer from the devil rather than God—The devil comes in and portrays himself as God and deceives the people by speaking in a fake version of God's voice: 'And no marvel; for Satan himself is transformed into an angel of light' (See 2Corinthians 11:14).

➢ They don't pray fervent and effectual prayers— Their prayers aren't piercing the dark veil of the 2nd Heaven, which is the realm of the devil, so they don't really get through to God. Faithful, passionate, powerful prayers avail much (See James 5:16).

On a side note, the Christian Broadcasting Network (CBN) mentions seven basic ways that people hear from God (Buseck, 2016):

➢ *Scripture:* "All Scripture is given by inspiration of God, and is profitable for doctrine, for reproof, for correction, for instruction in righteousness, that the man of God may be complete, thoroughly equipped for every good work" (See 2Timothy 3:16-17).

➢ *The Holy Spirit speaking to our heart:* "For this is the covenant that I will make with the house of Israel after those days, says the Lord: I will put my laws into their minds, and I will write them on their hearts: and I will be their God, and they shall be my people. And they shall not teach everyone his fellow citizen, and everyone his brother, saying, 'know the Lord,' for all will know Me, from the least to the greatest of them" (See Hebrews 8:10-11).

➤ *The Prophetic (word of knowledge, word of wisdom, personal prophecy):* "Do not quench the Spirit; do not despise prophetic utterances. But examine everything carefully; hold fast to that which is good" (See 1Thessalonians 5:19-21).

➤ *Godly counsel:* "Where no counsel is, the people fall: but in the multitude of counselors there is safety" (See Proverbs 11:14).

➤ *Confirmation:* "By the mouth of two or three witnesses every fact may be confirmed" (See Matthew 18:16).

➤ *The peace of God:* "Let the peace of Christ rule in your hearts, to which indeed you were called in one body; and be thankful" (See Colossians 3:15).

➤ *Circumstances/Timing:* "After these things he (Paul) left Athens and went to Corinth. And he found a certain Jew named Aquila, a native of Pontus, having recently come from Italy with his wife Priscilla, because Claudius had commanded all the Jews to leave Rome. He came to them, and because he was of the same trade, he stayed with them and they were working; for by trade they were tent-makers" (See Acts 18:1-3 – this relationship between Paul, Aquila and Priscilla—which happened as a result of circumstances—became one of the most important strategic partnerships in the book of Acts).

Were former believers but fell out of the faith:

In "How Will The Shocking Decline Of Christianity In America Affect The Future Of This Nation?" Michael Snyder (2012) says that "Over the past few decades, the percentage of Christians in America has been steadily declining (para. 1)." Snyder says that millions upon millions of Americans don't believe in the fundamentals of Christianity any longer. For example, Lifeway Research found that 46 percent of all Americans "never think about whether they will go to Heaven or not" (para. 7). In addition, while 86% of all Americans considered themselves Christian in 1990, that number dropped to only 76% by 2008. Dave Olson, director of Church planting for Evangelical Covenant Church says that only 18.7% of Americans regularly attend church right now. By 2050, that number is expected to drop by 50%. Lifeway found some other startling statistics on the attrition rate. For instance, 65% rarely pray with others, 38% almost never pray by themselves, 65% rarely or never attend worship services, and 67% don't read the Bible on a regular basis.

Are unsure of their life purpose:

In "God Guides, We Decide", Kevin and Kay Brenfleck (2016), National Certified Career Counselors, and contributors to CBN, claim that the Holy Spirit within us makes it possible for a person to find their life purpose. In addition, they say that people may also hire counselors, who are led by Biblical principles, to guide them to God's will for their lives.

Have doubts about their future:

Warner Huston, a columnist for breitbart.com, says according to a nationwide poll (US) of graduating college students, 51% of the students were unsure about their futures after graduation. Moreover, many students felt their lives would not be as good as past generations (Huston, 2014).

Doubt isn't the opposite of faith; it is an element of faith. It's quite normal to have doubts about some things concerning God. Being a precursor to faith, doubt essentially helps God stretch and test your faith. However, it's only by reaching out to God more and more, and trusting Him that you can overcome doubt.

Living outside of God's blessings:

A World Student Christian Federation (WSCF) article found that 1.4 billion people in the world were living below the poverty line, $1.25 or less per day, according to the World Bank (Source: Crome, 2013).

Cooper Abrams, a contributor to bible-truth.org states, "The truth that obedience to God brings blessing, is the first principle in understanding what it means to be a child of God" (2015, para. 1). It's quite possible that many people living on less than $1.25 per day, do not know God, particularly in the case of them being from countries that don't serve the God of Israel.

Don't believe 100% in the Bible:

In its Fourth Annual State of the Bible survey, American Bible Society claimed that 19% of about 2000 respondents were skeptical of the Bible. In addition, 79% of adults and 64% of millenials (age 18 to 29) were less likely to view the Bible as sacred. Another 50% of adults and 35% of millenials were less likely to believe the Bible contains everything a person needs to know to live a meaningful life. And in terms of being likely to never read the Bible, that number stood at 26% for adults and 39% for millenials (Source: American Bible Society State of the Bible, 2016).

On The Essential Bible Blog, Whitney Kuniholm (2015), lists the top 10 reasons the Bible is true:

- ➢ manuscript evidence
- ➢ archaeological evidence
- ➢ eyewitness accounts
- ➢ corroborating accounts
- ➢ literary consistency (66 books written over 1,500 years by 40 different writers but it tells one "big story" of God's plan of salvation that culminated in Jesus Christ)
- ➢ prophetic consistency
- ➢ expert scrutiny
- ➢ leader acceptance
- ➢ global influence
- ➢ changed lives

Despite the overwhelming evidence that support the credibility of scripture, some people are still unbelieving. According to Pastor Rod Parsley of World Harvest Church in Columbus, Ohio, "The only part of the Bible that works for you is the part you believe!"

Don't feel really connected to God:

All things considered, anyone that goes inside of a church should come out feeling like they are truly connected to God.

As an aside, there are a number of simple ways you can improve your relationship with God. The most important way is to have faith. Without faith it's impossible to please God. But with faith, it's impossible to miss Him. If you don't feel connected to God, you can build your faith up by obtaining information about God, and learning to trust Him. The best source of information about God is the Bible. I suggest you read the Word daily, and as you do the Holy Spirit will reveal more and more about God and His Word and His will to you. After all, that's what He (the Holy Spirit) does, reveals God to you. By reading, meditating on, and studying the Word regularly, God will draw closer and closer to you.

Once you develop your faith, you can do other things to develop a deeper connection with God, such as praising God, praying to God, asking God questions, having regular conversations with Him, and above all, listening to Him.

There are also other things you can do to deepen your connection with God. For example, get rid of the sins in your life, and turn away from everything and everyone that separates you from Him. If people or places or things or your lifestyle keeps you away from God, you need to make some serious changes. God has a desire to conform you into His image. So as you seek to become more intimate with the LORD, He will slowly help you uproot anything in you that is not right with Him.

Don't know how to pray and get answers through prayer:

Bob Smietana (2014), of LifeWay Research, discussed how 1137 Americans surveyed felt about the effectiveness of their prayers. Only 25% of those surveyed felt like their prayers were always answered by God. The results speak volumes: the vast majority of people just don't know how to pray. They may know how to pray and go through the rituals of prayer (clasping hands, getting down on their knees, etc.), but they don't know how to get prayers up to Heaven, and get answers back from God. I can't help but think of James 5:16 again here: "The effectual, fervent prayer of a righteous man availeth much.' Are you praying effectual, fervent prayers? If not, there are some things you can do to get more of your prayers answered.

Craig Buseck (2015), a writer for CBN, details three things that enables believers to see answers to their prayers. They are being *persistent*, *purposeful*, and *personal*. Being persistent is to say "hold fast to" or hold on tightly to His promises. Do not be overcome by disappointment; instead keep the faith. To be purposeful in prayer is to share your heart with God. Let him know of your deepest needs, concerns, and desires. Finally, to be personal is to have a relationship with God. It takes a bit of time to develop a close relationship with God just as it would with any other relationship. However, by opening up to God and allowing Him in every aspect of your life, and seeking His guidance and companionship, you will naturally get close to Him. God hears and answers the prayers of those who are in Him. It's a privilege to have access to the throne of God through Jesus Christ. Don't take it for granted. And whenever you get answers to prayers, be sure to thank God.

Don't know about spiritual gifts:

The BarnaGroup conducted another survey of about 3000 people to assess whether or not people were aware of their spiritual gifts (See 1Corinthians 12). Two-thirds (68%) said they heard of spiritual gifts. Yet, that leaves about 32% of them being unaware.

"Like everything else in the Christian walk, intellectual understanding is not enough. The truth of it must go deep down into the spirit; be "shone"...and "engrafted" into our spiritual nature" (Source: Seargent, 2015).

Don't think that there is life after death:

State of the Kingdom Address

I've heard of many people not believing in life after death. Not only will everyone on earth find out that there is an afterlife, they will also be judged by the Almighty who will decide whether they make it to Heaven. It's unfathomable to think that anyone in a relationship with God would deny that there is life after death. More than likely the people who don't believe in an afterlife are unsaved.

Don't believe there are penalties when you die unsaved:

Some people believe that hell is just a representation of a bad outcome after death. They don't believe it's a literal place of pain, suffering, torment, and eternal separation from God. To believe that there are no penalties for those that die unsaved is to call God an unjust judge. If the LORD so punishes evildoers on earth for their wrong deeds, how much more will He punish them in eternity? If He did not punish those that did not accept His Son, everyone will enter Heaven. That would make the death and resurrection of Jesus in vain. He died to save sinners that repented and accepted Him, from eternal fire.

Don't believe the Bible is the inspired Word of God:

According to Jonathan Petersen, writer for Bible Gateway, a searchable bible website, a recent Gallup poll showed that three in four Americans believed the Bible was the inspired word of God. The other 21% of survey respondents felt like the Bible was simply "fables and history" (Source: Petersen, 2014).

I have to go back to a point made earlier in this section. The Bible is not just a single book. It's a collection of over 66 books called the *canon of scriptures*. Those books were written by more than 40 different authors over the course of 1500 years, in three different languages (Hebrew, Greek, and Aramaic), on three different continents (Africa,

Asia, and Europe). Yet, all of the accounts share the same storyline, message, and theme. That is nothing short of a miracle. Only God, the divine, supernatural being, could coordinate such a complex web of writers, time periods, events, languages, and locations to produce a unified work, which is the Holy Bible.

Believe in purgatory or someplace other than heaven and hell in the afterlife:

In "What's Afterlife?" Sarah Sharp, a writer for US Catholic Magazine, cited a survey conducted by pewforums.org, where roughly 73% of Catholics believed in purgatory (Source: Sharp, 2014)

According to the Catholic religion, purgatory is "a place or condition of temporal punishment for those who, departing this life in God's grace, are not entirely free from venial faults, or have not fully paid the satisfaction due to their transgressions."

To believe in this theory makes the name, blood, death, and resurrection of Jesus of none effect. As the apostle Paul said in the book of Romans, "For as by one man's disobedience many were made sinners, so by the obedience of one shall many be made righteous" (See Romans 5:19). Believers are made righteous through Christ. He suffered and died for our sins. There is no need for anyone to re-suffer or get punished for their sins on earth if they repented and accepted Jesus as their Lord.

Let's shoot for 100%

As evidenced from the previous section, there are a lot of people misinformed about God and His Kingdom. It's time we work harder to get 100% of the people believing 100% of God's Word and receiving 100% of His blessings, including salvation, as a result. Sure,

State of the Kingdom Address

100% of anything sounds impossible. However, it's at least worth the effort. Who knows, we may be able to get 80% of the people left on earth saved, delivered, and set free from bondage and *death* without Christ.

REASSESS YOUR LIFE

If you struggle with any of the aforementioned issues above, it's time to reassess your life and make sure that you are living in accordance with God's will. It's better to have a paradigm shift in your thoughts, actions, and lifestyle at the price of a broken spirit than it is to continue living the way you've been living and thinking the same way you've been thinking. God is merciful, and willing to forgive: 'The sacrifices of God are a broken spirit: a broken and a contrite heart' (See Psalms 51:17).

CHAPTER 11: ARMED FOR BATTLE

And God is able to make all grace abound toward you; that ye, always having all sufficiency in all things, may abound to every good work. - 2Corinthians 9:8

I love what Revelation 5:12 says about what Jesus died to receive: 'Worthy is the Lamb that was slain to receive power, and riches, and wisdom, and strength, and honour, and glory, and blessing'. Jesus not only died for you to receive eternal life, but also to receive power, riches, wisdom, strength, honour, glory, and blessing. God has covered all of your needs through Christ. If there are any seemingly unmet needs in your life, the word *blessing*, in the verse above covers it all. God has given you everything you could need to be a great success in life and to achieve your purpose.

YOU HAVE EVERYTHING YOU NEED

It's time to get all that God has for you. God has made everything in His Kingdom available to you, both spiritually and materially. That includes the victory, power, favor, authority, wisdom, knowledge, understanding, deliverance, wealth, faith, honor, health, great relationships, marriages, children, and others. He has also made it possible for you to experience Him more intimately. He has given you the ability to hear Him, see Him, feel Him, talk with Him, call on angels, see angels, see the Heavens open, experience miracles, see signs and wonders in nature, get insider secrets to the Kingdom, call on God for business advice, get help with major decisions, find the right spouse, and develop new ideas through divine inspiration. The LORD has given all of Himself to the world for the times in which we're living. Nothing is left on the table, and everything that God gave you is to be used for His glory.

Benefits of the Kingdom as a joint heir with Christ

Consider a few of the many benefits of God's Kingdom that you have been granted:

Riches, as an heir to the Kingdom:

You were born royalty. You get to inherit everything that Jesus inherited. It doesn't matter where you were born, or how you were born, or how you were raised, or what you have. As a child of the King of Kings, you were born royalty. God sees you as a king, arrayed in royal apparel, wearing His spirit upon you, having His stuff at your disposal, being the person that inherits His Father's blessings. Learn to experience life more fully and abundantly. Think higher. Act like you came from a King.

Access to God Almighty:

As a child of God, you have the ability to go to His throne. In ancient Biblical times, there was a veil that stood between the outer court and the Holy of holies in the temple (See Matthew 27:51). However, Jesus came to wash away our sins and make it possible for us to have direct access to the holy throne of God. Whereas, in times past, the high priest was the only individual who could go beyond the veil of the temple to access God (on behalf of the people), today you have that same ability. That's because Jesus, your High Priest, is the bridge between you and God, presenting you to the LORD as righteous in Christ: 'Seeing then that we have a great high priest, that is passed into the heavens, Jesus the Son of God, let us hold fast our profession' (See Hebrews 4:14). In short, when you go to the throne of God, He accepts you on behalf of Jesus.

Personal relationship with God:

I had an interesting conversation with God a couple years ago. I was feeling sick at the time. I wasn't eating healthy, and my body responded. I was always tired, and feeling down. My diet consisted of fast food and junk food, rarely, if ever, eating any fruits or vegetables. Then, one day, I prayed for God to make me feel better. God told me explicitly to start eating more fruits and vegetables. I wasn't sure that was the right thing to do, nor if that would make me feel better. I'm not the most health conscious person, but still, I thought there was much more to feeling better than simply eating more healthy foods. After I prayed to God and He told me to eat healthier, God instructed me to go to the book of Genesis, where it talks about how He created the earth. I went there. Then, God told me to find the part where He made the animals and vegetation (See Genesis 1:11-12). I went there, and found that scripture. Then God asked me bluntly, "Which came first, the animals or the vegetation?" I then responded, "The vegetation came first." "Yes. That's true, David, because I always make the most important things first. Vegetables are much more important than meat. Eat more vegetables and you will feel better." I figured that junk food really didn't fit into any category, so I began to eat much less of them. I also began eating more fruits and vegetables. As I did, I began to feel better. I had more energy, was less weighed-down, and I just felt fresh overall. It was good to be feeling better. It was even better to know that God was involved in every area of my life. I had a personal relationship with Him, such that I could even call on Him to plan my meals. God is just as much there for you as He is for me. Every area of your life that you want God in,

State of the Kingdom Address

He will be there if you invite Him. You have the ability to have a real personal relationship with the Almighty God. That brings me to this scripture: 'Abraham believed God, and it was imputed unto him for righteousness: and he was called the Friend of God' (See James 2:23). God wants to be your friend today. Invite Him into your life, or in deeper than He already is.

Ability to spend intimate time with Jesus:

There are countless stories all over the Internet and television of people having personal one-on-one encounters with Jesus. I've discussed earlier the near death experiences (NDEs) or outer body experiences (OBEs) where people saw Jesus face to face. Some have been taken up to Heaven in dreams where they got to see the Lord. Others have seen Him face-to-face, in spirit. I have even heard of stories where people have heard the voice of the Lord. He spoke to them in the same way that He spoke to Paul the Apostle on that Damascus road (as Paul was going out to persecute the Jews). I've personally heard the audible voice of God in a dream one night. The LORD's voice was not in my voice's tone, like when the Holy Spirit speaks to me, but it was God's individual, authentic voice that I heard. It was very powerful, deep, pronounced, yet calm, peaceful, and very clear.

Anna Rountree, in her book, *The Heavens Opened* (Source: Rountree, 1999), explained how she saw Jesus face-to-face when she was taken up to Heaven in a dream, often spending personal time with Him in a walled-garden in Heaven. In my upcoming book, *Diario Spirituali*™ (My Spiritual Diary), I mention several situations where I have seen the Lord face to face. I have seen Him coming down from the sky in the Rapture. I have seen Him dying on the Cross at Calvary. I have seen Him in the sky next to an angel as He was preparing to judge the earth (as mentioned in earlier chapters). And I have seen Him in Heaven adorned in a rich-red robe getting ready to come down and judge the earth. Know this, beloved: almost every time I saw Jesus in a prophetic dream, He was getting ready to do something extraordinary. He was either getting ready to die for our sins, rapture His Church, or judge the earth. I have also had many earthly experiences, where Jesus accompanied me, or even touched me. Every time He came to me He came in peace and love, and I felt Him all around me. Don't be surprised that if, during these end-times, Jesus manifests Himself to you face to face. As we get closer to the Lord's return, He is revealing Himself to more and more faithful believers, perhaps to build their faith, hope, and love toward Him.

Ability to call on angels:

In the same manner that the archangels Michael and Gabriel rescued me from hoards of devils I was battling one week (mentioned in Chapter 7), your faith can activate angels to work on your behalf. Think of that the next time you are involved in spiritual warfare, or if you just need a victory over your circumstances in life.

Power from on high:

I can't begin to tell you how much power I've seen the Holy Ghost exhibit through people. He is strong beyond belief. And the power that is in Him is in you. I will not bore you here with some of my own personal testimonies of walking in the power of the Holy Spirit. You can read more about that in Chapter 4, 7, or in *Diario Spirituali*™. The Holy Spirit is mighty in you. He is God's gift, your Comforter. He is every bit God, that God is God. Thank God for His gift of His Spirit, Who is here for you whenever you need Him.

State of the Kingdom Address

Favor of God upon you:

God favors you. Favor is the unmerited grace of God upon your life. Is there anything other than that that you need? I was talking to a friend several weeks ago about God's favor. We had a debate about the benefits of favor. My conclusion, which I still stand by today is that favor is better than fortune. Here is a good illustration of favor at work: Suppose somebody around you has a whole lot of good stuff (property, money, etc.). Now, suppose they might not be living in God, being unbelievers and worldly people. Now, suppose that God's favor rests upon you, not for anything you did, but for who He is as well as His ability to favor whoever He wants. God's favor upon you says this: "I know that person next to you has all that good stuff. I know they have the money you could be making. I know they have the property. I know they have the house and the car you want. But I like you so much, I'm going to give you their stuff." That's what favor does in the Kingdom of God. You see countless stories in the Bible of Kings and kingdoms topple due to God's favor on the children of Israel or His servants, and His anger against the people of the world. Here are just a few examples:

> ➤ Mordecai replaces Haman (See Esther 8:2)
> ➤ David replaces King Saul (See 1Samuel 13:14; 2Samuel 5:3)
> ➤ Solomon reigns instead of his brothers (See 1Kings 1:39)
> ➤ Esther replaces Queen Vashti (See Esther 2:17)

I believe that favor is good for everything, except another person with favor's territory. In short, I don't believe it's God's desire to give you another believer's birthright, especially if that person is righteous before God. He will bless you both with your own stuff, in the same way He divided up Canaan for the twelve tribes of Israel. However, in terms of unsaved people in the world, it's an open field. I see so many believers walking passively, almost afraid to take opportunities, victories, or gain that comes their way as a result of God having favor upon them, but rebuking someone else without favor, that you may be slated to replace. That's offensive to God. Let His favor rest upon who it may. The person you're replacing may be wicked. They could appear to be one way, but behind the scenes they could be living a double life. They could have also been given chance after chance after chance by God to get right, but refused. Favor can run out, just like it can run in, that is, into your life. Take the breakthrough that God has given you no matter who is on the losing end of the deal. The LORD needs righteous people in office, and now is your time. Walk in divine favor today.

Victory over the devil:

Famed televangelist, TB Joshua (2015), has some of the most miraculous healing and deliverance services I have ever seen. He is a minister from Nigeria and runs the Synagogue Church of All Nations (SCOAN). He and his staff of other ministers regularly deliver people possessed by demonic spirits. I have seen people delivered from all sorts of devils, including Beelzebub and the spirit of Jezebel. The devil is a defeated foe when you walk in the blood of Jesus and in the power of the Holy Spirit. Check out some of TB Joshua's deliverance services on YouTube when you get a chance. It's that type of power that's available to you through Christ.

Peace that passes all understanding:

Can you imagine that the apostle Paul wrote a great portion of the Bible from prison? That's incredible, especially given the fact that

Satan likely accompanied him there. In the same light, I think of how Moses wrote the Torah (the first 5 books of the Bible) from the wilderness, or even how David probably wrote many of the psalms under distress—in caves, in valleys, in exile, running for his life from King Saul, Absalom, or others. Man, that almost feels like my life. Writing this book was no cake walk for me, let me tell you. Anyway, there are other people in the Bible who persevered through difficult situations to do something for God, including Elijah, Jesus, the 12 apostles, and others. The one thing that all of them had in common was the peace of God. Sure, they had tough, turbulent times, but they could always resort back to the peace of resting in God and relying upon Him for their deliverance. While you go through any challenges you face in life, God offers you peace, so much peace that the world will be amazed at why you didn't cave in:

> ➢ "He should've given up a long time ago."
> ➢ "She should've lost her mind by now."
> ➢ "God hasn't given them a victory yet. Why are they acting like everything is okay?"
> ➢ "Why are they comfortable carrying that old heavy, rugged, inconvenient, humiliating, crucifying cross? I would have put it down by now."
> ➢ "Why haven't they given up on their purpose? There are other things in life that would make them so much more comfortable."

Or, in the case of Job's wife…

"Why don't they just curse God and die?"

You see, those people I mentioned from the Bible have developed peace that passes all understanding. They are fully confident that God has them covered and He will meet all their needs. Those types of people can abase or abound, they can be up or down, left or right. All they worried about was whether or not they were in God's will, and whether or not God was with them. People like Joshua and Caleb are of this sort. They could be born in the wilderness, spend 40 years there, eat manna from Heaven, eat quail from the sky, drink water from a rock, wear clothes for 40 years, wear shoes that didn't wear out, shout down the walls of Jericho and conquer it, or inherit the Promised Land and the wealth of it. The bottom line is that they trust God, and somehow find peace and confidence in every situation they face. Needless to say, that people of that Joshua, Caleb, Jesus, Paul, David, Gideon, Jacob caliber don't break. Why? It's because they have God. They rest in His shadow, as described in Psalms 91. They have come to the realization that God has a plan for their lives. They believed that God will see them through. They understood that their present position in life, if it is uncomfortable, is simply a point along the path to promise. If you track their lives, they had different points, some up, some down. However, they were only points along their path. And when you have a vision from God, understanding, and the faith to know that all things work together for your good, you can endure any hardships in life until you get to where God wants you. As I have said before, to whom much is given much is required. How much do you want out of life? If you want a lot, expect God to take you through a lot of training to equip you for a lot. You have to learn to be responsible with it when you get there. If you want little out of life, then expect little training. God will bless you wherever you are. Though, everyone that's in God is required to carry their cross. Learn to do it in peace. That's a token of a true relationship with God.

State of the Kingdom Address

Grace and mercy through the name of Jesus:

You can command all things in the name of Jesus, so long as they are a part of God's will. There is something about His name that causes earth to tremble and hell to run away. I go back to the story of the earthquake I dealt with a few years ago. I rebuked it in the name of Jesus, and it stopped just as quickly as it started. I encourage you to not underestimate the power in the name of Jesus, which gives you power over all circumstances in life.

Salvation, a gift that not even devils can receive:

If the devil could go back to the day he tried to get God's worship from the angels in Heaven...

If he could go back to the day he tried to take the throne from God...

If he could take back his attempted coup of the Most High...

Would he?

Probably not. He's intrinsically evil. He also should have known better than to try and overthrow God:

> ➢ He saw God's power and glory first hand.
> ➢ He knew Heaven was a holy place, and nothing less than holiness could remain there.
> ➢ He was a part of God's creation, which showed God as being the Supreme Ruler.
> ➢ He led the worship God received from all of Heaven, and bare witness of everyone and everything always worshipping God.

Even so, Satan still wanted to try his hand at getting praise that belonged to God. What's even worse is that he can never, ever, repent. He is eternally damned, destined for the Lake of Fire (See Revelation 20:10).

You, on the other hand, as a human being, have the privilege of repenting of all your sins, and coming into the blessings of God through the Messiah. You can accept Jesus as your Lord and Savior and one day enter Heaven. God has given you the free gift of salvation, a gift so coveted that the devil and every demon in hell hates you because you have the ability to enter Heaven through repentance. Although, they are forever cursed and suffering the torments of hell. Don't take that gift of salvation for granted. Repent of your sins and turn back to God.

Authority to reign as a king on earth:

Have you ever considered what a king eats during the course of a day? I was interested in that very topic a few months ago. So I decided to look it up. What does a king eat? I researched what the average king probably ate during the middle-ages or ancient times. Kings usually had very exquisite diets[4].

---

[4] Here is what I found from a question respondent on Yahoo Answers:

Among other things, Kings eat swan, peacock, or pheasant, exotic game birds like rail, bittern, crane , egret and young heron. They ate suckling rabbits, pigeons, and beef mutton. They ate a variety of meat and fish in rich spicy sauces. They ate all types of stews, pies, and fritters. Coloring was very important during feasts, and most dishes had some exotic color to them. In addition, a lot of their dishes were covered in silver or gold

State of the Kingdom Address

That is how a king ate back then. And that is how you should be eating now. God didn't just give you the authority to reign as a king in the spiritual realm. He gave you the power to reign in the physical realm as well. You should be thinking like a king, acting like a king, talking like a king, walking like a king, dressing like a king, eating like a king, going to the bathroom like a king, directing like a king, making decrees like a king, behaving like a king, being a king. It's time for you to act, look, talk like your Heavenly Father, the King of all kings. You came from Heaven; it's only right that you represent God on earth the right way: 'Behold, what manner of love the Father hath bestowed upon us, that we should be called the sons of God' (See 1John 3:1).

Financial blessings:

It amazes me that so many Christians in the world struggle financially. You may be one of them. If so, do you realize that you are a child of the Most High, God? God is not broke and neither should you be. I love the story of the prodigal son (See Luke 15:11). After receiving an inheritance from his father, the prodigal son spent his entire substance on riotous living. Broken, with nowhere else to go, the son returned to the father and begged the father to take him back into his home. The father received him gladly, not just taking him back, but giving the son a ring, shoes, a fatted calf, and a robe. The other son, who received his own inheritance from the father, did not waste it. However, he complained when the father took the other son back. The father told the complaining son that he was forever with him,

---

foil. Medieval feasts usually had two, three, or four courses, each course having many dishes in them (Source: Yahoo Answers, 2011).

and all that the father has is his. That's sort of like you, right? Everything that God has is yours. It's at your disposal. He meets your needs, and if there is anything you ask according to His will He will answer your prayer. In the case of the son that spent his substance on riotous living and came back to receive mercy from the father, that's also like you, right? You can spend your stuff on a whole bunch of wrongful living. Despite that, God, in His endless mercy, takes you back when you repent and return to Him. He then gives you access to His best stuff, His robe, His ring, His shoes, and His fatted calf, His very best. There is never a reason for you to be without. God has more than enough available to you as a child of the Kingdom. Whether you are like the first son in the prodigal son parable, who spent his substance on riotous living but returned to God, or like the second son, who always had access to the father's stuff, you live in financial blessings. God has given you financial resources beyond your wildest dream. You just have to go and get them by faith, works, and obedience to God, who guides you to blessings: 'The LORD is my shepherd; I shall not want' (See Psalms 23:1).

Divine health and healing:

Pastor Rod Parsley, of World Harvest Church discussed an incident a while ago, where a young girl was healed in the middle of the night of a severe back deformity. The girl had received a visitation from the LORD and saw the glory of God at the foot of her bed. Hardly able to move, let alone walk, the girl heard a voice from God that said, "Always remember…I didn't do this for you, but for me." God was about to heal her, and He wanted all the glory for it. The LORD eventually covered her body with His spirit, and twisted her back into its rightful place. It was a miracle. The girl that previously couldn't walk, and was well known to be an invalid, was able to walk days later. The entire town knew of her miracle, and people became more

State of the Kingdom Address

faithful about divine healing. As a Kingdom Kid, you have the ability to receive divine healing from God: 'And they cast out many devils, and anointed with oil many that were sick, and healed them' (See Mark 6:13).

The love of God:

The most quoted verse in the Bible is John 3:16: 'For God so loved the world, that he gave his only begotten Son, that whosoever believeth in him should not perish, but have everlasting life.' Can you believe how much love that is? That's love even when you're where you're not supposed to be. That's love even when you were not in God. That's love even if you mocked God and laughed at the Cross in the past. That's love that followed you in your darkest times, and pulled you out of dangerous situations. That's love that will follow you for eternity. God has given you all of His love.

The anointing and gifts to fully live your calling:

God placed His anointing on you the moment you were born. He predestined you for your call, according to the book of Jeremiah: 'Before I formed thee in the belly I knew thee; and before thou camest forth out of the womb I sanctified thee, and I ordained thee a prophet unto the nations' (See Jeremiah 1:5). God has set you apart and poured His spirit out upon you. You have His seal of approval, destining you to leave an indelible mark on His Kingdom and the world.

MOVE INTO YOUR GREATNESS

God has equipped you for greatness: 'Thou shalt increase my greatness, and comfort me on every side' (See Psalms 71:21). He has prepared you for the miraculous. Set your face like flint and do whatever it is He wants you to do. I don't know what that is; but you know. Rest assured that God has already gone before you, making the crooked ways straight (See Isaiah 45:2). You will prosper in all your work because there is no need left unmet by the LORD. Amen.

CHAPTER 12: BEAUTIFICATION

To appoint unto them that mourn in Zion, to give unto them beauty for ashes, the oil of joy for mourning, the garment of praise for the spirit of heaviness; that they might be called trees of righteousness, the planting of the LORD, that he might be glorified. -Isaiah 61:3

It's about seven days before Christmas, 2014, as I write this. I am sitting at a desk. As I overlook the surrounding community, through the hysteria of busy highways, outside chatter, and Christmas music from a local Catholic school, I see life. I imagined what God probably saw in Heaven the moment He decided to create the earth, and man to occupy it. The LORD may have seen the beauty of it all: Through man's fall, beauty; through the problems on earth, beauty; through the death and resurrection of Jesus, beauty.

While I grappled with what to write for this chapter, God spoke to me. He said, "Get them *beautified*. Help them prepare for My return." I could've just as easily blurted out, "But how, LORD?" I held my peace, and thought for a moment: "How should I proceed with this chapter on beautification?" Then it occurred to me: "Share with them what God shared with you. Empower them as the LORD empowered you." That made perfect sense. After all, beautification is "the process of making visual improvements to a person, place, or thing," according to Wikipedia. It's about getting you ready for Jesus. It's not about me or how beautiful I think you are and can be. It's about God's definition of beauty, which is way better than mine. God wants to adorn you in beauty. He wants the Church to look, feel, and be beautiful so that He can return to the perfect Bride. God wants to beautify you from the inside out. He wants your spirit to be the perfect representation of Him: 'But the fruit of the Spirit is love, joy, peace, longsuffering, gentleness, goodness, faith, meekness, temperance: against such there is no law'

(See Galatians 5:22-23). He wants your outward appearance to reflect Him too—wealth, health, strength, living in the right house, driving the right car, glorified, dignified, honorable, attractive, well-dressed, smelling right, radiant, clean, orderly, and well-organized. God wants you to be beautiful all around so that He can show you off to the world, and so He can set you up as a light unto the world. In the words of a business friend of mine, "If your lights are out, how can you lead anybody else to the light?"

IT'S TIME TO WAKE-UP

It's time, beloved. Perhaps you are like the many Christians around the world who accept the status quo. They become complacent and get comfortable living beneath God's best for them. They become satisfied with just enough of God to make it through the day. They are content with just enough faith to buy a Cheeseburger Happy Meal at McDonalds. They are alright with just enough money to avoid eviction or foreclosure for another month. They are fine with just enough blessings to get by until Jesus comes and 'beams them up'.

Listen, God is not a *just* God. He does not want to give you 'just enough' of anything. He wants to give you everything, as the apple of His eye. It's time for you to step up and step out, and start being that beautiful Church that God designed you to be. You're not a human wishing. You're a human being. It's time for you to start being who you are in God's eyes. You're supposed to be stronger spiritually. You're supposed to have more faith than you already have. You're supposed to be better off financially. You're supposed to be envied by the people around you. People ought to look at you and get a *lemon face*. That's that angry face people get that makes them look at you like they bit into a sour lemon. That's when God blessed you so good that your enemies get irritated by it! God has made you an enviable people. Jesus wants to come back to a blessed, beautiful, spotless Church. And quite frankly, we ain't there yet.

HOW TO PREPARE FOR JESUS

Over the course of about 20 years of a committed walk with God, I have learned so much about the LORD and His Kingdom. One of the most important things I learned is that He is getting us ready for something big. All of your life, everything you've been through, everything that you are, has been about God getting you ready. It's not just about you being ready to achieve your purpose, but being an active participant of this powerful movement on earth that prepares the way for the Lord's return. And He is coming real soon: 'The Lord is not slack concerning his promise, as some men count slackness; but is longsuffering to us-ward, not willing that any should perish, but that all should come to repentance' (See 2Peter 3:9).

Earlier in the book, I described dream where I saw Jesus face to face. My question to you is, if the Lord returned today, do you feel like you are being the person He would like to see? Have you accepted Him as your Lord and Savior? Are you walking in His Spirit? Are you working His harvest? If not, some changes are in order. You need to prepare for Him, as if He can show up any minute, because He can. Below are a few ideas to help you live up to your potential as a child of God. In the words I often use in my training business, "Let's go higher!" Let's get beautified for God! Here's how:

See yourself from God's eyes

God sees you as an eagle. As the parent eagle, the LORD has you in the nest, way up in the clefts of rocks somewhere. You're away from all the other birds, because that's where eagles ought to be. They soar above the norm. Furthermore, you're in the safety of the nest under

God's wings of protection. He knows your capabilities. He knows you can fly and you can float on winds at over 10,000 feet in the air. The LORD sees you for who He created you to be. You're an eagle and you were made to resemble God, the parent eagle. It's time for you to begin flying. Show off your wings. Leap from the nest, and fly. God will never allow you to crash against the ground if you fail.

The Esther Effect

In a book called *The Esther Effect*, author Dianna Booher (2008) encourages women to exhibit "pivotal decision-making and bold behavior". Booher identifies several modern-day Esthers that showed patience, prayer, and love in some of the most extreme conditions (just like the matriarch, Queen Esther, from the Bible). In addition to the character of Esther, the Church is required to go through the same preparation process as Esther had to go through to be prepared to marry King Ahasuerus (See Esther 2). Albeit, the Church has a much more important preparation at hand because it's preparing for a wedding feast with Jesus. You need to sanctify yourself this day. The wedding could be tomorrow.

Go get everything God has for you

The Church is hardly that glorious City set on a hill that God destined it to be. Believers are dirt poor. People are living in doubt and fear, scared to go forward into their calling. Sickness is having its way with the people of God. And some saints walk around discouraged and depressed all the time, as if God wasn't for them. This is not the image of a Church that would make the world want to become a part of it. I mean, why would anyone else want to be poor, sick, and discouraged? Sure, there are some believers holding onto the promises of God and living the life He wants them to live. But the vast majority are not. And you may be in that vast majority. I adjure you, if you are, it's time to go get everything God has for you. It's time for you to step up to the plate and step out of your comfort zone, and go take stuff back from the devil. God needs you prosperous because He needs you to share your prosperity with those in need. As a famous pastor once said, "We [the church] don't have a money problem. The money is just in the wrong hands." That blessed life is yours for the taking. Nonetheless, God will not take it for you. He has already given it to you; you simply have to take it by faith.

Give back to the world

You are not just called to get yourself ready for the Lord to come back to earth. You are called to get others ready. In short, you should be giving yourself back to the world. There are people out there who are believers, yet rarely do anything with that belief. They decided they will 'wait until Jesus comes to take them home'. My question is this: Wait, for what? A house to land on your head? A successful business to come blind-side you? People on earth to save themselves? People who have never heard the gospel to witness to themselves? People wait, and wait, and wait, for the Lord. What they should be doing is not waiting for Jesus to return, but working until Jesus returns. They should be helping to save souls, taking land from the devil for the Kingdom of God, being all God called them to be, ministering to the poor, sharing the love of God with others, and more. I say the same to you. If you're someone that is simply waiting for Jesus to return, you need to get out there and work for the Kingdom. You need to build the Body up and spread the gospel. The Lord will come back whenever He wants. He doesn't need you to be waiting. He needs you to be working. He needs you to be ready, and getting others ready.

Be an End-Time Warrior for God

You are an end-time warrior whether you like it or not. In the days of ancient Israel, any man over the age of 20 was required to go fight wars for Israel: 'From twenty years old and upward, all that are able to go forth to war in Israel: thou and Aaron shall number them by their armies' (See Numbers 1:3). In fact, even the Biblical patriarch, Joshua was sent to fight a war immediately upon meeting Moses, his mentor. There was no, "Hi Joshua, I'm Moses. Nice to meet you." There was simply, "Choose us out men, and go out, fight with Amalek" (See Exodus 17:9). You are in the same type of situation. You are an end-time warrior, in the army of the Most High God. As you accept Jesus as your Lord and Savior, you enlisted yourself as a soldier in the battle against Satan and his forces. Accordingly, you should be going out to destroy every work of the devil in the same way he intends to destroy you. Your mission should be to advance the Kingdom of God. If you feel like you've been reluctant to step out in faith and go after the vision God planted in you, now is the time for change.

Beauty for ashes

Like the opening scripture to this chapter (See Isaiah 61:3), God wants to give you beauty for ashes. Every area of your life that has been destroyed by the fire of pain, lack, loss, hurt, depression, discouragement, or affliction, God wants to restore. He wants to make it beautiful, once again. Whatever the devil meant for bad, God has purposed for good. Trust that God is able to make right everything that is wrong in your life.

Enjoy the beautification process

Wherever you are in life right now is a part of your beautification process. Whether you're a successful business owner or an entry level office clerk, you are simply at a phase in your process of getting pretty for God. He's fixing you up spiritually, teaching you to take on His character. He does that through life experiences. Whether good or bad, everything you go through is an object lesson. God has a plan to make you even better and better, more prosperous and blessed, day by day in all that you do. Until you get to the place of beauty that God sees you in, you must stay in the process. God is working a work in you.

State of the Kingdom Address

Consider a piece of clay on a potter's wheel. The potter has to rub it, pinch it, pull it, grab it, and so forth. It's being processed. That potter knows what he's doing to and with that piece of clay. He already had a beautiful vessel in mind before He even created it. God is the same way with you and your life. You are on a potter's wheel. God is pulling you, pinching, discarding excess clay, throwing a part of you aside, putting more clay on you, watering you, squeezing you in every which way He has to in order to make you the vessel He envisioned you being before He made you. Just like impatient children, people try to run away from the Father before He is done fixing us up. They want to escape the process of being made, of beautification. But it's the process that leads to the promise.

Your challenges, victories, defeats, and experiences in life were simply a part of that process of God preparing you for Him in Heaven. You want to get off the wheel at times, but God says, "No. Not yet. I'm not done." You want God to stop pressing and pinching you, but God says, "If you leave now you will be unfinished." You want to completely give up at times, but God says, "Just one more second. I'm almost done."

Beloved of God, you may have long been on the wheel. You may have gotten used to life as it is and thought you would always just be a regular old piece of clay. You may have accepted your life as being a simple process of pinches, pulls, casting aside, discomforts, hurts, and pains. In fact, you may even be of the other type, who thinks that they have arrived already, like they have it all together. Either way, God has a plan for you. He wants you to do more for His Kingdom than what you're doing now. He wants to use you mightily to do His work. God wants you to be a sign (a symbol) and an ensign (a standard) of His grace. And He wants you to usher in the return of Jesus Christ. It's time for you to thrive, and go out as the beautiful vessel of glory that God made you. It's time for you to be who the LORD called you to be. Reign as royalty. Fly as an eagle. Walk out as a joint-heir with Christ. You are destined to be a ruler on earth. Rule right from where you are. Destroy the works of the devil. Cast aside any weight holding you from the divine purpose of the Almighty. Take a leap of faith. Be beautiful. Prepare ye the way of the Lord.

PRAYER OF RELEASE:

God, take your beloved child into the palm of your hands. Let them know how deep and profound your love is for them. LORD, forgive them for all their sins and trespasses against you. Restore anything that they have lost due to sin. And heal their land, Oh, God.

Show them that you have destined them for beauty and not ashes, victory and not defeat. Reveal to them your plan for their lives, and the part they play in preparing the way for your return.

God, I ask that you guide them in all paths of righteousness, and away from temptation. Let your strength, blessings, favor, grace, and mercy follow them wherever they go. Help them be the vessels of honor that you created them to be from the foundations of the world. And may their positive influence on others around them increase forever and ever, for your name's sake. In Jesus Christ's name. Amen.

CHAPTER 13: THUS SAITH THE LORD...

So shall my word be that goeth forth out of my mouth: it shall not return unto me void, but it shall accomplish that which I please, and it shall prosper in the thing whereto I sent it. -Isaiah 55:11

> How long will you tarry, my child? How long will you wait for me? You wait as if I'm going to do something new to you or for you. I have done what I would do to you. Since the beginning, I created you for my glory. I destined you for purpose. And I gave myself to you for your work. I gave you everything you need in life to thrive. Yet, my people still wait.

> The LORD is not slack concerning His promises. But they are yes and amen to those that believe! Why then, do you allow the enemy to take from you what I have given you? Why do you disannul the Word of God and make it of none effect? For the promise is yours, saith the LORD. Yea, the fullness of the Kingdom is yours for the taking. But as a thief in the night, the devil comes and robs you of my blessings.

> My child, it is not for me to take away from you. For I am a giving God, providing for my children, even better than an earthly father. I don't withhold my mighty right hand from saving my beloved. I don't withhold the blessings that I have

for you. I give until they are overflowing. I pour out, when there seems to be nothing left to give.

For the LORD is not low on resources, nor is His power limited that He cannot deliver. I am the everlasting God!

I am mighty in all my ways. The LORD has no enemies, and devils flee at the mere mention of my name. It is for you, my beloved, to walk in lock step unison with me. It is for you, and not Satan. I have selected you as a joint-heir with me and have seated you in high places.

Yet, my people have left their first love. They have forgotten the joys we have had together. They have forsaken the LORD to fulfill vain glory, selfish pride, and lusts of the flesh. It is only by returning to me, my love, that you will become once again filled with the peace and provision that you seek. I am the LORD. There is none like me. And though many may promise you love, and treasures on earth, they cannot compare to my endless love and treasures which are in Heaven.

Put first, therefore, my ways. Put my will before man, and you will experience my passion. For it is to save you, and romance you, even as a husband, his beloved wife. Yet, my Body has deprived me of the opportunity to love! They have left me, and take away the one thing I need, the ability to express my love to my people.

Return, therefore, Oh child of the Most High. I am a good and gracious God. I am merciful from generation to generation. I am that I am. You are my blessed one. Though

State of the Kingdom Address

I have many children, you are an only child to me. Give me the chance, saith the LORD. Give me the chance to love you and lead you once more. Leave the world behind and come to me. Come to my Kingdom, for it is full of abundance and love.

I cry daily. My loves have gone astray. They have trampled under foot my Word, and have placed it at the bottom of all their desires. This is even done in the Church. I cry, that you have discarded my Word. Oh, that you would embrace my Son, and taste the blood that He has spilled for you! It is He that is the Word, and you have replaced Him with your worldly desires.

It is for this reason, saith the LORD, that I am awakening you. It is for this reason that I had to intervene in your life at this moment. It is not for your sake. Nor is it for my sake. But it's for my Son's sake, who continually feels the pain of his wounds each time a believer rejects Him or lives outside of His blood covenant.

Arise, Ye mighty! And pick up your swords, ye treacherous ones! For the LORD is raising up His people as a thorn in the side of the enemy. I will not raise them up like in times past. I will not do what you have seen or experienced before. I will not do it like it's being done now. But I am doing a new thing, saith the Almighty.

It is time, child. It is time for you to cast away every weight that is holding you back from my perfect promises.

It is time for you to be who I created you to be. Let the weak say, I am strong. And let the faithful say, Amen.

Now is the land before you. However, Satan guards it, daring you to come forth to knock him off. How insulting this is to me! For I have not given him the power, nor the victory. But it is for you, my sheep. It's for you, the flock of my fold.

So do not wait any longer. The blessing is not here, but there. You must go forth, my child. You must go forth to advance my army against the forces of darkness. You must take back the land that the enemy is holding, and bring it into the treasury of God.

As you advance, then will you see the power of the Most High God manifested on earth. For I will do a mighty work through you, saith the LORD. Though a million men were told of the incredible exploits I will do through you, not one of them will believe. You are that generation that I have saved for myself. You are the people that I will cause to shock the world. Men and women will marvel at the blessings that I shower you with.

Oh, that I had warriors to advance my army! What joy would it bring me to see my Davids, Joshuas, Gideons, Deborahs, Pauls, Peters, Elijahs and others walk on earth, even in this day. Though they are here with me, I have preserved their spirit to be alive and well for these times.

Walk, therefore, ye beloved. Go in the power of the ancient ones. For you have me with you, saith the LORD. My

State of the Kingdom Address

blood is more than sufficient to get you the victory. Turn not to the left hand nor the right. But go straight forth in my mighty name, which is above every name.

Do what I lead you to do. Go where I guide you. For the LORD has great blessings ahead for the Redeemed. My Church will be glorified. My name will be exalted. My way will be prepared. And the earth shall once again see the Lord, in great power and glory. Amen.

ABOUT THE AUTHOR

David Newby is a well-respected Global Developer, End-Time Revivalist, Life Strategist, trainer, speaker, author, business developer, philanthropist, leader, and motivator, among other things.

Since high school, David has been on a quest to grow closer to God, excel in business, and revolutionize the world through his work. He is well en route to achieving all three. David attended schools such as University of Maryland College Park and Morgan State University, before graduating from University of Phoenix with both a BS in Business/Public Administration and a MBA in Global Management.

However, it was during a time at University of Maryland, that David had an epiphany, leading him to God. Almost 20 years since that experience, David has become a highly sought after Christian leader, business executive, and humanitarian. He has started a number of companies, including Global Innovations and Development, DGN Training, Exchange Pro, and others.

He is known for his outside of the box thinking, and his gift of inspiring and motivating people worldwide. David has learned from some of the biggest names in the personal development industry, including John Maxwell, Zig Ziglar, Les Brown, Tony Robbins, Dani Johnson, and Jack Canfield. He has also been featured on TV, radio, magazines, blogs, and other forums like The BusinessMakers TV Show with Russ Capper, alongside the likes of people like George Foreman, University of Phoenix *Phoenix Focus* Alumni Magazine, *Living Day By Day Magazine*, Survival Radio Network, and many more.

State of the Kingdom Address

He has written for organizations like CBS and Examiner to name a few. He has also trained and consulted tens of thousands of people around the world, including well known celebrities and business leaders through his programs, products, services, and online communities such as his group, The Empowerment Zone on LinkedIn.

David is an esteemed influencer and 'leader of leaders', according to some. However, these days he tries his best to be a servant of God and of others. He presently spends his time working God's harvest, growing his own businesses, consulting other leaders and business owners, traveling, writing, hanging out with family and friends, and enjoying life.

He offers speaking engagements, group training, and limited one on one training to corporations, business executives, associations, churches, colleges and universities, church leaders, government officials, educators, and working professionals.

To find out more about David, or to inquire about his availability as a speaker, or trainer, please visit http://belovedhq.com or call (410) 575-4356.

Please be sure to leave a review of this book on Amazon at **http://amzn.to/2j1Xeh0**

SPONSORSHIP OPPORTUNITY

We want to get this book out to over 1 billion people worldwide! But we need your help! If you or your organization would like to sponsor our marketing and promotion program, or make a contribution, please contact us for more info.

Call (410) 575-4356 or visit us at http://belovedhq.com!

To find out more about the various sponsorship packages, please visit us at http://belovedhq.com or call 410-575-4356.

State of the Kingdom Address

PERMISSIONS

We would like to thank all the publishers and individuals that granted us the permission to reprint the cited material:

Pastor Yong Doo Kim, www.baptizingfire.com

Reverend Robert Evans, www.revivals.arkangles.com/study-oldtestament.php

SHARE THIS INFORMATION WITH OTHERS

It's our duty as Christians to spread the gospel and help get the world ready for Jesus' return. How many people do you know that would benefit from this book? Will you meet them face to face and encourage them to get a copy? Will you call them on the phone and turn them onto the book? Will you share a few posts on social media, informing your network of where they can buy SOKA? If there are people you know that are not in a position to buy it themselves, will you buy them a personal copy of *State of the Kingdom Address*? Maybe you could teach a seminar at work or at your local church on the major topics of the book. For example, with private label rights, you can create your own course or program from the material in *State of the Kingdom Address*—without having to worry about copyright issues. You can find out more about our Private Label Rights at http://belovedhq.com. You don't have to be a master at every subject in this book to share it with others. We teach you, through our free study guide, that will help you learn the information in SOKA. You just have to be a willing participant in getting the important messages in SOKA out to the masses. That way, you can help save souls and earn money by teaching some of the principles outlined in the book. The point is, we want you as a marketing and promotional partner so we can get the word out about SOKA. And there are numerous ways for you to join us.

JV AND AFFILIATE PARTNERS

We are also working with JV partners and affiliates to get *State of the Kingdom Address* to as many people in the world as possible. Our joint venture partners (JVs) and affiliates can earn up to 50% commission on every book or other one of my training products, services, or programs that they sell through their affiliate link. This includes both physical and digital copies of SOKA. You can make hundreds, thousands, or even tens of thousands or more per month by helping us sell *State of the Kingdom Address* to people and organizations in your network. Better yet, we provide all the marketing materials you will need to sell the book, including email messages, articles, banners, social media posts, videos, audios, and more! To find out more about our partnership program and to apply to become a JV or affiliate, please visit http://belovedhq.com/partners.

Finally, it may even behoove you to lead a discussion on the topics in *State of the Kingdom Address* around your dinner table with your family. The bottom line is to help us get the word out as quickly as possible and to reach as many people as possible with this content.

LEAVE YOUR MARK, ESTABLISH YOUR LEGACY

Think about that–churches, governments, businesses, communities, and people worldwide getting themselves ready for Jesus' returning, and walking in the blessings of the Almighty God in the meantime. That's exactly what would happen as you help us get *State of the Kingdom Address* in the hands of people all around the world. Business executives will change the way they do business. Governments will glorify God. More people will come to the Kingdom. The Church will become that glorious City set on a hill that God wants it to be. People will become empowered to walk in total victory over the devil. The world will turn to God and His Word. And by you helping us spread the message by sharing SOKA with others, you will play a huge part in this revolution…this revival coming upon the earth!

So my question to you is, "How will you help us?" If not you, then who? If not NOW, then when? Time is of the essence, and souls are in the balance. Please reach out to us at http://belovedhq.com to find out how you can become a marketing and promotional partner with us through SOKA. We are a part of an unprecedented end-time movement on earth. And you play a pivotal role in preparing the world for the return of the Lord. You have come to the Kingdom for such a time as this…

GIVE AND IT SHALL BE GIVEN

There's something about the law of giving that can't be put into words. As you pour out into the lives of others, God pours out into your life. He lines up the universe, the situations, the earthly resources, the time, and everything else that needs to be lined up, to bless you. That is one of the invaluable benefits of helping God get His Word out to the public through *State of the Kingdom Address*: the LORD will bless you for all you do for His Kingdom. And it's all because you're helping lead people to Him and His perfect will for their lives and the Church.

JOIN THE MOVEMENT

If you want to go fast go alone; if you want to go far go with others. – African Proverb

State of the Kingdom Address

State of the Kingdom Address is not just another book. It's a movement! Even better, it's a catalyst of God's end-time movement on earth. Our goal with SOKA is to reach as many people as possible as quickly as possible with the Word of God and the power of the revelation in *SOKA*.

I envision a world where all people will at least have a chance to hear the gospel, and learn about the LORD. I believe that by hearing the words in this book, and applying the principles to their lives and their work, they will not only dramatically transform their lives, they will help to dramatically transform the Body of Christ. The Church will become that light of the world that will make us an enviable entity.

Naturally, we want *State of the Kingdom Address* embraced by the Church. We want it shared amongst government leaders. We want it discussed at business meetings with Fortune 500 executives and between leaders in some of our most successful organizations of today. We want SOKA taught in public school systems. We want it taught in remote Indian villages. We want people to walk in the power of the Holy Ghost, and to be effective end-time warriors against the works of the devil.

I've trained countless world renowned business leaders the principles in SOKA. I have appeared on radio, magazines, TV, and have been featured on some of the most popular blogs in personal development. I have created online courses, training programs, and have worked with some of the biggest names in the personal development industry. I have built and led online communities of more than 10,000 people strong, very successful people, based on the strategies and content in this book. By the grace of God, everything taught in SOKA has been effective at getting people where they belong in God's Kingdom.

I would love to have you as a marketing and promotional partner of *State of the Kingdom Address*. Let's get the book out to everyone in the world. Let's start a movement! If you'd like to join us and help spread the gospel, please visit us at http://belovedhq.com/partners and signup to be a JV or affiliate, or inquire about our private label rights. Grab your affiliate link and marketing materials. Then, think of all the major companies you know that could benefit from this book. Think of the company insiders you know personally. How can we get them to share it with their employees and stakeholders. What government officials can you reach out to right now to get them a copy of SOKA? How many speaking engagements do you have coming up? How many of your audience members can you tell about the book, and how they can purchase it? How can you get them to share SOKA? What about your family, friends, colleagues, and neighbors? Could they benefit from reading the book? Please make a list today of 20 to 30 names of people you can reach out to about SOKA. Tell them about the book and how it's impacted your life. Encourage them to get a copy for themselves. We appreciate you helping us advance God's Kingdom on earth through *State of the Kingdom Address*.

BOOK DAVID FOR SPEAKING

Want to book David for a speaking engagement for your business, association, church, college, university, or other organization or event?

Contact us at http://belovedhq.com, email dnvm22@gmail.com, or call (410) 575-4356 to book him.

FREE PERSONAL DEVELOPMENT TOOLS, TIPS, STRATEGIES, AND INFORMATION

FREE *Life Success System* Mindmap…helps you create a mindmap to get you from where you are in life to where you want to be. This mindmap helps you achieve all of your major life goals, both spiritual and nonspiritual. Short-term and long-term goals are accounted for in this mindmap, which helps you become more productive and leads you to the results that you want in life. (Mindmap template)

FREE *Spiritual Success Strategies* Audio…gives you spiritual strategies of success in a brief, inspiring audio that you can listen to at home in your office, in your car while driving to work, or at the gym while working out. Listen to it enough and the strategies will become life transforming habits. (60 minutes)

FREE *Spiritual Words of Wisdom* eCourse…learn from the spiritual experiences of David Newby that took him from first learning about God to where he is now. See how he became the spiritual leader that he is today. David advises you not only on the things you need to do to improve your life and your walk with God, but the things you need to avoid doing to remain in God's cloud of blessings. (30 Day eCourse)

FREE *Bigger, Badder Better Breakthroughs* Training Session…limited time only! Get a free 30-minute *Bigger, Badder, Better Breakthroughs* Training Session with David Newby. Find out what you have to do in life to have the biggest, baddest, best breakthroughs imaginable. Get off of your plateau, and do the right things today that will take you places tomorrow in which your competition can never get. (30-Minutes)

Find out more here>>> **http://belovedhq.com**!

SOKA SUCCESS STRATEGIES 90-DAY CHALLENGE™

You have a chance to win up to thousands of dollars in cash or prizes by taking the SOKA Success Strategies 90-Day Challenge. In this challenge, you will be required to video chronicle your journey of applying key strategies of success outlined in Chapter 8 of SOKA. You must show a before shot of where you were before you started the challenge, and an after shot of where you ended after the challenge. You can challenge yourself in any area of life, whether spiritually, financially, physically, in weight loss, relationships, and others. You must have at least 10 minutes of recordings per week, whether a couple minutes per day, or one 10-minute video at the end of the week. The videos will document your journey. The person with the most compelling, inspirational, and verifiable story of transformation by applying the principles in SOKA will win the challenge. All stories will be verified, and proof of a transformation must be substantiated, either by people, testimonies, letters, visual evidence (such as scales or physical appearance for weightloss, etc.). The winner will get up to thousands of dollars in prizes, PLUS a special bonus gift. The contest will run from October 1, 2018 to January 1, 2019. Please visit http://belovedhq.com/sokacontest to enter.

ACKNOWLEDGEMENTS

Writing and marketing this book took a great deal of support from people around me. I could not have done it without you. And I am forever indebted to you. I send a special thanks and gratitude to:

The Lord, Jesus, who has been my best friend and adviser throughout this whole entire project. He encouraged me when I needed encouragement, and directed me at times I felt lost. All praises and honor due to your name, Lord.

My family, blood and nonblood relatives. My mother, brothers, sisters, aunts, uncles, cousins, and others. I thank God for you, and love you with all my soul!

To my friends, followers, and fans, thank you! Your support makes me want to keep doing what I do…but even harder. I love you and can't wait to see you on your big stage! I believe in you. Believe in yourself.

Apostles Craig and Colette Toach and AMI, who are like my spiritual parents. We have never met in person, but I can't begin to tell you how much you and Apostolic Movement International have helped me come into the spiritual man that I am today. You taught me to recognize my high calling, and walk in the power of the Almighty God. Your work is not in vain. I doubt seriously that you have the slightest inkling of how many people you are impacting. I love you. May God continue to shake up the heavens, and destroy the plans of the devil through the work that you do!

The Empowerment Zone Group on LinkedIn, you're the best. The best group. The best supporters. The best community. The best human beings I've come across in a long time. I'm humbled to be associated with such high-achievers, and positive minded people of God. I love you. Although I may not know you all personally, the fact that you comment, share, and like my posts goes a long way. Your encouragement helped me to stay focus and keep the plow moving even when I felt like quitting at times.

Winners Chapel, never discount your work and the impact of your ministry on the masses. So empowering, authentic, alive are your services. May God continue to prosper you and your founder, Bishop David Oyedepo. You made me like church again. Peace and love to the winners family…internationally.

To my marketing partners out there, too many to count. Radio personalities, TV Hosts, magazine publishers, writers, coaches, consultants, PR professionals, JVs, affiliates, friends, family, colleagues, promoters, and others. Each of you was a pivotal part in helping me bring visibility to SOKA. I couldn't have done it without you. Thank you…from the bottom of my heart!

To the coaches and consultants, that helped me become better at what I do. Thank you sincerely, to people like L. Hall, Apostle Colette Toach, Apostle Craig Toach, John Maxwell, Dani Johnson, Robert Kiyosaki, Tony Robbins, the late Zig Ziglar, Les Brown, Jack Canfield, Steve Harrison, and so many more. You taught me lessons in business, leadership, marketing, and so many other things. May continued blessings and peace abound upon you and yours.

To all those I missed, may the favor of God rest upon you. May His love follow you wherever you go. May God make your life an example of what the blessings of the LORD looks like. I love and adore you. There is not enough space, nor time to give every single person who helped me with this project thanks. Either directly, or indirectly, what you did for me is recorded in Heaven. May God have mercy on you and your household for all that you helped Him do on earth by supporting this project. Praise the LORD!

SET APART BY GOD - A VERY SPECIAL THANK YOU

Dawn Designs

Design and Marketing Consultancy

Philippines

http://dawndesigns.ph

I wanted to give a certain individual special attention, and a very special Thank You. Rather, God wanted to acknowledge them and their character. God told me to tell the people that read my book, "She is a sign and an ensign of how I want my people to operate on earth in these days!" If you look up the words "sign" and "ensign", you will notice that "sign" is a symbol or signal. "Ensign" is a standard. Church, April Dawn Loranzo is a symbol, and a standard of service to God and His work on earth, and the subsequent blessings that come with it! If you're doing anything less than what she did recently, and how she did it, you're not doing it right. Months ago at the time of this writing, I needed a logo designed for this end-time movement I created called REVIVE!, at revive-movement.com. Its mission is to usher in a revival worldwide by turning people back to God. Now, being strapped for cash at the time, I didn't want to pay too much for the logo. In fact, I had already identified several websites that I could probably get a nice logo for well under $100. But God stopped me from purchasing a logo. Instead, He told me to reach out to the people in my network, my connections on LinkedIn at the time, and see who would design the logo. I was hesitant at first because I figured, "Who in their right mind would design it for free?" and "Why wouldn't I want to pay someone for their services? Wouldn't they deserve payment if they designed it?" I thought. Then, God showed me a few things. One, this end-time movement, and His work on earth cannot, and will not be done by me alone. It's a team thing, and God expects all of His people to be involved. Two, I have to learn how to lead by delegation at times, as placing all of the work, cost, and responsibility on me would render it unsuccessful, and at the very least, wear me out and make the ministry, in this case, the REVIVE! movement, ineffective. By the way, the book that you just read is a part of the REVIVE! movement. Three, God wants all of His people to give to His Kingdom, in finances, in time, in talent, in resources, in support, in benevolence, and so forth. It's His stuff He gives us. We are His, and everything of us, including our finances, time, knowledge, position, and social networks belong to Him, and for the work of the ministry. Finally, God wanted to show me that He will bless us as we give. So, I sent out the call. I asked people in my network if they knew of any good graphic designers who could do a great logo. I got a number of responses. To this day, people are still responding to the original LinkedIn thread. Yet, all of them wanted money. I explained the situation, and told them I would mention their business, and help market their services to my network, both online and offline. I never mentioned I would place them in my book. However, they all wanted money. I got messages on LinkedIn, and emails, and comments on my original thread. But it all revolved around money. Not one of the "money-seekers" was willing to look at the bigger picture, and the opportunity in front of them...a chance to reach hundreds, thousands, or millions or more people with their business, while helping God advance His Kingdom on earth through the REVIVE! movement. Instead, they all wanted payment for services rendered. They all, to this day, are probably getting paid for services rendered...all $100 dollars of it for one logo… competing with each other for crumbs. Yet, one woman stood apart, separated herself from the "norm", and got a special blessing. She is not on the "plateau" as

State of the Kingdom Address

many of the rest of them. Instead, she left it...simply by serving...by giving! Dawn April Loranzo, thank you greatly for designing our logo! You are a perfect example of goodness and service in God's eyes. May this mention in my book memorialize your business and your service to God's work. May your name go down in history as being an ordinary woman, who, as small as it may seem to people, stepped up in an extraordinary way. Dawn, you have a great cloud of witnesses in heaven watching you. God looks down from Heaven and smiles upon you with great delight! May your business continue to prosper, and may God endow you with special favor from on high. LORD, shower her with grace, mercy, and goodness, that she may bring honor to your name. Hear my prayer, and do not let my words fall to the ground. But let them prosper, exceedingly, according to your will. Friends, God has singled out Dawn for blessings. What you do in darkness will be revealed in the light! Through one small act of kindness, she has received a special mention in my book in a space usually reserved for sponsors. That, to the tune of several hundred, or thousands of dollars normally. Further, her name and story will be read or heard in all lands where my book goes. She will doubtless be known of by millions of people worldwide. In the same compassion and grace that Dawn had toward me and the Kingdom of God by creating a logo free of charge, I ask you to follow her example. Be compassionate toward her business needs by checking out her design and marketing services. Dawn does logos, websites, and many more things, which will help you start or grow your business, ministry, brand, project, program, or movement. Give her the opportunity to serve you. I was very well pleased with my logo. It turned out to be very clean and professional! It was delivered within a day or two, and she even offered me free revisions if I was not satisfied! What a spectacular service! Now, wherever I go on earth, in this ubiquitous REVIVE! movement, people all over will know that Dawn Loranzo, a good-natured, small woman from the Philippines, with a big heart, created our logo. She could have easily charged me hundreds of dollars for a logo. But God would have otherwise. He wanted a chance to bless Dawn! He did. He gave her a chance to exponentially increase her income, gain more visibility, and tell more people about her business, all while honoring her. That, my friend, is worth much more than $200 for a logo design! "Where there is no vision, the people perish!" God has blessed dawn with the heart of a servant, the vision of an eagle, and an outcome that will far exceed her former income. Will He not do the same for you? Please visit Dawn's site at http://dawndesigns.ph and check out some of her design and marketing services. Thank you sincerely for your consideration. God bless! Let's go higher, David Newby, Founder, REVIVE!

SOKA SUCCESS SEMINARS™

A certain amount of spiritual leverage and positioning is achieved when you live in accordance with the Word of God. *State of the Kingdom Address* helps you live the Word, applying scripture to your everyday life so that you and or your organization can be at the forefront of God's movement on earth. That means being ahead of your business competition, getting the deals they wanted. It means being first in line for promotion at your job, being chosen over someone else, only because you have the favor of God upon you and they don't.

Now, we are offering seminars where we teach you many of the principles detailed in SOKA. You will learn the strategies, tactics, and tips you need to thrive during God's end-time revival on earth. There is no better place to be than ahead of the curve—ahead of what God is about to do on earth.

Our SOKA Success Seminars™ provides success tools and customizable training programs for each client. Whether you're part of a small group, or a large organization, our company can create the right training system for you and your colleagues or associates.

The SOKA Success Seminars™ are ideal for:

- ➢ Christians
- ➢ Business executives
- ➢ Fortune 500 companies
- ➢ Churches
- ➢ Church leaders
- ➢ Government officials

- Working professionals
- Sales professionals
- Small business owners
- Associations
- Educators
- Students
- Military personnel
- Small mastermind groups
- Think tanks
- And more…

Contact us today at http://belovedhq.com to find out more about our SOKA Success Seminars™!

WORK WITH DAVID NEWBY AND HIS TEAM

TRAINING PROGRAMS

As a Life Development Strategist, David develops high-impact, high influence, extraordinary Christian men and women and empowers them to become revolutionaries in their fields.

He equips them with the strategies, tools, tips, resources, and information they need to not only become more successful, but to help advance God's Kingdom on earth through the incredible work that they do.

Now you can work with David Newby and his team to totally transform your life. Through the following training programs, David helps you have a bigger impact on the world...

REVIVE! Inner Circle Program

Get the training you need to become a leader in God's end-time revival on earth. By becoming a part of the REVIVE! Movement's Inner Circle, you get to work closely with David and his high-performance, revival-minded, God-dedicated, devout team of men and women of faith for an entire year to help lead the world to revival. You will get life-changing strategies to not only help you stay in alignment with God's new, unprecedented move on earth, but to help you become much more successful and rise to the top of your field. You also get to ride our robust marketing system with the REVIVE! Movement to help promote your products or services. Finally, get lifetime designation as a REVIVE! Founding Member, a classification that will do wonders for your business, brand, or ministry. Find out more about this program at revive-movement.com or in our Facebook group at bit.ly/revivemovement

Revival Survival Course

Learn the fundamental principles you need to survive and thrive during the end-time revival. Look at the end-time revival as God's new play for His fourth quarter people, His closers. If you are like most people, you are probably operating from the old play book. You know, what's typically taught in church, what gets you to where you currently are, what helps you make it in the traditional, status quo system. There's a new thing that God is doing, and it requires new principles, a new perspective, new mind, new heart, and new way of doing things. You can't keep putting new wine in old bottles and hoping for different results. The Revival Survival program helps to break your mind, and equip you with a new, more powerful, successful, victorious way of thinking, moving, and living so you can really rule and reign with Christ. You will be thriving during the end-time revival, whereas many people around you may be struggling to figure out what keeps them stuck, how to deal with the devil and spiritual attacks, how to navigate this new unchartered landscape, and how to leverage their position in Christ for optimal results. David and his team helps you with all of that and more in this course! Find out more about this program at revive-movement.com or in our Facebook group at bit.ly/revivemovement

Success Strategies™ Program

Learn the fundamental strategies of life success. You have heard of a few of them already. Let David and his team explain them in depth, and help you implement each one. David will also share strategies that he has never revealed to the public. And when you apply them, they will catapult you to levels of success that may otherwise take you 10 to 20 years to achieve on your own. This program is a premium extension of the free audio recording by the same name. However, it goes much more in depth, and shares some profound truths about success and how to achieve it in accordance with God's will for you. Find out more at http://belovedhq.com/training.

Conqueror Training™ Program

David teaches you how to be an effective Conqueror in Christ. Many of us hear that phrase and believe it. But do we do what's necessary to reign on earth as a conqueror? Are we really conquering new territory? Are we driving out devils and ruling as mighty kings? Get in this program and you will be able to drive Satan and his subordinates off your territory simply by showing up to battle. There are a lot of soldiers in God's Kingdom. There are very few conquerors. Find out how you can be one, by enrolling in our Conqueror Training Program™. Find out more at http://belovedhq.com/training.

Revolutionary Impact™ Program

What does it take to have a revolutionary impact in this world? Well, not everybody is built to be a revolutionary. Revolutionaries account for less than 1 out of every 100,000 people. Nonetheless, when they get out there, they get out there in a big, big, way. They are world changers. They are pioneers. They are who they are, and they leave an indelible mark on the planet. Are you a revolutionary? There's only one way to find out. The Revolutionary Impact program helps you determine whether you have been called by God to be a revolutionary. And if so, our team will equip you with the training and information you need to be effective at living your calling. Find out more at http://belovedhq.com/training.

Let's Go Higher™ 1-on-1 Training Program

Need a more customized training program? Do you find it more beneficial to go one on one with David and his team? The *Let's Go Higher* training program is intended to do just that—take you higher in life by giving you direct access to David or one of his top trainers. This program is only available to a select few. As a rule of thumb, David only considers working one on one with people that he feels has a very high calling, and who are anointed by God to do incredible exploits on earth. Find out more at http://belovedhq.com/training.

GET HUGE DISCOUNTS ON THE *STATE OF THE KINGDOM ADDRESS*™ BOOK OR THE AUDIO PROGRAM WHEN YOU BUY IN BULK FOR YOUR EMPLOYEES…

Take full advantage of bulk purchases of SOKA and get tremendous savings. Now, you can empower your entire team to walk in the blessings of God, while preparing their souls and their households for the ultimate return of Jesus. And it won't cost you the retail value of the book or audio program. Whether your team likes to read the book or listen to the audio, you can make sure everyone has a copy without breaking your bank.

Not only will *State of the Kingdom Address* equip them to improve their individual lives, but it will also help them be more effective at work. That translates into an incredible competitive advantage for your organization by way of God's favor, increased productivity, greater accountability, self confidence, faith, determination, better financial management, and the like.

Allow SOKA to equip your staff with the strategies for sustainable success that will place them light years ahead of the competition. You can teach them in company meetings. Incorporate them in your training material. Place them in your employee handbook. Discuss them at lunch with a colleague. Talk to other leaders in your organization about how to make SOKA a part of your culture. Strategize ways to make sure your entire staff has had a chance to hear the gospel and personally know Jesus.

Applying just a few of these principles will lead to a dramatic change in the spirit, mind, and actions of your team, which results in long term success for you and your organization:

- ➢ Knowing God
- ➢ Understanding spiritual warfare
- ➢ Removing spiritual blockages
- ➢ Dealing with wickedness in high places
- ➢ Attracting the favor of God
- ➢ Be positioned for unstoppable wealth
- ➢ And more

Whether you represent a private or public organization, we can provide you with a substantial discount on SOKA when you buy in quantity. Please contact us at http://belovedhq.com/training for more info.

To purchase the *State of the Kingdom Address*™ book or Audio Program in bulk, visit www.belovedhq.com and use the Contact form. For bulk orders via phone, call (410) 575-4356.

COMING SOON

STAY TUNED FOR UPCOMING RELEASES…

David has a number of new books being released in the near future. They are expected to be available to the public within the next four years, some sooner than others. If you would like to preorder any of the books, or get on our early notification list, please browse our Upcoming Releases page at http://belovedhq.com/upcomingreleases. Here are just a few titles you can look out for…

- State of the Kingdom Address 2020™ (Coming January 2020)
- Spiritual Warfare Manifesto™ (TBD)
- Diario Spirituali™ (TBD)
- Hunger Pangs™ (TBD)
- Life Success Manual™ (TBD)

ALSO LOOK OUT FOR THESE SOKA SEQUELS…

- SOKA for Church Leaders™
- SOKA for Government Officials™
- SOKA for Business Executives™
- SOKA for Working Professionals™
- SOKA for Everyday People™
- SOKA: The Lost Files™

LET'S CONNECT FURTHER…

Visit my main website: http://revive-movement.com

Visit my personal website: http://belovedhq.com

Connect on LinkedIn: https://www.linkedin.com/in/davidgnewby

Join my LinkedIn group, The Empowerment Zone: http://bit.ly/jointheez

Find me on Facebook: https://www.facebook.com/DNvm2

LIKE my Facebook page: https://www.facebook.com/DavidGNewby/

Join my Facebook group, REVIVE! Movement: http://bit.ly/revivemovement

Subscribe to my YouTube channel: https://www.youtube.com/user/DNvm2

Follow me on Twitter: https://twitter.com/DavidGNewby

Find me on Instagram: https://www.instagram.com/dnvm22/

ADDITIONAL RESOURCES FOR SUCCESS

TRAINING PROGRAMS

The information in *State of the Kingdom Address* is designed to propel you forward in the Kingdom of God and get you prepared for the return of Jesus Christ. I want you to apply the material in SOKA to your life so that you can prosper spiritually and otherwise.

David's Training

The following training programs help you have a bigger impact on the world through the work that you do in the Kingdom of God.

Our premier training programs are:

- REVIVE! Inner Circle
- Revival Survival eCourse
- Success Strategies™ Program
- Conqueror Training™ Program
- Revolutionary Impact™ Program
- Let's Go Higher™ 1-on-1 Training Program

Check them out today at http://belovedhq.com/training or http://revive-movement.com to see if we are running any special promotional offers!

I've also found other programs extremely helpful to me or my clients, in terms of improving our lives spiritually, professionally, personally, financially, physically, or in some other area.

Disclaimer

As a disclaimer, please note that below, we are simply providing additional resources that may help you grow your life. Individual results may vary. By enrolling in any program or course, or by purchasing any product or service below, you indemnify us of any potential damages.

Some of the programs suggested are secular in nature, meaning that they may be based on best success practices from a worldly or practical standpoint. I believe they have great significance to your overall success.

Albeit, I would strongly recommend that you always place spiritual things, in particular, things of God before any worldly practice or advice. Put simply, if whatever specific practice you follow doesn't line up with the word of God, or is in any way contrary to the will of God for you, discard it.

With that said, here are a few resources that may be of interest to you...

APOSTOLIC MOVEMENT INTERNATIONAL (AMI) FIVEFOLD TRAINING

AMI has a powerful Fivefold Training program that raises up Apostles, Prophets, Pastors, Evangelists, and Teachers in the Church. The ministry is designed to go and prepare the Body of Christ for the final move of God. Perhaps unbeknownst to them, AMI is largely responsible for my personal spiritual growth and development over the past several years. In fact, I would go as far as to say, that it's because of the amazing team at AMI, Apostle Colette Toach, Apostle Craig Toach, Les Crause, and others, that I even decided to move forward with SOKA and my other work in the Kingdom. They have helped me come up in leadership, ministry, and success, not to mention the multiplied millions of other people they've helped throughout the world. You can find out more about AMI and their programs at http://apostolic-movement.com.

ET THE HIP HOP PREACHER

Eric Thomas, *ET the Hip Hop Preacher*, is an incredible inspiration to me. He has been impacting the lives of millions worldwide with his positive, never-give-up attitude about success. His focus and determination to be the best he can be is infectious. He is one of those guys that just make you believe you can achieve anything. I strongly recommend you check out some of his material on his website at

http://shop.etinspires.com/#_a_Dnewby.

100-DAY CHALLENGE

Gary Ryan Blair has an incredible goal achievement program available that he has been using to help people and organizations achieve their goals more effectively. The program is called the 100-Day Challenge. I've used it for the past several years, and it has been a great help in enabling me to write, market, and launch this book on time. I implore you to try the challenge out for yourself. It could help you in a number of areas, including business, finances, health, relationships, project management, and others. You can take the 100-Day Challenge at http://bit.ly/100newyou

DANIJOHNSON.COM

Dani Johnson is one of my favorite mentors in business and personal development. Dani strikes a great balance between spirituality and practicality in her coaching. As a result, she empowers people to trust and obey God, but also to do their part to achieve their dreams. Check out two of her premier programs below. Also, be sure to visit her site at http://danijohnson.com for some of her success products and services.

- ➢ First Steps to Success
- ➢ Creating a Dynasty

ROBERT KIYOSAKI

Robert Kiyosaki is one of the world's most sophisticated financial minds out there. Robert is best known for his book, *Rich Dad, Poor Dad* in which he appeared on the Oprah Winfrey show years ago to discuss. Robert has been teaching people worldwide how to become financially successful, applying tips and strategies they don't typically teach you in school. You can learn more about Robert at http://richdad.com

State of the Kingdom Address

MATTHEW MIGLIN

Matthew Miglin has been featured on CBS, NBC, ABC, Fox, and more for his business-transforming coaching. He is a well-known business expert, and helps both startups and established businesses become more profitable. Get his business resources for startups (http://bit.ly/2HYkbJo), or those for current businesses (http://bit.ly/2KCXsV3). You can also find out about his groundbreaking financial strategies at voiceofprosperity.com.

OTHER RESOURCES

THE BIBLE

E-Sword Digital Bible:

http://e-sword.net

Blue Letter Bible:

https://www.blueletterbible.org/

MOVIES

The Success Principles DVD at http://bit.ly/4moresuccess

BOOKS

- *The Success Principles 10th Anniversary Edition* at http://bit.ly/10yearsofsuccess
- *Rich Dad, Poor Dad*
- *Think and Grow Rich*
- *How to Win Friends and Influence People*
- *Heaven Awaits the Bride*
- *Baptize By Blazing Fire*
- *The Harbinger*
- *The Esther Effect*

COMMUNITIES

The Empowerment Zone, empowerment group: http://bit.ly/jointheez

REVIVE! Movement, end-time revival group: http://bit.ly/revivemovement

NOTES AND REFERENCES

Chapter 3: Anna Rountree, *Heaven Awaits the Bride* (Lake Mary, FL: Charisma House; 3rd printing edition, 2007).

Chapter 3: Reverend Robert Evans. Revivals in the Bible – The Old Testament. Retrieved February 2, 2016 from http://revivals.arkangles.com/study-oldtestament.php

Chapter 4: Crause, Les. Apostolic Movement International. (2016). Retrieved April 1, 2016 from http://apostolic-movement.com

Chapter 4: Benny Hinn, "Your Supernatural Wealth Transfer Is Coming", accessed February 15, 2015, http://www.bennyhinn.org/articles/7574/your-supernatural-wealth-transfer-is-coming

Chapter 5: David J. Stewart, "Billions of People are Going to Hell!" (2016). Accessed April 2, 2016 from http://www.jesus-is-savior.com/billions_of_people_going_to_hell.htm

Chapter 5: Dominique Mosbergen, "How Many U.S. Christians Believe Christ's 'Second Coming' Will Happen Soon? More Than You May Think (SURVEY)." (2013). *Huffington Religion*. Retrieved April 19, 2016 from

http://www.huffingtonpost.com/2013/04/01/christ-second-coming-survey_n_2993218.html

Chapter 6: Apostolic Movement International. (2016). Accessed April 2, 2016 from http://apostolic-movement.com/

Chapter 6: BBC News. Paris attacks: What happened on the night. (December 2015). Retrieved April 2, 2016 from http://www.bbc.com/news/world-europe-34818994

Chapter 6: Jonathan Cahn. *Mystery of the Shemitah*. Lake Mary, FL: Frontline, 2014. Print.

Chapter 6: Real Thing TV. (2013, November 19). 4 blood moons coming 2014-2015 Jesus coming [Video file]. Retrieved from https://www.youtube.com/watch?v=WDn2ZxWIjOI

Chapter 6: Sid Roth's It's Supernatural! (2014, September 14). Blood moons: What's coming in 2015? [Video file]. Retrieved April 2, 2016 from http://bit.ly/1XTTMlM

Chapter 6: "Jonathan Cahn: The Harbinger," The Christian Broadcasting Network. (2016). Accessed February 15, 2015, http://www.cbn.com/tv/1471942971001

Chapter 6: Jonathan Cahn. The Harbinger: The Ancient Mystery that Holds the Secret of America's Future. Lake Mary, FL. Charisma Media, 2012. Print.

Chapter 6: "Tom Daschle 9/12/2012," C-SPAN, accessed February 15, 2015, http://www.c-span.org/video/?c4032478/tom-daschle-9122012

Chapter 6: National Archives: The Center for Legislative Archives. George Washington's Inaugural Address, April 30, 1789, accessed February 15, 2015, http://www.archives.gov/legislative/features/gw-inauguration/

State of the Kingdom Address

Chapter 6: "Harbinger author says loss of Tree of Hope a warning," World News Daily, August 9, 2014, http://www.wnd.com/2014/08/harbinger-author-says-loss-of-tree-of-hope-a-warning/

Chapter 6: "Remarks of President Barack Obama – As Prepared for Delivery Address to Joint Session of Congress," The White House, accessed February 15, 2015, http://www.whitehouse.gov/the_press_office/Remarks-of-President-Barack-Obama-Address-to-Joint-Session-of-Congress/

Chapter 6: "CIA Insider Warns: 25-Year Great Depression is About to Strike America", Money Morning, accessed February 15, 2015, http://moneymorning.com/ext/articles/rickards/25-year-great-depression.php?iris=254985

Chapter 6: Sid Roth's It's Supernatural, accessed February 15, 2015, http://sidroth.org/television/tv-archives/jonathan-cahn

Chapter 6: The Temple Institute. (2016). Accessed February 15, 2015, https://www.templeinstitute.org/

Chapter 6: The Temple Institute, accessed February 15, 2015, https://www.templeinstitute.org/table_showbread.htm

Chapter 7: Kim Yong-Doo, *Baptized By Blazing Fire* (Lake Mary, FL: Creation House, 2009)

Chapter 7: Divine Revelations, accessed February 15, 2015, http://bit.ly/1CBNbBS

Chapter 8: Black Christian News Network. (2016). "25 Million "Middle Class" Families in America Live Paycheck to Paycheck". Retrieved April 2, 2016 from http://www.blackchristiannews.com/2014/04/25-million-middle-class-families-in-america-live-paycheck-to-paycheck/

Chapter 8: Anup Shah. (2013). Global Issues. Poverty facts and statistics. Retrieved April 2, 2016 from http://www.globalissues.org/article/26/poverty-facts-and-stats

Chapter 8: Darren Hardy. (2015). "Darren Hardy shares secrets of great achievers." YouTube. Retrieved April 2, 2016 from https://www.youtube.com/watch?v=X-CC3JO8L3o

Chapter 8: Jack Canfield. The Success Principles: How to get from where you are to where you want to be. New York: William Morrow Paperbacks, 2004.

Chapter 8: John Maxwell. (2016). The John Maxwell Company. Retrieved April 2, 2016 from http://www.johnmaxwell.com/

Chapter 8: Statistic Brain. (2016). Retrieved April 2, 2016 from http://www.statisticbrain.com/world-poverty-statistics/

Chapter 8: Tami Luhby, "25 Million Middle Class Families in America Live Paycheck to Paycheck," April 27, 2014, http://www.blackchristiannews.com/2014/04/25-million-middle-class-families-in-america-live-paycheck-to-paycheck/

State of the Kingdom Address

Chapter 8: Anup Shah, "Poverty Facts and Stats", Global Issues, accessed February 15, 2015, http://www.globalissues.org/article/26/poverty-facts-and-stats

Chapter 8: Jack Canfield, *The Success Principles*, William Morrow Paperbacks. 512 pages. 2006.

Chapter 8: Michael C. Mankins, *Harvard Business Review*, Stop wasting valuable time. 2004. https://hbr.org/2004/09/stop-wasting-valuable-time

Chapter 9: Apostolic Movement International. (2016). Retrieved April 1, 2016 from http://apostolic-movement.com

Chapter 9: BBC News. (2013). How many Roman Catholics are there in the world? Retrieved April 2, 2016 from http://www.bbc.com/news/world-21443313

Chapter 9: Colette Toach, "Identifying the Fivefold Ministry," Apostolic Movement International, accessed February 15, 2015, http://apostolic-movement.com/show.php?t=Identifying%20the%20Fivefold%20Ministry&ref=78&button=

Chapter 9: David Johnston. (2016). Red Letter Living. Retrieved April 2, 2016 from http://redletterliving.org/

Chapter 9: Gallup. (2016). Religion. Retrieved April 2, 2016 from http://www.gallup.com/

Chapter 9: Reverend Robert Evans, OAM. Revivals in the Bible – The Old Testament. Retrieved January 30, 2016 from http://revivals.arkangles.com/study-oldtestament.php

Chapter 9: Emily Canal. January 13, 2016. Joe Biden's Mission To Cure Cancer Has A $5.2 Billion Head Start. *Forbes*. Retrieved January 17, 2016 from
http://www.forbes.com/sites/emilycanal/2016/01/13/joe-biden-cure-cancer-5-billion/?utm_campaign=Forbes&utm_source=LINKEDIN_COMPANY&utm_medium=social&utm_channel=Business&linkId=20343760#3139ff0c2cc71a44ee5b2cc7

Chapter 9: "Fast Facts About American Religion," Hartford Institute For Religion Research, accessed February 15, 2015, http://hirr.hartsem.edu/research/fastfacts/fast_facts.html#sizecong

Chapter 9: John Hunter. World Peace and Other 4th Grade Achievements. Boston: Houghton Mifflin Harcourt, 2013. Print.

Chapter 9: Michael Lipka. (2015). Muslims and Islam: Key findings in the U.S. and around the world. Pew Research Center. Retrieved April 2, 2016 from http://www.pewresearch.org/fact-tank/2015/12/07/muslims-and-islam-key-findings-in-the-u-s-and-around-the-world/

Chapter 9: Robinson, comment on "How many atheists in the world?", accessed February 15, 2015, http://wiki.answers.com/Q/How_many_atheists_in_nthe_world#slide=15

Chapter 9: Pastor Roosevelt, Living Faith Christian Center, http://www.lfccnj.com/pages/about.php

Chapter 9: Gabe Lyons, *UnChristian* (Ada, MI: Baker Books)

Chapter 9: Antonia Blumberg. "China On Track To Become World's Largest Christian Country By 2025, Experts Say," The Huffington Post, accessed February 15, 2015, http://www.huffingtonpost.com/2014/04/22/china-largest-christian-country_n_5191910.html

Chapter 9: Pew Research Center. (2015). The Future of World Religions: Population Growth Projections, 2010-2050. Retrieved April 2, 2016 from http://www.pewforum.org/2015/04/02/religious-projections-2010-2050/

Chapter 9: Danny Shea. (2010). Pat Robertson: Haiti 'Cursed' By 'Pact To The Devil' (VIDEO). HuffPost Media. Retrieved April 2, 2016 from http://www.huffingtonpost.com/2010/01/13/pat-robertson-haiti-curse_n_422099.html

Chapter 9: Sickles, Jason. 2016. Lottery veterans question Tennessee family's behavior before claiming Powerball winnings. Retrieved January 17, 2016 from http://news.yahoo.com/lottery-veterans-question-tennessee-familys-escapades-before-claiming-powerball-winnings-165008074.html

Chapter 9: Flake, Jeff. *Wastebook: The Farce Awakens.* (2015). Retrieved 1/18/16 from http://1.usa.gov/1SYwZ3N

Chapter 9: National Alliance to End Homelessness. Fact sheet: Veteran homelessness. (2015). Retrieved April 22, 2015 from http://bit.ly/1ZHdfXy

Chapter 9: Tony Robbins. (2016). Retrieved April 2, 2016 from http://tonyrobbins.com

Chapter 9: Travel China Guide. (2016). Religion and beliefs in China. Retrieved April 2, 2016 from https://www.travelchinaguide.com/intro/religion/

Chapter 10: Divine Revelations, accessed February 15, 2015, http://bit.ly/1CBNbBS

Chapter 10: DivineRevelations Spiritlessons. (2011, August 22). Heaven and hell - 1000 to 1, by Pastor Park [Video file]. Retrieved from https://www.youtube.com/watch?v=HR1sFtFug38

Chapter 10: Mike Holmes. "What Would Happen If the Church Tithed?" *Relevant Magazine.* 8 Mar. 2016. Online.

Chapter 10: Mary Baxter. *A Divine Revelation of Hell.* New Kensington, PA: Whitaker House, 1993. Print.

State of the Kingdom Address

Chapter 10: "What is the Romans Road to salvation?" Accessed February 15, 2015, http://www.gotquestions.org/Romans-road-salvation.html

Chapter 10: Mike Holmes, "What Would Happen if the Church Tithed?" *Relevant Magazine*, July 10, 2013, http://www.relevantmagazine.com/god/church/what-would-happen-if-church-tithed

Chapter 10: T.M. Luhrmann, "My Take: If you hear God speak audibly, you (usually) aren't crazy", CNN, December 29, 2012, http://religion.blogs.cnn.com/2012/12/29/my-take-if-you-hear-god-speak-audibly-you-usually-arent-crazy/

Chapter 10: Michael Snyder, "How Will The Shocking Decline Of Christianity In America Affect The Future Of This Nation?", End Of The American Dream, January 18, 2012, http://endoftheamericandream.com/archives/how-will-the-shocking-decline-of-christianity-in-america-affect-the-future-of-this-nation

Chapter 10: Chris Turner, "Ultimate Purpose and Meaning: Some Say They Pursue It, Others Do Not", Lifeway Research, December 27, 2011, http://www.lifeway.com/Article/Research-Ultimate-purpose-and-meaning

Chapter 10: Dave Olson, as cited in Justin Taylor, "How Many Americans Attend Church Each Week?", The Gospel Coalition, February 15, 2015, http://www.thegospelcoalition.org/blogs/justintaylor/2007/03/01/how-many-americans-attend-church-each/

Chapter 10: "Nones On the Rise", Pew Research Center, October 9, 2012, http://www.pewforum.org/2012/10/09/nones-on-the-rise/

Chapter 10: Kevin and Kay Brenfleck, "God Guides, We Decide", The Christian Broadcasting Network, accessed February 15, 2015, http://www.cbn.com/finance/brennflecks_godguides.aspx

Chapter 10: Warner Huston, "51% of Millennials Have Grave Doubts About Their Futures", Breitbart, May 24, 2014, http://cdn.breitbart.com/Big-Government/2014/05/23/51-of-Millennials-Have-Grave-Doubts-About-Their-Future

Chapter 10: Paul Tillich quote: Tillich, Good Reads, accessed February 15, 2015, http://www.goodreads.com/quotes/129557-doubt-isn-t-the-opposite-of-faith-it-is-an-element

Chapter 10: Paul Crome, "Living Below the Line", World Student Christian Federation Europe, January 15, 2013, http://wscf-europe.org/mozaik-issues/living-below-the-line/

Chapter 10: Cooper Abrams, "Obedience Brings Blessings", Bible Truth, accessed February 15, 2015, http://bible-truth.org/msg19.html

Chapter 10: Barna Group, "State of the Bible 2014", American Bible Society's State of the Bible, accessed February 15, 2015, http://www.americanbible.org/features/state-of-the-bible-research-2014

Chapter 10: Whitney Kuniholm, "Top 10 Reasons the Bible is True", Essential Bible Blog, accessed February 15, 2015, http://www.essentialbibleblog.com/2013/03/top-10-reasons-bible-is-true.html

Chapter 10: "What People Experience In Churches", Barna Group, accessed February 15, 2015, https://www.barna.org/congregations-articles/556-what-people-experience-in-churches

Chapter 10: "Americans Pray for Friends and Family, but Rarely for Celebrities or Sports Teams", Lifeway Research, October 1, 2014, http://www.lifewayresearch.com/2014/10/01/americanspray forfriendsandfamily-2/

Chapter 10: Craig von Buseck, "Three Keys To Answered Prayer", The Christian Broadcasting Network, accessed February 15, 2015, http://www.cbn.com/spirituallife/BibleStudyAndTheology/Discipleship/vonBuseck_ThreeKeysPrayer.aspx

Chapter 10: Craig von Buseck. "Seven keys to hearing God's voice." The Christian Broadcasting Network, accessed April 2, 2016 from http://www1.cbn.com/prayer/seven-keys-to-hearing-god

Chapter 10: David Seargent, "Spiritual Unity Awakening", Christianity Oasis, accessed February 15, 2015, http://www.christianityoasis.com/Puritypublications/5015/SpiritualUnityAwakening.htm

Chapter 10: "Americans Describe Their Views About Life After Death", Barna Group, accessed February 15, 2015, https://www.barna.org/barna-update/article/5-barna-update/128-americans-describe-their-views-about-life-after-death#.VOEv1ObF-RN

Chapter 10: Jonathan Petersen, "75% in USA Believe the Bible is in Some Way Connected to God", Bible Gateway Blog, June 10, 2014, https://www.biblegateway.com/blog/2014/06/75-in-usa-believe-the-bible-is-in-some-way-connected-to-god/

Chapter 10: Sarah Sharp, "What's after life?", U.S. Catholic, accessed February 15, 2015, http://www.uscatholic.org/church/scripture-and-theology/2009/03/whats-after-life

Chapter 11: Anna Rountree, *The Heavens Opened: Revealing a Fresh Vision of God's Love for You* (Lake Mary, FL: Charisma House; 1st edition, 1999)

Chapter 11: TB Joshua, The Synagogue Church of All Nations (SCOAN), accessed February 15, 2015, http://www.scoan.org/

Chapter 11: Louise, comment on "What did Kings eat in the Medieval Ages?", accessed February 15, 2015, https://au.answers.yahoo.com/question/index?qid=20110811053449AAJPYjR

Chapter 11: Yahoo Answers. What did kings eat in the medieval ages? Retrieved April 2, 2016 from

State of the Kingdom Address

https://au.answers.yahoo.com/question/index?qid=20110811053449AAJPYjR

Chapter 12: Dianna Booher, *The Esther Effect* (Nashville: Thomas Nelson, 2008)

All Biblical references have been taken from E-Sword Electronic Bible, King James Version, http://www.e-sword.net/

www.ingramcontent.com/pod-product-compliance
Lightning Source LLC
Chambersburg PA
CBHW071853290426
44110CB00013B/1127